MW01028921

ACTS

A Commentary for Bible Students

PHILIP A. BENCE

General Publisher: Nathan Birky
General Editor: Ray E. Barnwell
Senior Editor: David Higle
Managing Editor: Russell Gunsalus
Editor: Kelly Trennepohl

CONTENTS

EDITOR'S PREFACE

This book is part of a series of commentaries seeking to interpret the books of the Bible from a Wesleyan perspective. It is designed primarily for laypeople, especially teachers of Sunday school and leaders of Bible studies. Pastors will also find this series very helpful. In addition, this series is for people who want to read and study on their own for spiritual edification.

Each book of the Bible will be explained paragraph by paragraph. This "wide-angle lens" approach helps the reader to follow the primary flow of thought in each passage. This, in turn, will help the reader to avoid "missing the forest because of the trees," a problem many people encounter when reading commentaries.

At the same time, the authors slow down often to examine particular details and concepts that are important for understanding the bigger picture. Where there are alternative understandings of key passages, the authors acknowledge these so the reader will experience a broader knowledge of the various theological traditions and how the Wesleyan perspective relates to them.

These commentaries follow the New International Version and are intended to be read with your Bible open. With this in mind, the biblical text is not reproduced in full, but appears in bold type throughout the discussion of each passage. Greater insight will be gained by reading along in your Bible as you read the commentaries.

These volumes do not replace the valuable technical commentaries that offer in-depth grammatical and textual analysis. What they do offer is an interpretation of the Bible that we hope will lead to a greater understanding of what the Bible says, its significance for our lives today, and further transformation into the image of Christ.

David A. Higle
Senior Editor

AUTHOR'S PREFACE

As always, God had a plan. The editors of this series had asked my nephew to write this volume. Jack saw that he was too busy to do the job well. I was in a slow transition between ministries. As a workaholic (yes, I am seeking freedom from this addiction), I did not feel busy enough. My nephew and I laughed at our predicaments. If the series editors agreed, the decision seemed like a no-brainer. They did agree, and I have had a grand time working through the book of Acts.

The material was not new to me. I have heard stories of the early church since before I could read. I give credit to my parents, my Sunday school teachers, and my Houghton College and Asbury Theological Seminary professors for making the Kingdom stories more familiar through their words and their lives. I thank Kingsley College of Melbourne, Australia, for my opportunity to teach Acts to its students. Those students, too, helped enrich my understanding of the book.

I offer you the written results of my acquaintance with Acts—what I have written in this book. I hope that it will help you learn more about our Lord's first followers. You will review the events in which He disclosed himself to them. Through hearing the old stories once again, perhaps you will come to know their Lord better. The same Spirit given at Pentecost indwells God's church—you and me—today.

I have occasionally asked groups of Christians which one of the early congregations they consider to be the model church. It usually takes them a period of head scratching before they offer the answer I am looking for: Antioch of Syria. Because we have no letters written by Paul to this church, it often receives a minor place in our memories of the first century. Antioch deserves better than this. While believers in that community "were worshiping the Lord and fasting, the Holy Spirit" spoke and they heard (Acts 13:2). They obeyed His instructions. And the world has never been the same. If we will worship and fast, the Spirit will again speak to us. Through us, He can continue changing our world, bringing the Kingdom "on earth as it is in heaven" (Matthew 6:10).

Philip A. Bence
1998

INTRODUCTION

We thank God for the book of Acts. Without it, our knowledge of the first-century church would be dramatically reduced. Acts is a unique aid to understanding the New Testament and its time period. When we want to know about the life of Christ, we can look to four different inspired records (the Gospels[1]). But Luke alone wrote a history of the next thirty years. Jesus' life, death, and resurrection changed history forever. On one hand,[2] those dramatic events offer the finished work of Christ. On the other hand, Jesus was just beginning His ministry of reaching the world. Without Acts, we would be cut off from any record of how Christ *continued* the ministry He *began* during His earthly ministry. The Epistles would give us hints,[2] but those hints would produce more questions than information. Similarly, Acts gives information that enables us to better understand the New Testament epistles, their writers and readers, and many of the issues which these books address. We thank God for Luke and his work which remains for us to read.

Was Luke thinking of Christians at the turn of the second millennium when he wrote? Probably not. What first-century factors motivated Luke to write the book of Acts? (Of course, the Holy Spirit inspired Luke to write the book. But the Spirit did not dominate the biblical writers, nor did He dictate words to them. Rather, the Spirit used human circumstances [for example, a conflict in the church at Corinth] as the means to leading Jesus' first followers to write. So, while we do not wish to downplay God's inspiration of Luke's writings, it is still appropriate and helpful to ask why Luke wrote.) As Luke thought of his first-century readers, what were the big questions he hoped to answer? Before we rush to consider what God, through Acts, says to the church *today*, it is good to see what Luke hoped to communicate to his *first* readers.

Why did Luke write the book of Acts? The first and most obvious answer to this question is that he was providing a history of the early church. (What Luke wrote in the introduction to his gospel would apply equally well to Acts: Luke wished "to write an orderly account," so that others "may know" with "certainty" what happened [Luke 1:3-4]). Without Luke's record, it would be difficult to piece together how the church grew so rapidly from a tiny gathering, at one corner of the Roman Empire, to a movement powerful enough to attract the emperor Nero's attention.

Acts 1:8 provides a significant clue to Luke's purpose for writing his history. Jesus told His followers, "You will be my witnesses in Jerusalem, and in all Judea and Samaria, and to the ends of the earth" (1:8b). It is quite likely that Luke quotes, at the beginning of Acts, these words from Jesus as a summary of all that is to follow. This verse serves as a framework for one possible outline of the book: Jesus' followers would be witnesses to (1) Jerusalem (1:1–8:3); (2) Judea and Samaria (8:4–11:18); and the ends of the earth (11:19–28:31).

Even so, Luke does not give us a detailed history of *everything* that happened along the way from "Jerusalem . . . to the ends of the earth." Luke faced the same problem that John described at the end of his gospel: "If every[thing the early Christians did] were written down, I suppose that even the whole world would not have room for the books that would be written" (John 21:25b). There are several potential topics that Luke all but ignores.

At the beginning of the book, Luke lists the names of all eleven remaining apostles (see Acts 1:13; Judas had committed suicide [1:18]). But nine of them receive no more individual attention. As a group, they appear several times, at least until chapter 15. But after 1:13, Luke mentions individual actions of only Peter and John. (Luke speaks of the death of James the apostle in 12:2.)

Luke tells his readers almost nothing of how the church spread *east* and *south* from Jerusalem. He gives little attention to the spread of the gospel southwest to Africa, and mentions significant ministry to Africans only twice: Africans were present on the day of Pentecost (see Acts 2:10)[3]; and Philip offered the good news to an Ethiopian eunuch (8:26-39). Likewise, Luke gives little information on how Christians reached northeast to Babylon and Persia (except the mention of people at Pentecost from these locations [see 2:9]). Arabia, to the southeast, receives no mention at all.

Other ancient church traditions tell us that ten of the first twelve apostles traveled the world as Jesus' witnesses. We know of many areas in which they ministered. Thomas, for example, went to India. John Mark, the junior partner whom Paul at one time rejected (see Acts 15:38), eventually turned out well. Ancient records tell us that John Mark preached Jesus in Egypt. Other first-century believers reportedly took the good news to the small Eastern nation of Edessa. Luke does not describe these missionary trips. In this sense, his history is quite limited. For whatever reasons, Luke focuses his attention on one quarter of the geographical pie of which Jerusalem is the center, accenting how the church moved north and then east toward Rome.

In his gospel, Luke portrays how much of Jesus' ministry occurred in Galilee. How much attention does the church in Jesus' home area receive in Luke's second volume, Acts? Would you believe, only brief mention in one verse (see Acts 9:31)? It would be interesting to know how the church developed in Capernaum and Nazareth, but this news did not, for whatever reasons, fit Luke's purposes.

Luke focuses his attention on only a few of the church's leaders: Peter, Paul, Stephen, Philip, Barnabas, and James. One man, Paul, receives center stage for over half the book (see Acts 9; 13–28).

Luke did want to write a history of the early church, but it does look like he had particular goals in mind. What might these goals have been? Some good possibilities include the following:

Personal. Luke or his readers obviously felt a special interest in Peter and Paul, the book's two central figures. One quite simple outline for the book builds on personal interest: Peter—chapters 1 through 12; Paul—chapters 13 through 28.

Peter became the leader of the twelve disciples during Jesus' ministry. Among the eleven disciples remaining after Jesus' death and resurrection, Peter continued in the roles of initiator and spokesman for several years after Jesus' ascension (see Acts 1:15; 2:14; 3:6-7; 4:8; 5:3, 29). His words and actions help to summarize the activity of the Jerusalem church in the days when it served as the unquestioned headquarters of the Christian church.

But, in Luke's record, Peter fades away, and Paul appears as the missionary of Olympic stature (F. F. Bruce calls Paul "Luke's hero"[4]). Paul, as the Apostle to the Gentiles, complemented Peter's ministry among the Jews. It's no wonder that Luke describes Paul's ministry in great detail, but might there not have been other apostles whose ministry attained equal effectiveness? And there is the puzzling question of why Luke felt it important to include the information contained in the last quarter of his book, which he devoted to Paul's arrest, imprisonments, trials, and travel to the supreme court in Rome. During that time, Paul planted no new churches and, as far as Luke tells us, won only a few converts. Within the last few chapters, Luke twice repeats the story of Paul's conversion, which already dominates chapter 9.

Why this focus on Paul's ministry and preliminary trials? Perhaps Luke wrote Acts (and his gospel as well) as a defense brief for Paul's trial in Rome. Or, one can broaden that thinking. Paul may have been the one officially on trial. At the same time, however, Christianity as a system also may have been "facing charges." If that were the case, Roman government officials would benefit from an account of the founding of Christianity, its survival despite its founder's death, and its spread from Jerusalem across the Empire. If Acts were a defense brief specifically for Paul, then it would be appropriate to highlight the part Paul played in Christianity's movement toward Rome. (To further support the theory that Luke wrote Acts as a defense brief for Paul, note how many times Luke quotes local government officials in stating their views that Christianity and its representative, Paul, had done nothing to harm the welfare of the Empire [see, for example, 18:14-15; 19:37-39; 25:25; 26:32].)

How does Luke's apparent interest in the lives of Peter and Paul relate to us today? After all, not only has Peter been dead for two thousand years, but he moved out of Jerusalem church leadership even during his own lifetime. (Luke alludes to the fact that James, the brother of Jesus, was Peter's apparent successor [see 12:17; 15:13; also Galatians 2:12). Paul may have been the greatest missionary in the history of Christianity, but he lived two thousand years ago. What relevance does he have for our lives today? The answer to these questions is quite simple. Like Peter and Paul in centuries past, we today seek to serve Jesus effectively. The model of Peter and Paul always challenges us toward greater faithfulness.

Geographical. Christian witness radiating in every direction from Jerusalem may have fascinated Luke the *believer*. But Luke the *writer* knew of his readers' special interest in the Roman Empire and in the gospel's movement toward the Empire's capital. If Luke's books (Luke and Acts) were written as a defense brief for Paul, then their first readers could have been part of the Roman legal establishment. Luke may have gloried in the gospel's ripple effect in every direction ("to the ends of the earth" [Acts 1:8]), but apparently saw the move toward Rome as most relevant to his purposes for writing these documents.

How do these emphases relate to us? Paul's trial dropped out of the news centuries ago. Rome is not our capital. But, for many people, the verdict on Christianity is still out. Perhaps you can use Luke and Acts as effective tools today. People considering a decision for Christ need to understand the origins and early days of the movement they might join.

Another related question which the church needs to be asking today is how Christianity made such an impact during the thirty-year period described in Acts. Christianity leapt across several urban centers of the

Empire. Individual lives and entire communities were transformed. Many in the first century sacrificed lifelong traditions to join the cause of Christ. At the same time, others rejected the Jesus movement and fought Christianity fiercely. But people living in places such as Corinth, Ephesus, and even Rome could hardly ignore the followers of "the Way" (24:14; this was an early name for the church).

Christians were "turning the world upside down" (17:6 NRSV). A small percentage of the population made a dramatic impact. It might be good for Christians today to ask why the evangelical church, with a large percentage of the North American population in its membership, is not affecting its society in larger ways. What was the dynamic in the early church that took it from Jerusalem to Rome? Can we receive that same power today? The Holy Spirit empowered the believers of the first century. He still offers himself to Christians today.

Cultural. The history of Christianity's movement from Jerusalem through Judea and Samaria, and then on toward Rome, illustrates how the gospel transcends human boundaries. Today, the Christian church faces tensions relating to cultural diversity. How does the gospel best move across ethnic, linguistic, religious, and other cultural barriers? Many non-Christians, and some people within the church, are asking on what basis Christians should be attempting to export their faith to groups of other backgrounds. Are these questions new? No. The first-century Roman world faced the same diversity experienced in any major Western city today. The modern situation includes new factors: the universal television network, the ease of transportation, and computer-enabled communication. These make it possible for the nations of the world to interact as a "global village." Yet, we still face one significant question that is twenty centuries old: Is it legitimate to believe that the Christian faith is superior to other world religions? Assuming the answer is yes, *how* do we market it most sensitively and effectively? The actions of the first-century Christians give us helpful insight.

Theological. What was the good news that Jesus and His followers announced to the world? Did it truly meet the needs of people both inside and outside the Jewish tradition? Luke records several early church sermons. In them, he allows the preachers to summarize the content of the Christian faith. Listen to the requests of early seekers scattered through the book of Acts and across the Roman Empire. Jews in Jerusalem asked, "Brothers, what shall we do?" (2:37). A religious Roman officer living on the Palestinian coast addressed Peter: "We are all here in the presence of God to listen to everything the Lord has commanded you to tell us" (10:33b). A pagan European Gentile asked, "What must I do to be saved?" (16:30). Residents of Rome spoke to Paul: "We want to hear what your views [on the hope of Israel] are" (28:22a). Each of these openers gave Peter or Paul opportunity to witness about Jesus and salvation.

You likely have a good grasp of your beliefs. It is always good, however, to go back to the source. Compare your ideas of Jesus, who He is, what He offers, and what He demands, with the views of the inspired apostles. Seek to share your faith accurately and boldly as they did.

As he thought about writing his two-volume set, Luke could well have selected all five of these goals: historical, personal, geographical, cultural, and theological. In first-century scenarios, as well as contemporary situations, these factors raise crucial questions. Who shares the faith? To whom should the church preach the gospel? What factors ease or hinder the transmission of the gospel? How are the barriers to be overcome? What factors distinguish believers from nonbelievers? How do these distinctions give unity to all Christians? How much diversity is permitted, or even desired, within the overall church? How does Jesus meet the needs of people from all backgrounds? How does God, through the unique gifts He offers the church, impact the world?

Readers of Acts, then and now, find clues which help to answer these questions.

Luke sought to write an explanation of the gospel of Jesus Christ and its spread toward Rome. He did so in order to defend the Christian truth and its proponents. It is possible that Luke wrote a defense brief for Paul's trials. In any case, the book of Acts continues to be useful long afterward. Christians from the second half of the first century to today have found Acts to be not only a fascinating historical account, but also a testimony to God's sovereignty. Christians, then and now, have asked, "Why *should* I, and how *can* I, continue to serve God in a world that resists Him?" Paul answered those questions with letters. Luke chose to respond with a series of stories. But these men proclaimed the same message: Nothing can "separate us from the love of God that is in Christ Jesus our Lord" (Rom. 8:39). Likewise, nothing can imprison the word of the Lord (see 2 Timothy 2:9).

Pagan Romans may have felt that Christianity threatened the peace of society. Luke wrote for these skeptics, too. He points out that the Christians do nothing to harm life and do much to help it. The God who made and who loves the world is behind . . . better yet, is *in* . . . the

Christians. God, through them, wishes to give His peace to all people. As first-century skeptics and seekers read Acts, those who sincerely sought the truth came to better understand God's way. Many no doubt followed that way.

Luke wrote to present and defend the faith. As you work your way through this commentary and the book of Acts, notice how Luke accomplished those goals. Find security in the truth which he and the apostles proclaimed. Follow their model in proclaiming it to today's world, which needs the good news of Jesus as much as Luke's world did.

Before turning to Luke's record, we can benefit from answering several more preliminary questions. Who was Luke? How do we know he wrote Acts? Who was Theophilus, the named recipient of the books we call "Luke" and "Acts"? How do these two books relate to each other? How did Luke research material for his books? Can we trust the accuracy of his history?

AUTHORSHIP

Who was Luke? We know only a few crucial facts about this man. Paul mentions Luke three times in his epistles[5] (see Colossians 4:14; 2 Timothy 4:11; Philemon 24). Let's consider what these verses tell us.

Crucial fact #1: Luke was a Gentile. In Colossians 4:10-11, Paul mentions Aristarchus, John Mark, and Jesus, also called Justus, as being "the only Jews among [his] fellow workers." Paul then goes on to describe three more colleagues, including Luke, who must have been Gentiles. Among all the New Testament writers, Luke was the only one who had *not* descended from Abraham. Luke was an "adopted member" of God's family, and yet he wrote a larger proportion of the New Testament than any other inspired writer. The grace God gave to Luke, He still gives to us.

Crucial fact #2: Luke was Paul's companion over a period of years. Luke was present with Paul during Paul's first Roman imprisonment (see Colossians 4:14; this is the imprisonment with which Acts ends), and also his second Roman imprisonment (see 2 Timothy 4:11; during this imprisonment Paul wrote the three Pastoral Epistles—the two to Timothy and one to Titus).

Crucial fact #3: Paul saw Luke as a faithful fellow worker (see Philemon 24). In Paul's last letter (2 Timothy), as he faced death, he told how others had deserted him, while Luke had stayed close. Luke risked his own life by associating with a condemned political prisoner. It's no wonder that Paul describes Luke as his "dear friend" (Col. 4:14).

Crucial fact #4: Luke was a medical doctor. Obviously, today's physicians view ancient medical knowledge and training as quite primitive. Even so, skills of observation and attention to detail would have served the ancient doctor as much as his contemporary counterpart. Luke's medical training would have prepared him for his primary career as well as for work in historical research and writing.

Crucial fact #5: In two of the three epistles where Luke appears, he is sending greetings to believers elsewhere. Luke became a well-known figure, loved not only by Paul, but by Christians across the area of Paul's previous ministry.

Like Paul, I would rejoice to have such a personal physician and friend.

How do we know that Luke wrote Acts? Scholars have had to play detective here, for nowhere in the book does Luke identify himself as its author. Their task, however, has not been dreadfully difficult.

All of the ancient writers who mention any author for Acts identify that writer as Luke.

The evidence within the contents of Acts does nothing to contradict, and offers some support for, that same conclusion. Within the book, the author appears to have been one of Paul's companions and faithful coworkers. At several points in the second half of the book, the author switches from saying, "They did this," to "We did this." The "we" sections are Acts 16:10-17; 20:5–21:18; and 27:1–28:16. Within these blocks, we see that the writer accompanied Paul in ministry and travel.

The book indicates that the author was one of Paul's traveling partners, but does not tell us which one. By process of elimination, we can rule out most of Paul's other ministry companions.

For example, if the author of Acts described himself via the use of the word "we," this seemingly rules out, as author, any of Paul's coworkers which Acts specifically names, such as Barnabas, John Mark, Timothy, Tychicus, Trophimus, Aristarchus, and others.

Does Luke's name appear anywhere in Acts? No. This seems odd, if Luke truly was Paul's well-known "dear friend" and faithful fellow worker (Col. 4:14; Philem. 24). That, in itself, might wrap up our investigation, but Paul names several other coworkers who, like Luke, do not appear by name in Acts. One is Demas, but he is not a likely author for the book. Would the church have revered the writings of a man who loved the world too much and deserted Paul near his end (see 2 Timothy 4:10)? Epaphras, Epaphroditus, and Titus are other possibilities. They faithfully served alongside Paul, but do not appear by name in Acts.

Could one of them have written Acts? Another factor likely rules them out. The author of Acts traveled with Paul on the shipwreck journey to Rome recorded in Acts 27. Epaphras and Epaphroditus did not travel to Rome with Paul on that occasion. They went to Rome later. (Epaphras likely went later, as a messenger from Colossae, to visit Paul in Rome [see Colossians 1:7-8; 4:12]. Epaphroditus traveled to Rome as a representative of the church at Philippi [see Philippians 2:25].) That leaves Titus, but there is no biblical evidence that he was ever in Rome with Paul. Jesus Justus remains another possibility (see Colossians 4:11). But he evidently was a figure of smaller prominence than Luke. Putting all the evidence together, Luke stands alone as the likely author of Acts (and the Gospel that bears Luke's name).

RECIPIENTS

Who was Theophilus, the named recipient of both volumes of the two-volume set of Luke and Acts (see Luke 1:3; Acts 1:1)? His identity remains one of the puzzles of biblical history. Biblical scholars have been able to offer nothing but guesses. The only solid hint Luke gives us is the honor that he gave to Theophilus, calling him "most excellent" (Luke 1:3). The only other New Testament people to receive such acclaim were the Roman governors Felix and Festus (see Acts 23:26; 26:25; in the first of these references, the New International Version editors translate the phrase with the English words "His Excellency," but in Luke's Greek original, the phrases in both references are the same). Luke saw Theophilus as one deserving great respect.

The name Theophilus is derived from two Greek words meaning "God" and "love." Either from his parents' early hopes, or by his own personal piety, Theophilus was described as a "God-lover."

Who was he? A high government official involved in Paul's Roman trial? Perhaps. A wealthy benefactor of the church who "commissioned" the two-volume writing? Maybe. Or, possibly, Theophilus was a seeker whom Luke hoped to win to the faith. It's also possible that Theophilus might not have been a single person, but a "code name" for any person who truly sought God and found Luke's writings a help in that process. It was certainly Luke's hope that *all* of his readers would progress in their love for God.

RELATIONSHIP OF ACTS TO THE GOSPEL OF LUKE

How do the two volumes—the Gospel of Luke and its sequel, Acts— relate to each other? To best understand Acts, readers should see it as the second half of a two-volume set. Luke makes this clear, in Acts 1:1, both by his reference to his "former book" and by addressing the second volume to the same recipient, Theophilus.[6] Note also the words with which Luke summarizes his gospel. He says that he wrote that work to describe what "Jesus began to do and to teach" (Acts 1:1). Acts, in one sense, does not describe a new story, but the continuation or the fulfillment of Jesus' three-year ministry. While the writers of the other Gospels saw Jesus' resurrection as the confirmation of His lordship, Luke offers further evidence: God's Spirit empowered Jesus' followers to take the good news "to the ends of the earth" (Acts 1:8).

One can see other parallels between Luke's gospel and Acts. Both open with chapters that set the stage for what follows. Luke begins his gospel with the birth of Jesus and events leading up to it (see Luke 1–2). Acts, likewise, begins with the birth of the church and events preceding it (Acts 1–2). Middle portions of both books show the gospel proclaimed at an increasing number of sites (Luke 3:1–8:50; Acts 3:1–21:16). Both books move on with their respective heroes each making a final journey toward a city where a momentous trial would occur (Luke 8:51–19:28; Acts 27:1–28:14). Both books finish on a note of victory (Luke 24:50-52; Acts 28:30-31).

How did Luke research material for his books? Since the books of Luke and Acts comprise one single work, the introduction to the Gospel (see Luke 1:1-4), then, refers to both volumes that follow. In that introduction, Luke describes his overall research methods. He grasped the significance of the Jesus events that had occurred in the first two-thirds of his century. Witnesses to these events had described what they saw. But, then as now, the rumor mill had done its thing. Various accounts were floating everywhere. Some, undoubtedly, were quite accurate; other "records of the minutes" needed additions and corrections.

Luke undertook his own investigation. He read written reports. (Nearly all scholars feel that Luke had at least the Gospel of Mark before him when he wrote his own gospel.) He interviewed witnesses. (For example, Luke was not a member of the group gathered together on the day of Pentecost. But he surely spoke with some who were.) In many instances, Luke reviewed his own memory of the events he had witnessed, offering such detailed accounts at times that scholars believe he must have been keeping a diary. That diary certainly would have been one of his sources as he wrote a more public record of those events. Many theorize that during Paul's two-year imprisonment in Caesarea (see Acts 24:27), Luke might have spent time interviewing witnesses to events that had occurred in Palestine before his own involvement in the Christian movement.

How do we know that we can trust the accuracy of Luke's history? Perhaps the best response to this question is another question: Are there any reasons to *doubt* the truthfulness of Luke's record? Some scholars have suggested possible problems.

Some feel that Luke's picture of Paul does not correspond with the epistles Paul wrote.[7] On one hand, we see an apostle who strongly reprimanded the Galatians for falling back into Jewish practices (see Galatians 3:1-5, 10-13). On the other hand, Luke shows a Paul who allowed Timothy to be circumcised and who submitted to the Jewish rituals (see Acts 16:3; 21:26). Can these pictures both accurately portray the same man?

This conflict finds fairly simple resolution. When the Galatians toyed with returning to circumcision, they did so because they feared it was necessary for salvation. Paul did not have Timothy circumcised so that Timothy could go to heaven. Paul merely wanted to avoid needless conflict with the Jews to whom Timothy would be ministering. Timothy's circumcision was a pragmatic matter, not a theological necessity. What about Paul's own submission to Jewish practice? The critics here seem to have forgotten Paul's statement to the Corinthians: "I have become all things to all men so that . . . I might save some" (1 Cor. 9:22).

Others doubt Luke's accuracy on another point related to the Galatian epistle. Luke refers to three occasions, after Paul's conversion, on which Paul visited Jerusalem (see Acts 9:26; 11:30; 15:4). In Galatians, Paul quite strongly says that he made only two trips to the Jewish capital (see Galatians 1:17-18, 20; 2:1). But these statements raise a problem only if one dates the Galatian epistle after the Jerusalem Council. Many scholars feel that Paul wrote to the Galatian church just after his first missionary trip, which was *before* Paul made this third trip to Jerusalem for the Council (see chapter 13 of the commentary).

Another possible problem relates to the speeches in Acts. The longest of the recorded speeches can be read in just a few minutes. Some ask, "How can anyone claim that Luke wrote an accurate history when he obviously did not quote the apostles exactly?" This attack seems rather pointless. To give an accurate account of what Peter said at Pentecost, for example, Luke did not have to give a complete manuscript of Peter's sermon. (Contemporary newspapers rarely print full quotations of Washington speeches, and yet readers accept the accuracy of their summaries.) Some offer a stronger critique of Luke's record at this point. They feel that Luke *invented* the speeches, placing within Peter's or Paul's mouth what Luke felt would have been appropriate for the occasion. There is no way that Luke can win this one. Because Luke's speeches appear to fit the occasions, the critics see this as evidence that Luke concocted some appropriate words. If Luke's speeches did not fit the occasions, the critics would cite this as evidence that Luke invented the speeches.

Now, to be fair, it has been documented that some other ancient secular historians did invent the speeches they included in their accounts.[8] But, that in itself is not evidence that Luke did so. It is equally possible that Luke consulted people who heard (or even gave) the speeches he records in Acts.

Is there evidence to support the accuracy of the history Luke records? A century ago, a British historian set out to prove that Acts was a second-century "fictional account." Sir William Ramsay's research, to his great surprise, revealed just the opposite. Ramsay concluded that Luke was a first-century author of a work which offers a trustworthy picture of the events it describes. Ramsay was particularly impressed with Luke's awareness of first-century political situations. Luke accurately notes the titles of various local government officials. These include the following:[9]

Cyprus	proconsul	Acts 13:7
Philippi	magistrates	Acts 16:20
Thessalonica	city officials	Acts 17:6
Ephesus	officials of the province	Acts 19:31
	city clerk	Acts 19:35
Malta	chief official	Acts 28:7

If Luke was so careful to record these political terms correctly, then would he not have given equal care to the other information he included in Acts?[10]

At the end of this introduction to the commentary, the reader can find a detailed outline for the book of Acts. The text of this commentary explains and justifies that outline in more detail. At this point, a quick overview might be helpful.

This outline highlights two primary features of the book.

First, the book of Acts is a history of what God did in the middle portion of the first century. Without God's supervision and participation, Luke would not have written Acts. More importantly, there would have been no great story to record. Through Peter, Paul, Luke, and others, God was fulfilling His plan for the church then, and was providing us with knowledge of Christianity's early spread. (Today, God's people can do much to impress themselves and others. But they can accomplish nothing of eternal value unless they, too, live in submission to the power of the Holy Spirit.)

Second, the book of Acts describes God's acting in a progressive manner. Each section of the book (and the history it records) shares a significant overlap with its neighbors. The last three-quarters of Acts successively show how God has moved His people one large step farther along in the plan.

Part I shows the birth and establishment of the Christian church in Jerusalem. Part II overlaps with Part I in its focus on the ongoing life of the Jerusalem church. The step forward? In this quarter of Acts, the emphasis is not merely on the growth of the church itself, but on God's preparing that church for mission "to the ends of the earth" (Acts 1:8). Part III overlaps with Part II in its emphasis on missions. But in Part III, the church is no longer *preparing* for worldwide missions; under Paul's leadership, the church moves out to the distant lands in the Roman Empire. Part IV shares with Part III the emphasis on Paul, the missionary. But this final section portrays Paul's evangelistic work as largely complete. What's left? Paul's reaching one more goal: ministry in Rome, the Empire's capital.

In the lives of His people today, God continually wants to do that which is new. But He rarely works in individual lives or in great movements of people in a way that does not build on their previous history. God calls us ever to look forward to the future He has planned. But that vision for what's ahead never negates the need to live purposefully in the present, the only time ever available to us.

ENDNOTES

[1]The Gospels include the New Testament books of Matthew, Mark, Luke, and John.

[2]The Epistles are comprised of the New Testament books of Romans; 1 and 2 Corinthians; Galatians; Ephesians; Philippians; Colossians; 1 and 2 Thessalonians; 1 and 2 Timothy; Titus; Philemon; Hebrews; James; 1 and 2 Peter; 1, 2 and 3 John; and Jude. The books of James; 1 and 2 Peter; 1, 2, and 3 John; and Jude are called General Epistles because they are books or letters written to broad groups of people, rather than being addressed to specific individuals or churches the way that, say, Paul's letters to the Corinthians were.

[3]In the New Testament, Pentecost primarily refers to the event when the Holy Spirit was given to the church; this occurred on the day of Pentecost. The Greek term *Pentecost* comes from means "fiftieth" or "the fiftieth day" and is literally the fiftieth day after the end of the Passover. It is also known as the Jewish Feast of Weeks. This day is part of the Jewish observances, and was the beginning of the offering of first fruits.

[4]F. F. Bruce, *The Book of the Acts* (Grand Rapids, Michigan: Wm. B. Eerdmans Publishing Co., 1988), p. 15.

[5]Paul's epistles are comprised of the New Testament books of Romans, 1 and 2 Corinthians, Galatians, Ephesians, Philippians, Colossians, 1 and 2 Thessalonians, 1 and 2 Timothy, Titus, and Philemon (some consider Paul to be the unknown author of Hebrews as well). Paul's epistles include two categories: the Pastoral Epistles—1 and 2 Timothy, Titus; and the Prison Epistles—Ephesians, Philippians, Colossians, and Philemon (these letters were most likely written during the Roman imprisonment Luke describes in Acts 28:30).

[6]Ralph Martin, *New Testament Foundations,* vol. 2 (Grand Rapids, Michigan: Wm. B. Eerdmans Publishing Co., 1978), p. 67. In addition to the material cited in this paragraph is the scholarly conclusion that the two books were written with similar style and vocabulary. Likewise, they share common themes: for example, participation of women in the Christian movement, and interest in outreach to Gentiles.

[7]See endnote 5.

[8]Donald Guthrie, *New Testament Introduction* (Downers Grove, Illinois: InterVarsity Press, 1970), p. 360.

[9]Ibid., pp. 354–55. To best see the accuracy of Luke's political terminology, one would have to see the ancient words written in their original language. The New International Version translators have done their best to give modern approximations of the ancient phrases. For another evaluation of how Luke portrays first-century life, you may consult a book by an expert in Roman society and law who sees Luke's record as politically accurate: *Roman Society and Roman Law in the New Testament,* by A. N. Sherwin-White (Grand Rapids, Michigan: Baker Book House, 1963).

[10]I. Howard Marshall, *Luke: Historian and Theologian* (Grand Rapids, Michigan: Zondervan Publishing House, 1971), p. 69.

ACTS OUTLINE

I. God Establishes the Church in Jerusalem 1:1–8:1a
A. Background 1:1-26
   1. The Preface Containing the Promise 1:1-11
   2. Setting Up Shop 1:12-26
B. Pentecost 2:1-47
   1. Before the Sermon 2:1-13
   2. The First Christian Sermon 2:14-40
   3. After the Sermon 2:41-47
C. Peter and John Heal a Man 3:1–4:31
   1. Leap, Ye Lame, for Joy 3:1-10
   2. All the Prophets Predicted Jesus 3:11-26
   3. Two Different Responses 4:1-7
   4. The First Round Goes to the Christians 4:8-22
   5. The Shaken Church Meeting 4:23-31
D. Two Trials 4:32–5:42
   1. God Puts a Husband and Wife on Trial 4:32–5:11
   2. The Jews Again Try the Apostles 5:12-42
E. Stephen, the First Martyr 6:1–8:1a
   1. The Widows' Controversy 6:1-7
   2. The Ministry and Death of Stephen 6:8–8:1a

II. God Prepares the Church to Take the Gospel to the Gentiles 8:1b–12:25
A. Setting the Stage 8:1b-4
B. The Ministry of Philip 8:5-40
   1. The Gospel to the Samaritans 8:5-25
   2. The Gospel Moves Toward Africa 8:26-40
C. The Conversion of Saul 9:1-31
D. The Ministry of Peter 9:32–11:18
   1. Peter Heals Two in Judea 9:32-43
   2. God Prepares Cornelius and Peter 10:1-23a
   3. God Welcomes Gentiles 10:23b-48
   4. The Home Church Settles Some Questions 11:1-18
E. A New Church in Antioch 11:19-30
F. Peter's Arrest and Miraculous Release 12:1-25

III. Paul: God's Messenger to the Gentiles 13:1–21:16
    A. The First Missionary Trip 13:1–14:28
        1. The Antioch Church Sends Missionaries 13:1-3
        2. Salamis 13:4-5
        3. Paphos 13:6-12
        4. Pisidian Antioch 13:14-52
        5. Iconium 14:1-6a
        6. Lystra 14:6b-20a
        7. Derbe 14:20b-21a
        8. The Return Journey and Arrival Home 14:21b-28
    B. The Jerusalem Council 15:1-35
    C. The Second Missionary Trip 15:36–18:18a
        1. Paul Sets Out Again 15:36–16:10
        2. Philippi 16:11-40
        3. Thessalonica and Berea 17:1-15
        4. Athens 17:16-34
        5. Corinth 18:1-18a
    D. Summary of Travel and Ministry 18:18b-28
    E. The Third Missionary Trip 19:1–21:16
        1. Ephesus 19:1–20:1
        2. From Ephesus to "Ephesus" 20:2-15
        3. A Review of Paul's Ministry 20:16-38
        4. The Final Journey to Jerusalem 21:1-16

IV. God Enables Paul Safely to Reach Rome 21:17–28:31
    A. Paul in Jerusalem 21:17–23:11
        1. Paul's Arrest 21:17-36
        2. Paul Speaks to Jerusalem 21:37–22:22
        3. The Trial Before the Sanhedrin 22:23–23:11
    B. Paul in Caesarea 23:12–26:32
        1. Paul Is Moved to Caesarea 23:12-35
        2. The Trial Before Felix 24:1-27
        3. The Trial Before Festus 25:1-22
        4. The Trial Before Agrippa 25:23–26:32
    C. Paul Reaches Rome 27:1–28:31
        1. Paul Travels to Rome 27:1–28:14a
        2. Paul Arrives in the Capital 28:14b-31

Part One

GOD ESTABLISHES THE CHURCH IN JERUSALEM

Acts 1:1–8:1a

In the years after Jesus' ascension, God wanted His church to take the gospel **to the ends of the earth** (Acts 1:8). But, before the church could move out, there needed to be a church. God established it and helped it to become firmly grounded in its faith. Luke, in the first seven chapters of Acts, describes key events in that process.

First, God came to dwell among His people. The Holy Spirit's presence in the church revolutionized the believers and empowered them for ministry (see Acts 2).

Second, the church faced increasing questions and persecution from the Jerusalem Jews. This resistance steeled the church for the challenges it would subsequently face (see Acts 3–4; 5:12-42).

Third, the church dealt with internal impurity and dissent. With God's help, the church overcame these first barriers in ways that taught it how to handle such situations in the future (see Acts 5:1-11; 6:1-7).

Fourth, the church came to see itself not merely as a revival movement within Judaism, but as a new building set upon the foundation of Judaism[1] (see Acts 6:8–8:1a).

Each of these events provided the church with necessary preparation for the rich, but often difficult, ministry that lay ahead.

ENDNOTE

¹Judaism is the life and belief system of the Jewish people and involves a covenant relationship with God. Though there are various branches of Judaism, the underlying theme among them has been monotheism and a recognition of the Law, or the Torah. The Hebrew word from which *Torah* comes is translated *law* and refers to divine instruction and guidance. The Torah is comprised of the instructions and directions given to Israel by God. Torah is another name for the Pentateuch (the first five books of the Old Testament: Genesis, Exodus, Leviticus, Numbers, and Deuteronomy), also known as the Law of Moses. It is considered the most important division in the Jewish Scriptures, with highest authority, since it was traditionally thought to have been written by Moses, the only biblical hero to have spoken with God face-to-face.

1

BACKGROUND

Acts 1:1-26

L uke did not begin his gospel with the birth of Christ. He saved that for a bit later, in what ultimately became chapter 2. The Gospel of Luke begins with introductory material that foreshadows the Bethlehem event. Likewise, Luke chose not to begin Acts, his second volume, with the birth of the church, that is, the coming of the third member of the Trinity—the Holy Spirit. Acts, like Luke's gospel, begins with material that sets up the reader for the big event which follows—in this case, Pentecost.[1]

1. THE PREFACE CONTAINING THE PROMISE 1:1-11

Volume 1 of Luke's set deals with roughly the first third of the first century; the second volume describes events which occurred in the next thirty years. The last verses of the Gospel and the first verses of Acts cover the same events. Why did Luke include this overlap? Luke wanted both books to help his readers look back to previous events and to underline the importance of future events.

You have probably watched a television miniseries. The first minutes of the second and subsequent episodes give a synopsis of how the story has developed to that point. This overlap both helps viewers to remember what has happened and prepares them to watch the story further unfold. Luke wished to accomplish the same goals. People picking up his second volume would need to know they were moving into the middle of a story.

What are the key factors in the overlapping material? The central unifying factor is Jesus. Luke summarizes the first twenty-one chapters of his gospel with less than a verse (see Acts 1:1). But in those words, notice the word **began**: The Gospel recounted **all that Jesus _began_ to do and to teach** (my emphasis). With that key word, Luke states the central tie between the two books. What Jesus had begun (the Gospels[2]),

He would now continue (Acts). The church may have called this book "The Acts of the Apostles," but Luke saw it as a record of what *Jesus continued* **to do and to teach.** The church today may still be finishing the record of what Jesus continues to do and teach.

In the opening verses of Acts, Luke gives specific examples of Jesus' previous actions, highlighting His death and resurrection. These events not only climaxed the Gospel account, but served as the center of the early church preaching which Luke includes in Acts (see, for example, Acts 2:23-24; 3:15). Everything in the Gospels moves toward that holy weekend. Everything in Acts builds on Calvary and the empty tomb. In the Gospels, everything Jesus did helped to move Him *toward* Jerusalem. In Acts, Jesus, through the church, moved *out from* Jerusalem.

Luke also highlights the overlap between the Gospel and the early church in the continuity of Jesus' teaching. Notice how the last words Jesus spoke in the Gospel (see Luke 24:45-49) parallel the first words Jesus spoke in Acts (see Acts 1:4-5, 8): "You should stay in Jerusalem. You will receive power from God. You will be witnesses. Through you, the nations will hear the good news."

Why does Luke include this repetition? To tie the two books together. The same Jesus who was the central figure before His own death remained the central figure after His resurrection.

At the beginning of Acts, Luke mentions one more key concept that ties the two books together: **the kingdom of God** (1:3). Luke was the only Evangelist (a special name for the four writers of the Gospels) who included the story of Jesus walking with two disciples to Emmaus the first Easter evening. To Cleopas and his friend Jesus "explained . . . what was said in all the Scriptures concerning himself" (Luke 24:27). During those next forty days, Jesus likely gave that same seminar, and more, to larger groups of His disciples. His topic? The Old Testament predictions of the coming of the Messiah, and the kingdom of God that He would bring.

Now, of course, God had been King of His world from the moment He created it. Even after the Fall, God remained ultimately in charge. But God inspired His prophets with visions of a coming day when a man sent especially from God would enable the world to return to its original splendor. This "Day of the Lord" would bring peace between nations, between people and the environment, and, underlying all this harmony, between God and humanity. While God had always retained His rule, the Old Testament prophets helped God's people to anticipate a day when a much larger number would recognize God as King and would freely submit to Him.

Jesus, in His inaugural preaching, had announced that the Kingdom had come (see Mark 1:15; also Luke 4:14, 18, 21). Throughout His earthly ministry, Jesus continued to explain the implications of that statement, particularly to His disciples. The disciples were slow to grasp Jesus' teaching. We can partially excuse their misunderstanding. They, along with the Jews of the previous centuries, had interpreted the teaching of the prophets to mean that the end times, the Day of the Lord, would come in a single moment. Despite having the best teacher the world has ever seen, the disciples were slow to take in the fact that God had at least a two-stage plan for the coming of the Kingdom. (In Jesus, the Kingdom had come in *reality;* not until His second coming would it arrive in *totality*.)

Even after those last forty days, with Jesus continuing to explain the Kingdom to them, the disciples still asked Jesus, **Lord, are you at this time going to restore the kingdom to Israel?** (Acts 1:6). What were they saying? "If you really are the Messiah, then you have to do what we have always been told the Messiah would do: He's going to bring the end of time as we know it; He's going to put Israel back on top of the other nations. This is your chance. You have defeated death. Now finish the job."

They likely wanted Jesus to disclose His power once and for all to the whole world. It's also likely that they wanted Him to offer them positions on the King's council. During Jesus' ministry, at least James and John had sought this reward (see Mark 10:35-40). The disciples likely wanted power for themselves.

Jesus responded to the apostles' question with a classic: "Well, there's good news and bad news." The good news was that Jesus did offer them power. The bad news? What Jesus promised was not exactly that for which they were hoping: **You will receive power when the Holy Spirit comes on you** (Acts 1:8a). With these words, Jesus tried one last time to help His followers to understand the Kingdom. The Kingdom had come, although it did not bring an obvious change to Israel's political situation. The Kingdom brought a new form of life to all people from **Judea . . . to the ends of the earth** (1:8), no matter what their politics.

With the Great Commission, Luke subtly shifts the focus. Although he is still in the introductory overlap between his gospel and Acts, he turns the perspective of the reader from the past to the future (see Acts 1:8 for a summary of all that follows).

Who would receive the power of the Holy Spirit? Ordinary people— the same ones who in that very minute had misunderstood the clear teaching of the best teacher—would receive the Holy Spirit and His power. Those who receive the Holy Spirit also receive power. The two are not separate gifts. Those who possess true spiritual power are those who have received the Holy Spirit.

What would they do with that power? They would be witnesses. Those who are witnesses need not be clever or articulate. Witnesses merely describe what they have seen and heard.

Where would they be witnesses? To whom? They would be witnesses there in Judea, to people like themselves; in Samaria, to people who were quite different, and whom the Jews generally saw as unacceptable; and to the ends of the earth, to people who were far from the disciples in every way.

What faith Jesus displayed as He foresaw a small group of 120 acting as witnesses to the world! This same Jesus compared God's kingdom to a small seed which, when planted, would become a large tree (see Luke 13:18-19).

As Luke finishes the introduction to the book of Acts, he takes his readers beyond the ministry of the apostles and beyond the ends of the earth. Through his retelling of the Ascension story (another component of the overlap between Luke's gospel and Acts; see Luke 24:50-53), Luke, for a moment, offers a vision of the end of time and the world that exists outside time. Jesus left His disciples, who would soon receive the power and care of the Spirit, to return to His Father's right hand. (Evangelicals often do not pay adequate attention to the Ascension. This event proves that Jesus not only had risen again, but would not die a second time. He is Lord. He is therefore worthy of our worship.) The Ascension left the disciples feeling bereft; perhaps they still felt disappointed that the Kingdom had not come as they felt sure it would. God was gracious; He sent them angels to encourage them and to remind them that the One who had just left them in the clouds would return in the clouds to end all time. Although the end had not yet come, they should not give up. The angels invited the Eleven (and us) to believe that the kingdom of God had truly *invaded* this world. Likewise, they help us to anticipate the day when the kingdom of God will *replace* the kingdoms of this world.

The Spirit has come. Through His presence, we experience the power of God. We remain ordinary people, but we have access to extraordinary resources.

Jesus will come. This knowledge gives us perspective. The world in which we live remains a fallen world, but we can see that nothing will prevent the coming of the new world.

We chuckle at the disciples. How could they be so greedy, wanting earthly power as the King's henchmen? How could they be so impatient, wanting Jesus to put all the pieces together at once? How could they be so foolish, staring into the sky as if Jesus had merely zipped up to heaven for a coffee break with the Father before quickly returning to them?

These three questions elicit three answers. First, let any one of us who, in his or her relationship with God, has never been greedy, impatient or misunderstanding, throw the first stone. Second, the disciples had not yet received the Spirit; watch for the changes that occurred in these disciples after that great event. Third, they may not have been all that Jesus had hoped for, but they did obediently head back to Jerusalem and prepare themselves for what was coming.

2. SETTING UP SHOP 1:12-26

In his account, Luke could have moved directly from the Mount of Olives (see Acts 1:6-11) to the day of Pentecost (2:1). Had he done so, the reader would have lost nothing essential to the story. The events recorded in 1:12-26 don't appear to document any great movement forward. These paragraphs' primary event is the selection of Matthias as the replacement for Judas. But, after his elevation to the apostleship, Matthias (not to mention the rejected candidate, Joseph Barsabbas) disappears from the narrative. What is Luke's purpose in including these paragraphs? While the disciples here may not have done anything outstanding, it's hard to fault what they did, and nearly impossible to complain about the motivation behind their action.

They returned to Jerusalem . . . (1:12). No, that's not extraordinary. So they walked a few miles back to their base. Note, however, that they were doing exactly what Jesus had commanded (see 1:4).

In the city **. . . they went upstairs to the room where they were staying** (1:13a). Luke could be referring to any second-story room in the city, but the odds seem good that they returned to the same house (possibly the house of John Mark's mother; see 12:12) where they had met with Jesus on the night of His arrest, the same room where Jesus appeared to them after His resurrection. The room would have had wonderful memories for them. There, in a familiar place, it would have been easier to maintain the habits of interaction with God and each other that they had formed when Jesus was there with them.

They stayed together as a group. Waiting for the Spirit to come must have been hard enough ("How long will we have to wait? How will we know when He comes? What exactly will happen?"), even with all of the group together to encourage each other. If they had broken up, and each had returned to his own separate quarters, their patience would have worn down more quickly. "When the day of Pentecost came, they were [still] all together in one place" (2:1).

Not only did the Eleven stick together, but they recruited other faithful people—**the women and Mary the mother of Jesus, and . . . his brothers** (1:14b)—to join them. This influx added stability to the small, potentially wavering group of disciples. At the same time, the Eleven could then begin serving as witnesses, as they shared Jesus' last words with the others who had joined them. It was from the larger group that subsequent church leaders arose, such as Matthias and James, the brother of Jesus.

While waiting, **they all joined together constantly in prayer** (1:14a). They still had lots of unanswered questions. But, rather than fretting over that which they could not predict, they spoke to the One who knew the future. Contrast this consistent time in prayer with their failure in the garden of Gethsemane six weeks before. The disciples were making progress! Their openness to God enabled Him to prepare them for what was coming.

During their time of waiting, they demonstrated this desire to seek God and His plan, not only by prayer, but by reflection on Scripture. When Peter stood up to initiate the process of replacing Judas (see 1:15), he began by placing Judas's defection in the context of Old Testament Scripture. Peter continued his presentation by quoting from two psalms (Ps. 69:25; 109:8) which he felt mandated the selection of one to take Judas's place. Now, we must admit that it is difficult for us to see how Peter interpreted the verses he quoted, in their original context, to support his conclusion (**Therefore** . . . [Acts 1:21]). But this does not negate the fact that Peter was looking to Scripture for guidance. And there is, of course, the possibility that Jesus himself had pointed out these verses and had told the Eleven to find a replacement for Judas.

The fact that the larger group agreed with Peter's feeling that Judas should be replaced strongly indicates the faith of the Body in their continuing as a unit. The Eleven could have seen their gathering as one last reunion before returning to their hometowns: "Let's remember the good times. Let's help each other grieve the fact that we will never return to the glory days when Jesus was with us." Had they moved into this mindset, they would have given no thought to maintaining the full component of twelve apostles. No, they believed that they, as a group following a *living* Jesus, had a future that required preparation.

The qualifications for the new apostle? He must be one who had already been an "associate disciple," **one of the men who have been**

with us the whole time the Lord Jesus went in and out among us, from Jesus' baptism through His death, resurrection, and ascension (1:21). Why? So he could **become a witness with us of his resurrection** (1:22). At this point in time, Jesus' followers were spending their time waiting in an upper room. But they recognized that they would not stay there. They remembered Jesus' last words. They anticipated acting as His *witnesses*. Since Jesus' resurrection offered the single strongest sign of His identity as God's son, the eleven remaining apostles thought it crucial that Judas's replacement could serve with them as a witness of the Resurrection. In their prayer, they asked God to direct them to the one who would serve with in the apostolic ministry. They may have had lots of questions, but their faith was strong. God would not let them down.

Each of us, on occasion, faces times of waiting. God gives promises. We wait to see them fulfilled. Questions and doubts enter our minds. We grow impatient. The faith which these early followers of Jesus manifested during this time of waiting serves as an example to us.

One other question arising out of this passage deserves attention. Have you heard it said that today's church should follow the model of the early church? Next time you hear that sentiment, ask why our churches don't follow this particular New Testament example: After the group prayed for God's guidance, **they cast lots** in order to gain the insight they desired (1:26).[3] Today, the church elects leaders, appoints committee members or, more often, asks for volunteers, but have you ever seen people in a church meeting draw straws?

You may think this a trivial matter, but it does raise a broader issue in a consideration of the inspired church history which Luke records in Acts. In what way should today's church see actions taken by the apostolic church as *prescriptive?* Those who feel that Acts prescribes today's church policies might say, "If it's good enough for Peter and Paul, then it's good enough for us." You could do far worse than to follow their example in every instance.

An opposite perspective would say that Luke's record of the early church is merely *descriptive*. "They may have seen fit to draw straws, but that does not tell us how we should select our leaders." This sounds good, too, as long as you are speaking only of drawing straws. When William Carey, the founder of modern missions, suggested that the church of his day needed to obey the Great Commission, as recorded in Acts 1:8, people around him responded by saying in effect that Luke's portrayal of the apostles' missionary activity was only descriptive, and not prescriptive.

They saw the Great Commission as applicable only to the New Testament church, and not to churches of subsequent generations.

Should today's church follow *all* the patterns set by the early church? How do contemporary Christians know which ancient models to follow? If you have questions about any particular action of the early church, look toward the broader teaching of Scripture.[4] If the early church set a pattern, and Jesus or the apostles commanded that action, then it's best to step in line. Where you have only the example of the church, look for the motivation behind what was done. On what basis did the early church draw straws to choose Matthias? This group was earnestly seeking to discern God's choice; their prayer documents their motivation. I have attended democratic church business meetings where the elections were governed by lots of desires, but not the hope of finding *God's* person. You are safest when you look for the principles behind apostolic actions. They're not always easy to find, but do your best to find and then follow those principles.

ENDNOTES

[1] I. Howard Marshall makes this comparison in *Acts* (Grand Rapids, Michigan: Wm. B. Eerdmans Publishing Co., 1980), p. 67.

In the New Testament, Pentecost primarily refers to the event when the Holy Spirit was given to the church; this occurred on the day of Pentecost. The Greek term *Pentecost* comes from means "fiftieth" or "the fiftieth day" and is literally the fiftieth day after the end of the Passover. It is also known as the Jewish Feast of Weeks. This day is part of the Jewish observances, and was the beginning of the offering of first fruits.

[2] The Gospels include the New Testament books of Matthew, Mark, Luke, and John.

[3] Lot casting was a frequent method for choosing individuals for set tasks. See Luke 1:9.

[4] "Unless Scripture explicitly tells us we must do something, what is merely narrated or described can never function in a normative way" (Gordon Fee, *How to Read the Bible for All Its Worth* [Grand Rapids, Michigan: Zondervan Publishing House, 1982], p. 97).

2

PENTECOST

Acts 2:1-47

Without the coming of the Holy Spirit, there would be no Acts of the Apostles. The first believers might have had patience to wait in their upper room for weeks, possibly even months. But had the Holy Spirit not come upon them, in time they would have returned to their homes bewildered and disillusioned. The Holy Spirit, living in and transforming the core of believers, enabled the astounding progress of the early church.

Without the coming of the Holy Spirit, you would not be reading this book. No commentaries on the New Testament would have been written, for there would have been no New Testament without the coming of the Holy Spirit. The Holy Spirit's coming does not overshadow the history-changing coming of Jesus Christ. But it is the last and *essential* link in the chain of events we can see merging into one.

At the time they are occurring, a number of events in a series can appear quite distinct. Looking back after time has passed, an observer can see them all as one. People tend to speak of World War II as if it were a single event. However, those who lived through that devastating war can remember quite distinctly several key, individual days in that six-year period. So it is with the events surrounding the Incarnation. The first Christian Pentecost[1] finished what we see as the "Jesus event" by which God came to live with His people forever. In our minds and on our calendars we can separate Christmas, Good Friday, Easter, and Pentecost. But we should also try to see them as *one* divine plan which transformed interaction between God and His people. Pentecost is the final episode in the Jesus event.

Like the events of the first Christmas, Good Friday, and Easter, the coming of the Spirit upon God's people at the first Pentecost was a unique, unrepeatable event. Before that day, God gave His Spirit only to special individuals, for limited periods of time, for special purposes (see, for example, Exodus 31:1-5, where God told Moses of two skilled craftsmen, whom God specially filled with His Spirit for their work in the construction of the Tabernacle). Since the first Pentecost, God has freely offered His Spirit to all people for all time. The first Pentecost forever changed the history of the world.

The Old Testament prophet Isaiah looked forward to the day of Emmanuel, "God with us." With the coming of Jesus, God revealed himself to His people as He never had before. When God poured out His Holy Spirit on all people (see Acts 2:14-17), God stepped even closer to His ancient name, Emmanuel. Before Pentecost, God had interacted with people. After Pentecost, God lived in them. During Jesus' ministry, His disciples served Him. After the coming of the Spirit, Jesus' servants became the means by which Jesus served the world.[2]

Ironically, Luke, in his account of this day, passes rather quickly over the actual gift of the Spirit, devoting his attention to the reaction of the crowds and Peter's explanatory sermon. The sermon occupies the bulk of this chapter (Acts 2), neatly dividing it into three segments: before (2:1-13), during (2:14-39), and after the sermon (2:40-47).

In Luke's account, the outpouring of the Spirit and the immediate response of the people set the stage for the sermon. In his preaching, Peter explained the strange signs the people saw. He set these signs in the context of the broader "Jesus event." He concluded by calling his hearers to receive God's new gift and to join in the celebration. God's new party grew quite large; its rich celebration continues indefinitely.

What are the questions Luke answers with the material he includes in this chapter? There are several such questions. How did God empower His people for their mission? How did this empowerment transform the small group of believers? How did outsiders become part of God's mission? How did the enlarged group relate to itself and to others around it? Consider the answers to these questions as you study Acts 2.

1. BEFORE THE SERMON 2:1-13

When the day of Pentecost came, they were all together in one place (Acts 2:1). Pentecost was one of the ancient Jewish harvest festivals. Over time, the Jews also chose to commemorate at Pentecost God's giving of the Law to Moses at Mount Sinai.[3] Even though God's gift of the Law helped His people to know Him better, His gift of the Spirit was a far greater act of revelation. This gift led to an immediate harvest of three thousand new believers (see Acts 2:41).

Notice God's timing of His gift of the Spirit. The Pentecost celebration took place fifty (or "five tens of") days after Passover, the time of Christ's death and resurrection (the *pent-* in *Pentecost* represents "five," as in *pentagon*), and was a significant Jewish festival. Acts 1:3 tells us that Jesus was with His disciples after Passover for approximately forty days, at which time He ascended (see 1:4-11). This tells us that the group of 120 believers (see 1:15) waited together for roughly ten more days before anything happened. They likely continued to pray and reflect on the words of Jesus and the Old Testament Scriptures. They didn't know it at the time, but God had a reason to keep them waiting. At Pentecost, another significant Jewish festival, thousands of Jews from around the world would be visiting their holy city. At that time, with crowds there to observe, God set off fireworks that caught everyone's attention.

First, God sent the sound **of a violent wind** (2:2). In both Hebrew and Greek, the original languages behind the Old and New Testaments (respectively), a single word translates the concepts of "breath," "wind," and "spirit." At times, scholars are uncertain as to which English word they should use to translate this Hebrew or Greek word. We read in Genesis that at the creation of Adam, ". . . God . . . breathed into his nostrils the breath [or spirit] of life . . ." (Gen. 2:7). Ezekiel's vision of dry bones uses the Hebrew word several times in a manner that demonstrates how wind, breath, and God's Spirit are related concepts (see Ezekiel 37:1-14). Thus, the wind often served as a symbol for the Holy Spirit. Jesus, for example, used this pun to help Nicodemus understand the new birth: "The wind blows wherever it pleases. . . . So it is with everyone born of the Spirit" (John 3:8).

Second, if the disciples were puzzled over what the **wind** meant (Acts 2:2), God gave them the symbol of **fire** to convince them that He was acting in a miraculous way (2:3). Reflecting back on the experience, the apostles might have remembered God's other uses of fire to represent His presence. God used "a smoking firepot" to seal the covenant with Abraham (Gen. 15:17).[4] God appeared to Moses in a burning bush (see Exodus 3:2). And because of the association between Pentecost and the giving of the Law, the apostles certainly would have remembered God's descending on Mount Sinai "in fire" (Exod. 19:18). Perhaps God intended the **violent wind** to represent His power, while the **fire** manifested His purity (Acts 2:2-3). Both symbols also convey God's mystery and awesomeness.

But what could speaking **in other tongues** mean (2:4)? The God of power and purity is the same God who wishes to communicate himself to people. He wishes that they not only recognize His power and purity, but also experience these within themselves. Many scholars feel that the gift of tongues mentioned in 1 Corinthians 12 may have been an ecstatic prayer language. On Pentecost, however, the supernatural gift of tongues enabled the 120 believers to speak in languages readily understood by pilgrims present in Jerusalem for the festival.

Was this gift of languages necessary? Perhaps Aramaic or Greek would have done the job just as well, but God, at least at first, chose to let the crowds hear His word in the languages they spoke most frequently.

The miracle that God performed here raises an interesting question. Readers normally assume that God enabled the 120 disciples to *speak* in languages they did not know. The text leaves open the possibility that Peter and the others spoke in a single language, such as Aramaic. The miracle may have come in the hearing, and not in the speaking. Perhaps God enabled the crowds to *hear* the proclamation in their own languages. We can't quite be sure.

Before leaving the symbols behind, it is helpful to note the list of people who first experienced the symbols—wind and fire—and the Spirit they represented. Luke mentions that **they were all together** (Acts 2:1). Who were **they?** There's no reason to doubt that this was the full group of one hundred and twenty mentioned in 1:15. This included the eleven original apostles, as well as Matthias, "the women and Mary the mother of Jesus, and . . . [Jesus'] brothers" (1:14).

God was gracious to give himself to so many whom some might have considered undeserving. The Eleven had deserted Jesus at the time of His great need. His brothers had rejected Him as Messiah during the time of His ministry. The women? While Jewish society treated women better than most of the surrounding cultures, the Jews generally saw women as second-class citizens. Yet, Jesus poured the Spirit out upon **all of them** (2:4). **Tongues of fire** rested **on each of them** (2:3). God used each person there as His witness.

God transformed His people. Peter, who had refused to admit his "Jesus connection" to a servant girl (see Luke 22:56-57), on this day proclaimed it to thousands. The apostles, who six weeks before had hidden behind the locked doors of the Upper Room, found they could not restrain themselves from bursting out of that room in praise to God. Ten days before, these apostles had been confused about when the Kingdom was coming; now they fervently proclaimed that it had arrived.

In God's planning, visitors from every direction were present to experience the wonders and hear the Word. **God-fearing Jews** (2:5) from all three of the world's then-known continents—Africa, Asia, and Europe (see 2:9-11)—had crowded into Jerusalem for the festival. Some were likely visiting their ancient holy site for the first time. They probably felt awe as they entered the city whose heritage went back to King David. They participated in Temple worship, observing traditions going beyond David to Moses himself. They might have felt they had entered another world, one caught in timelessness. Imagine the shock of being brought back to the present, where they heard country folk from Galilee speaking not only the Latin of Rome or the Greek commonly spoken across the Empire, but *all* their hometown dialects! The foreigners had come to offer their sacrifices, to remember what God had done in the past. But this group of 120 men and women was proclaiming that God was doing something altogether new.

Luke describes the observers' responses. They experienced **bewilderment,** and were **amazed and perplexed** (2:6-7, 12). Some were cynical, calling the believers drunk (see 2:13). Others expressed more serious interest: **What does this mean?** (2:12).

God had empowered and transformed His people. He now gave Peter a large congregation, ready for the explanation God wanted to give. God wished not only to help the people understand His new gift, but also to offer them a chance to experience this Spirit for themselves.

2. THE FIRST CHRISTIAN SERMON 2:14-40

Had he chosen to, Luke could have written a third-person theological interpretation of what happened on the day of Pentecost. He chose, however, to continue in the pattern of retelling what happened, allowing the narrative to speak for itself. As God gave Peter the first opportunity to proclaim the coming of the Spirit, Luke's writing permits Peter to continue preaching that good news to his hearers centuries later.

An interpretive question arises here and several times in Acts. To what degree do Luke's words reproduce the actual words of the sermons included in his record? On one hand, it was quite common for ancient, secular historians to invent speeches they thought fit the occasion and speaker. Contemporary historical fiction follows this model. On the other hand, some might think a doctrine of biblical inerrancy might require an accurate word-for-word transcription of the sermons. The truth likely falls somewhere between these two extremes.

It is extremely doubtful that Luke was present at the first Pentecost. But the disciples who heard the sermon likely remembered it. Ancient people developed their memories far more than we do today. Luke could have consulted those present at the first Pentecost and the occasions of other speeches he included in his writing. He may have edited the material given to him. As recorded in Acts, the longest address there can be read in eight minutes.[5] Certainly, many of these sermons originally exceeded that length. At the same time, there is evidence that Luke remained faithful to the original speakers in his writing of Acts. For example, the Peter sermons include common Jewish phrases that appear nowhere in the Paul sermons.[6]

A quick analysis of Peter's sermon as a whole (see Acts 2:14-40) helps us to see how each part fits into the big picture. While it's often impossible to place biblical sermons into a contemporary framework of introduction-body-conclusion, Peter's Pentecost sermon seems to approach this pattern. His introduction (2:14-21) tied the extraordinary events of that day to an Old Testament prophecy. The last sentence of the introduction, the final words he quoted from Joel, served as the focal point (the text) for the sermon as a whole. Within the body of the sermon (2:22-35), he developed that text, leading to his conclusion (2:36). The response of the crowd brought out Peter's appeal and application (2:37-40).

His sermon introduction did not need to catch anyone's attention; the crowd's surprise at hearing their home languages already had everyone waiting for an explanation. Peter moved to answer the question they all had on their minds: "What's going on?" (2:12). A summary of Peter's answer reminds us of a subsequent line from the Apostle Paul: "We are not drunk with wine; we are filled with God's Spirit" (see Acts 2:15-17; also Ephesians 5:18). Peter's response shows how much he had changed. He now grasped that the "Kingdom days" had come. On the day of Jesus' ascension just ten days before, Peter and the other disciples still lived in a muddle. Because God's kingdom had not come in the way they expected (see Acts 1:7), they had not comprehended its coming at all. But, having received the Spirit, Peter proclaimed with certainty to all of Jerusalem that the great days which the Old Testament predicted had come!

Had Peter taken time that morning to evaluate and modify all his theological expectations? No, but perhaps all of Jesus' explanations of the Old Testament had finally clicked into place. More importantly, the Spirit of Jesus now lived within Peter and the others, giving them supernatural insight.

In his sermon introduction, Peter quoted Joel at length (see Joel 2:28-32). What were the key points, and how did they relate to Peter's day?

First, God had promised to **pour out [his] Spirit** (Acts 2:17; Joel 2:28). While God had given the Spirit to people in the past, He seemed to limit this gift to certain periods of time. The people of God eagerly hoped for the day when God would freely give the Spirit to remain with the people forever.

Second, God had promised **to pour out [his] Spirit** *on all people* (Acts 2:17; Joel 2:28, my emphasis)—men and women, young and old. No longer did the Father share His Spirit with only special individuals: the leaders who needed supernatural help for their unique tasks. Through Joel, God had promised that the day would come when women, as well as men, and young, as well as old—all God's people—would experience Him.

Third, not only would all sense God's presence within them, but all would be able to minister—**prophesy** (Acts 2:17-18; Joel 2:28)— powerfully on His behalf. The fulfillment of that prophecy no one present could dispute.

Fourth, special signs—**wonders** (Acts 2:19; Joel 2:30)—would accompany God's activity. While the disciples did not, on Pentecost, see all that Joel had described (for example, the sun's going dark and the moon's turning to blood; Joel 2:31), the signs everyone had seen proclaimed that the Day of the Lord had come in reality, if not in totality. God had come to live among and within His people!

Fifth, all who turn to God can join the party! The last words Peter took from the Joel passage served as his Scripture text for his sermon: **Everyone who calls on the name of the Lord will be saved** (Acts 2:21; Joel 2:32a). In other words, "All that we have experienced today, God offers to each of you, too."

Having tied the amazing wonders of the day to the gift of the Spirit, Peter then spoke of the givers: the Father and the Son. As Peter moved into the body of his sermon, what was his primary goal? He wished to identify Jesus Christ as the **Lord** upon whom they should call, hoping that the Spirit would inspire Peter's hearers to call on the Lord Jesus.

Peter faced a major obstacle to the accomplishment of this goal: the theology of his audience. The people before him were Jews who firmly held to the idea that there was only one Lord: Yahweh, the Lord God of Abraham, Isaac, and Jacob; the God who also had redeemed their forefathers and brought them safely from Egypt to the Promised Land. (The Jews were afraid they might take God's name in vain. To prevent this, they never said God's name. Whenever they read the Old Testament, they refused to pronounce God's revealed name, "Yahweh."

In such situations, the word "Lord" served as the most frequent substitute. When, in English versions of the Old Testament, you see the word "LORD" with a capital *L* and "ord" in small capitals, it indicates that in the original text stood the name "Yahweh." See, for example, Psalm 110:1, a verse Peter quoted in this sermon [Acts 2:34b-35]. Thus, *God* and *Lord,* for the Jews, came to be synonyms.) Peter found himself caught. He could not deny the Lord God of the Old Testament without alienating his audience and denying the truth. Yet, how could he help the Jews to see that the God of their nation had revealed himself in **Jesus of Nazareth** (Acts 2:22)?

If Peter had to overcome the hurdle of their theology, he saw no better tool than that same theology. The Jews saw the writings of the Old Testament as God's Word. Peter chose to argue his case from the life and writings of King David, included in the Old Testament which his hearers revered.

How and when did Peter prepare this sermon? He certainly received much of his "ammunition" from Jesus himself, who had, after His resurrection, helped His followers relate the Old Testament prophecies to Him. Or the Spirit himself likely inspired Peter's words. (Luke twice includes in his gospel the assurance from Jesus that, in times of stress, words would be given to His followers as God's Spirit spoke through them [see Luke 12:11-12; 21:15]).

Peter referred to three Old Testament passages relating to David, seeking to show that all three referred to one person, Jesus the Lord. First, Peter quoted Psalm 16:8-11 (see Acts 2:25-28). These verses refer to one who would survive death. Peter reminded everyone that David had not survived death and, therefore, must have been speaking of another person. Next, Peter mentioned a promise God gave to David, that God would place on His throne one of David's descendants (see Acts 2:30; 2 Samuel 7:8a, 11b-16). The hearers would have recognized the allusion to the time when God promised to "raise up [David's] offspring" and to "establish the throne of his kingdom forever" (2 Sam. 7:12-13). Last, Peter quoted the opening lines of Psalm 110, where David spoke of **the Lord** speaking to His **Lord** (Acts 2:34; see also Psalm 110:1). The Jews felt quite sure that Psalm 110 was a prophecy referring to the Messiah; Jesus had used this belief in His attempts to help them recognize Him (see Luke 20:41-44).

Put the three passages together. David spoke of one who would survive death. David knew one of his offspring would inherit an eternal throne. David spoke of the Messiah as his Lord.

If David, a respected leader from the past, could go so far as to call the Messiah "Lord," then Peter could argue that perhaps it would not be blasphemy for him to follow David's example. Peter potentially moved his hearers one significant step forward. He helped them to see that there could be another Lord, one apart from the Lord Yahweh.

He then needed to help them see that this Lord was Jesus. Once again, there was a major barrier to overcome. The Jews took quite literally the Old Testament passage which said that anyone hanged on a tree—that is, crucified—was considered cursed by God (see Deuteronomy 21:23; also Galatians 3:13). Obviously, no one under such a curse could be the Messiah; therefore, Jesus could not be considered a candidate.

A problem to Peter? No, for Peter included in his argument what he and other believers had seen. **Jesus** had been **accredited by God . . . by miracles, wonders and signs** (Acts 2:22). Although Jesus had been **handed over . . . to death. . . . God raised him from the dead. . . . to life, and we are all witnesses of the fact** (2:23-24, 32). Under ordinary circumstances, a crucified man might be cursed by God, but in Jesus' case, God rendered that curse worthless by raising Jesus from death to life.

Jesus' resurrection showed Him as the one who defeated death. He is, therefore, the one to whom David referred in Psalm 16, and is to be seen as the eternal king of 2 Samuel 7. **Therefore,** Peter concluded, **let all Israel be assured of this: God has made this Jesus, whom you crucified, both Lord and Christ** (Acts 2:36). (It is no coincidence that the statement "Jesus is Lord" later became an important credal statement of the church [see 1 Corinthians 12:3].)

It appears that the Holy Spirit then took over. Great numbers of people realized for the first time that Jesus was the one upon whom they should call for salvation. They began to see that Jesus, whom they had killed, was God's anointed Messiah, to be worshiped on the same level as the Lord God of Israel. As their earlier questions had given Peter a place to begin preaching, their subsequent questions led him to the sermon's climax. **Cut to the heart,** they asked, **"Brothers, what shall we do?"** (Acts 2:37). In other words, "How do we call on the name of Jesus?"

Before looking at Peter's answer to their question, it is helpful to observe that while Peter began and finished his sermon with reference to the Holy Spirit (see 2:17, 38), the body of his sermon dealt not with the Spirit or His manifestations, but with Jesus, the Lord. Peter pointed out that the Holy Spirit was the cause of the astounding signs the people had

45

seen and heard. He encouraged them to open themselves to God so they might **receive the gift of the Holy Spirit** (2:38). Yet, the core of Peter's sermon focused on Jesus. The Holy Spirit had come as God to live with His people, and yet, without the work of Jesus, the Holy Spirit could not have come.

We fall into heresy if we fail to see the Holy Spirit as an essential part of the eternal Trinity. But we must ensure that we do not seek the Holy Spirit in and of himself. We receive the gift of the Spirit when we enter into a proper relationship with God through His Son, Jesus.

Peter sought to bring his hearers into a true understanding of who Jesus was, in order that they might submit to Jesus as Lord. Today, we or others around us may not struggle with the same barrier as the Jews in ancient Jerusalem. We may face no mental blocks to seeing Jesus as God's equal. Other factors, however, may block our submission to Jesus as Lord. Robert Munger provides a helpful picture.[7] He portrays our lives as the houses we own. In order for Jesus truly to be Lord of our lives, we not only must invite Him into the house, but must give Him the keys to the front door and invite Him to clean out every corner, rearranging all the furniture as He wishes. Only when our houses become His can we truly call Him "Lord."

Peter's sermon also introduces a principle for our interaction with nonbelievers. As we survey the sermons of Acts, we see how each witness tailored his presentation for his hearers. Peter went straight to the questions that were on the minds of the people in front of him (for example, "How do these people know my language?" or "What is happening here?"). With the help of the Spirit, Peter knew that in order to present the gospel effectively he needed to understand the previous thoughts and emotions of his hearers, so as to help them respond. He couldn't change the gospel, but he knew that the Jews would find it difficult to see Jesus as Lord. Peter squarely faced that hurdle, and then used their belief system as a tool to help them climb over the barrier to belief.

3. AFTER THE SERMON 2:41-47

What were the further gifts God gave to the crowd that day? The rest of Acts 2 details several such gifts. In closing the account of Pentecost, Luke gives his broadest overview of first-century church life. He foreshadows later passages in the book where he will give greater attention to some of the gifts God gave to the church then and still gives to the church today.

- Repentance (Acts 2:38)—Peter invited people to **repent.** The Jerusalem church leaders later suggested that this ability to turn around and turn toward God, in life and action, was a gift from God (see 11:18).
- Baptism (Acts 2:38)—Jesus himself had mandated being **baptized,** a physical action which graphically demonstrates God's ability to wash a person on the inside (see Matthew 28:19).
- Forgiveness (Acts 2:38)—Through **the forgiveness of . . . sins,** God wipes away all guilt from the past.
- The Holy Spirit (Acts 2:38)—God gave himself to His people through **the gift of the Holy Spirit,** the one gift which enabled both the reception of all other gifts and the fulfillment of all God's commands.
- Salvation (Acts 2:40)—It sounds as if Peter asked the people to save themselves. However, in the original language, Peter's words, **Save yourselves . . . ,** were really asking the people to allow themselves to be saved or rescued from all that had kept them away from God.
- Teaching (Acts 2:42)—Peter had laid out enough for his hearers to believe in Christ. After making that decision, they were given much more **teaching** by the apostles about who Jesus was, what He offered, and what He asked of them. Jesus had instructed His disciples to teach new believers "everything [He had] commanded" (Matt. 28:20).
- Fellowship (Acts 2:42, 44-47)—God gave the new believers each other. True fellowship is so much more than having coffee and cookies together; it is life together, even at personal sacrifice. The first believers gave their time, their possessions, their money—themselves, their **fellowship**—to each other.
- Breaking of bread (Acts 2:42, 46)—This could refer to the sharing of the Lord's Supper, the symbolic meal commanded by the Lord the night before His death, or sharing food at daily meals, or both. One interesting interpretation of **the breaking of bread** suggests that at every meal the early Christians remembered Jesus' death. (We might wish that Luke had given a fuller description of the church's practice of the Lord's Supper. This is the only allusion to this sacrament in the book of Acts. Luke might have prevented much church controversy had he given us more information.)
- Prayer (Acts 2:42)—Acts 3:1 describes Peter and John as being on the way "to the temple at the time of prayer." Together with each other and, at least for a while, with their non-Christian Jewish friends, the first Christians continued in **prayer.**

- Ongoing miracles (Acts 2:43)—Just as "Jesus . . . was a man accredited by God . . . by miracles, wonders and signs" (2:22), the Spirit gave credibility to the apostles by their **wonders and miraculous signs.**
- Worship (Acts 2:47)—These people, so blessed by God, continued **praising** Him for His goodness to them.
- Witness (Acts 2:43, 47)—Three thousand new believers had entered the Christian community on Pentecost. As time went on, **the Lord added to their number daily those who were being saved.** The 120 undoubtedly continued their witness, but God gave that gift to all who had believed and received His Spirit. God engineered the outpouring of His Spirit on Pentecost, not only for the benefit of those who would be there, but for all who would hear in the future. The new believers from the three continents took the good news of Jesus home with them. Fortunately, the new life the Christians experienced was "for all whom the Lord . . . God" called to himself, even we who were yet unborn (2:39).

Luke highlights that, from the beginning, the early Christians spoke and acted as they did because they served Jesus as their Lord. When Jerusalem or Rome later saw this as a problem, conflict came. Under the direction and power of the Spirit, the believers could not turn back to their old ways. But the Christians' lifestyle did not subvert any true authority. The principles under which the early Christian community lived serve as a model for any nation.   .

ENDNOTES

[1]In the New Testament, Pentecost primarily refers to the event when the Holy Spirit was given to the church; this occurred on the day of Pentecost. The Greek term *Pentecost* comes from means "fiftieth" or "the fiftieth day" and is literally the fiftieth day after the end of the Passover. It is also known as the Jewish Feast of Weeks. This day is part of the Jewish observances, and was the beginning of the offering of first fruits.

[2]G. Campbell Morgan, *The Acts of the Apostles* (New York: Revell, 1924), p. 32.

[3]Law refers to either the Levitical Code (all God's rules and regulations), the Ten Commandments, or the Pentateuch (the first five books of the Old Testament: Genesis, Exodus, Leviticus, Numbers, and Deuteronomy); it is often capitalized when it means the Pentateuch or the Ten Commandments.

[4]A covenant is a solemn promise made binding by a pledge or vow, which may be either a verbal formula or a symbolic action. Covenant often referred to a legal obligation in ancient times. In Old Testament terms, the word was often used in describing the relationship between God and His chosen people, in which

their sacrifices of blood afforded them His atonement for sin, and in which their fulfillment of a promise to live in obedience to God was rewarded by His blessings. In New Testament terms, this relationship (the new covenant) was now made possible on a personal basis through Jesus Christ and His sacrifice of His own blood.

[5]Floyd Filson, *A New Testament History* (Philadelphia: The Westminster Press, 1969), p. 171.

[6]William Barclay, *Great Themes of the New Testament* (Philadelphia: The Westminster Press, 1979), p. 62.

[7]Robert Munger, *My Heart—Christ's Home* (Downers Grove, Illinois: InterVarsity Press, 1954).

PETER AND JOHN HEAL A MAN

Acts 3:1–4:31

"Many wonders and miraculous signs were done by the apostles" (Acts 2:43b). As Luke continues his narrative history of the early church, he gives one of these apostolic miracles special attention (see 3:1-10). But before we look at this narrative, we need to recognize a special feature in Luke's writing.

Luke appears to have painted the events of Acts 2 and Acts 3–4 with the same brush. Notice the lengthy list of similarities.

PENTECOST[1] Acts 2	HEALING OF LAME MAN Acts 3–4	SIMILARITY
"Wind," "fire," "other tongues"/languages (2:2-4)	The healing (3:2-8)	Sign(s) from God
"Utterly amazed" (2:7)	**Wonder and amazement. . . . astonished . . . surprise . . .** (3:10-12)	Amazement of crowds
". . . let me explain. . . . These men are not drunk . . ." (2:15)	**Why do you stare at us as if . . . we had made this man walk?** (3:12b)	Peter began his sermon, referring to the sign and its misinterpretation.
"You . . . put him to death . . ." (2:23b)	**You killed the author of life . . .** (3:15)	Peter cited them for the death of Jesus.
"God raised him . . ." (2:24)	**. . . God raised him . . .** (3:15)	Peter declared that God resurrected Jesus from the dead.

continued

PENTECOST Acts 2	HEALING OF LAME MAN Acts 3–4	SIMILARITY
"We are all witnesses . . ." (2:32b)	**We are witnesses of this** (3:15b)	Peter testified that he and the other disciples were eyewitnesses of the resurrection of Christ.
References to David and his psalms (2:25-31, 34-35)	**. . . God fulfilled what he had foretold . . .** (3:18; see also 3:22, 25)	Peter interpreted these events as the fulfillment of prophecy.
". . . Repent . . ." (2:38)	**Repent . . .** (3:19)	Peter called the crowds to repent.
". . . for the forgiveness of your sins" (2:38a)	**. . . so that your sins may be wiped out . . .** (3:19)	Peter gave the reason for repentance: so that God would cancel their sin.
". . . about three thousand were added . . ." (2:41)	**. . . the number of men grew to about five thousand** (4:4)	Many responded positively.
"wonders and miraculous signs" (2:43)	**. . . miraculous signs and wonders . . .** (4:30)	References to signs and wonders are made.
"They devoted themselves to the apostles' teaching" (2:42a).	". . . the apostles continued to testify to the resurrection . . ." (4:33)	The apostles followed up and continued teaching.
"Selling their possessions and goods, they gave . . ." (2:45)	". . . they shared everything they had" (4:32).	The disciples—new and old—shared their possessions to meet the needs of others.

   Why did Luke paint two pictures that appear so similar? What was he trying to accomplish? What truths was he underlining?

   First would be the fact that *God was in control*. In both situations, God engineered miracles that were undoubtedly beyond the apostles' powers.

   Second, while in both situations the signs had grabbed the people's attention, Peter did not focus his preaching on the signs, but rather on Jesus. In both sermons, Peter focused on the *crucial facts of Jesus' death and resurrection*. Peter called his hearers not to glory in signs, but to repent and turn to God.

Third, Luke was showing the *courage of the apostles*. In both of Peter's sermons, the finger of guilt for Jesus' death was pointed at the Jews. But Peter did not accuse them of merely killing an innocent Galilean prophet; he said they had **disowned the Holy and Righteous One. . . . the author of life . . .** (3:14-15). In doing so, Peter risked his own life as well.

The events of Acts 2 and Acts 3–4 offer many similarities, but these two chapters do not end on the same note. Where the Pentecost sermon produced "favor" among "all the people" (2:47), this second sermon **disturbed** the Jewish leaders (4:2) and led to the jailing of Peter and John. We must be careful not to antagonize nonbelievers without good cause. At the same time, we need to hear the words of our Master: Beware "when all men speak well of you" (Luke 6:26).

1. LEAP, YE LAME, FOR JOY[2] 3:1-10

Luke may have chosen to include in his gospel account the miracle of the lame man's healing because of its spectacular nature. No one could doubt its authenticity. The man Peter helped up had never walked; he'd been **crippled from birth** (Acts 3:2), a period of over forty years. Also, his face would have been familiar to most of Jerusalem's population, since he was **put every day** outside **the temple gate called Beautiful** (3:2; see also 3:10; 4:16).[3]

Luke likely chose this incident because it was the catalyst to significant events which followed on that day and the next. As the miracle of languages had attracted a crowd on Pentecost, so this miracle of healing astonished those in the Temple that day and gave Peter another opportunity to proclaim Jesus to crowds of curious listeners.

In writing chapters 3 and 4 (the account of the crippled man's healing and its aftermath), Luke follows a story model established in chapter 2. In writing the first ten verses of chapter 3 (the healing account, narrowly speaking), Luke reverts to a pattern he used several times in writing his gospel. For example, the apostles' healing of the lame man in Acts 3 parallels Jesus' healing of a blind man (see Luke 18:35-43). In both accounts, a physically impaired beggar asks for help from those passing by, which they give. God's servants remove the beggar's impairment, and the beggar follows them, praising God. The miracle astonishes other witnesses, who join in worship. Luke surely saw the similarities.

It is equally certain that Peter and John, even as they were interacting with the lame man, were remembering their Master in similar situations.

How else would they have been able to exercise the faith required to offer healing? Peter and John sensed that the power which Jesus had displayed had come to live in them. Notice the primary difference, however, between the two accounts. Jesus manifested His own divine power. Peter and John, both during and after the encounter with the lame man, clearly stated that the healing power which had passed through them had its source in God.

Today, we who read the miracles of the Gospels[4] and Acts often wonder why we don't see more such miracles in our time. Such a question leads to several possible answers. God may choose to perform fewer miracles now than in the New Testament era; God may have had special reasons which required greater frequency of miracles at critical points in biblical history. Perhaps the church today is responsible; we might not be asking or believing for miracles as God's previous servants did. Or maybe the church today overestimates the frequency of first-century miracles, or underestimates the frequency of miracles in our time. There might be truth in all of these answers.

It is possible that, during the period of the incarnation and establishment of the church, God strengthened His servants with miracle power as a special sign of the new Kingdom which had come (see Matthew 11:4-6; Luke 10:9). It is likely that, in our Western overdependence on forces we can see, we don't truly believe that God can answer our prayers for miracles. This potential lack of faith is not limited to today's Christians; the early church in Jerusalem apparently did not believe that God could miraculously release Peter from prison (see Acts 12:14-16). Do we overestimate the number of miracles during the first century? Luke chose to include many accounts of miraculous signs, but the Jerusalem church faced its routine and its tragic days as well. Miracles today? We, too, face routine days and tragic days, but those days do not negate the miracles we have seen. Today's church lives in the Kingdom just as Peter and John did. We, too, can believe God for miraculous healings.

We should continue to bring our needs before God, as Jesus commanded us. We all are tempted to grumble about miracles which God does not perform. But, even on the days when God performed great miracles for the early church, its leaders focused not on the signs, but on the God behind the signs. We can learn from these early believers.

2. ALL THE PROPHETS PREDICTED JESUS 3:11-26

Peter's first sermon tied Jesus to two Old Testament figures: Joel and David. In this second recorded sermon, Peter broadened his Old Testament base. He still focused on Jesus, by whose power the lame man had been healed (see Acts 3:13-16), but worked to show how **all the prophets** (3:18, 24; see also 3:21) had looked forward to Jesus and the events which were occurring in Jerusalem during the decade in which Jesus ministered. Peter told his hearers that they, in Jesus' death and resurrection, and in the gift of the Holy Spirit, were witnessing the events their fathers had longed to see.

Look at the list of Old Testament figures Peter included in this brief, apparently unfinished sermon (see 4:1). To forestall any possibility that some might think he was proclaiming a new god in opposition to the God of ancient Israel, Peter clearly placed Jesus in the line of **Abraham, Isaac and Jacob** (3:13), the fathers of the twelve tribes of Israel. Peter singled out Abraham, noting God's promise that **through [Abraham's] offspring all peoples on earth will be blessed** (3:25). What offspring? Peter saw Jesus as Abraham's descendent who would touch the whole world.

If that weren't enough, Jesus was the one whom Moses—who led the Israelite tribes out of captivity in Egypt—predicted as his successor. Samuel, who helped establish the monarchy of Israel and who was the first of the Old Testament prophets, was brought in as a witness to Jesus. In case there could be any doubt remaining, Peter called on the whole company of God's Old Testament spokesmen: **All the prophets . . . , as many as have spoken, have foretold these days** (3:24).

Could all of these past leaders somehow have been misguided? Peter ruled out that possibility, too! It was **the *God* of Abraham, Isaac and Jacob** who **glorified . . . Jesus** (3:13, my emphasis). *God* wanted to fulfill **what he had foretold through all the prophets** (3:18). Peter had become convinced that to deny Jesus was to deny God (see 3:23). The Jews could no longer rest in their bloodline, for they had **disowned** Jesus, handing **him over to be killed** (3:13). Apart from a change in heart, there was no hope. If they would **repent . . . and turn to God,** their tragic **sins** would **be wiped out** (3:19).

How do we relate to the Old Testament and its God? For first-century Jews (and Christians), the Old Testament *was* the Bible. Thus, Peter could appeal to the Old Testament's history as evidence for the lordship of Jesus. Peter attempted to convince the Jews that Jesus was a teammate to the God of the Old Testament.

Today, our struggle is precisely the opposite. For some of us who have come to accept Jesus as Lord on bases other than Old Testament prophecy, these first two-thirds of the Bible cause a problem. Sometimes we can't quite see how the God of Israel is the same God who sent Jesus. In one era, He commanded the slaughter of all the Amalekites; in another era, He instructed His followers to love their enemies. Some have wondered if God "got saved" sometime during the period between the Testaments. What do we do with such questions?

There are no foolproof answers. It might be helpful to realize that we have company in our misery. As early as the second century, a Christian heretic named Marcion decided that Jesus had come from the "true" God, and not the "fallen" God of the Old Testament. (Marcion ruled Acts out of his canon [his list of inspired books]; perhaps it too clearly tied the two Testaments together.) But Peter's sermon (and the entire New Testament) rules out that easy answer. Jesus is God's servant (see Acts 3:13, 26); we cannot place the two on opposite sides of the playing field. Although Jesus surpassed all the prophets, fulfilling their words, He followed in an ancient line of people who also belonged to God. The prophets are **[God's] holy prophets** (3:21).

All of those prophets looked forward to the day when God would fulfill **what he had foretold through** them (3:18). Even now, after the coming of Jesus, the world still must wait **until the time comes for God to restore everything** (3:21). During these periods before the final restoration, the world remains fallen. All of God's interaction with a fallen world (the Amalekites of the Old Testament, for example) is not easy to understand. We may wonder if even God sometimes struggles with knowing how best to interact with His fallen world. It's probably best to admit that there are some questions we cannot yet answer.

What about the Old Testament? The God of the New Testament was active then. We cut ourselves off from so much that helps us to know Him better if we limit our study to the last one-third of the Bible.

3. TWO DIFFERENT RESPONSES 4:1-7

On the day he healed the lame man, Peter preached one sermon. Two different groups heard what he said. One group listened and responded positively. Another group may have heard, but they appear not to have listened.

Who were those who truly listened? **Many,** at least another two thousand, **who heard the message believed** (Acts 4:4). The Holy Spirit worked in their lives, enabling them to "repent . . . and turn to God" (3:19). They did so, despite the opposition of that "deaf" group—those with political and religious power.

This spiritually deaf group *heard* what Peter said. They recognized that Peter was proclaiming in Jesus the resurrection of the dead. But they did not truly *listen.* When they brought Peter and John before them, they asked a question that Peter had clearly answered in his sermon: **By what power or what name did you do this** [heal the lame man] (4:7)? If they had been listening to Peter's sermon, they would have heard him give that information: "It is Jesus' name . . . that has given this complete healing . . ." (3:16).

Why did this group play dumb? Because they had already rejected Jesus. Even if they had killed Jesus "in ignorance" (3:17), accepting Peter's message would have involved admitting that Jesus had been right and they had been wrong in dismissing His claims. Such humility does not come easily.

Peter preached only one message. The same Holy Spirit sought to work in the lives of all the hearers. One group hung onto its self-righteous ideas and power; the other group, however, entered God's kingdom. "People whose hearts are hungry for God are wiser than those whose lives are devoted to religion."[5]

What other factors led the religious leaders away from receiving Peter's message? They did not believe in *any* resurrection from the dead (see Luke 20:27; Acts 23:8). Thus, the resurrection of Jesus, a central theme of Peter's sermon, would have pushed their theological hot buttons.

But, on this day, politics may have weighed more than theology. These religious leaders were Sadducees; the leading Sadducees formed the core of the Sanhedrin, the Jewish body to which the Romans gave limited power of government over Judea. The Sanhedrin could retain its power only as long as it served the Romans by maintaining peace. In Palestine, this was not an easy job. The Jews were living in a window of peace between a period of bloody uprisings ending about 30 B.C., and a rebellion which led to the Roman destruction of Jerusalem in A.D. 70. The Sanhedrin sought to quell any movement of the people that might develop into a threat to the status quo.

This Jewish hierarchy had seen Jesus and His followers as a particular threat to their power and the stability of the nation. (To give Caiaphas, the high priest, the benefit of the doubt, he was speaking what he thought best for all Jews when he said, ". . . It is better . . . that one man die . . . than that the whole nation perish" [John 11:50].) But the Sadducees came to see that although they had killed Jesus, His movement refused to die! They struggled with how to handle His unschooled disciples who spoke with such fervor, and were provoking a large response (thousands of people) within the city.

So the Sadducees pretended they had not heard Peter preach. They invited Peter and John to speak again, hoping they would incriminate themselves and give the Sanhedrin grounds to do away with them, too. Caiaphas, still present (see Acts 4:6), likely had not changed his overall strategy. He would, if necessary, sacrifice two men for the long-term security of the Sanhedrin and the nation.

No matter how powerfully Christians present the gospel, and no matter how active the Holy Spirit may be, there will always be those who reject the truth. Peter and John did not take the Sanhedrin's negative response as a sign that they were wrong. Jesus had predicted that those who persecuted Him would mistreat His followers, too (see John 15:19-20). Peter and John no longer ran from danger; they now accepted it as part of their calling.

4. THE FIRST ROUND GOES TO THE CHRISTIANS 4:8-22

It is not easy for us, reading Luke's account two thousand years later, to feel what Peter and John must have felt as they were ushered into a packed room the morning after the healing. Luke paints the picture quite solidly. In one corner were "the rulers, elders and teachers of the law.[6] . . . the high priest . . . and the other men of the high priest's family" (Acts 4:5-6). In the other corner were two **unschooled, ordinary men** (4:13).

We have read the end of the story. We know that David once again stymied Goliath. We know that once again Shadrach, Meshach, and Abednego walked out of the fire unscathed. But for all Peter and John knew, they were facing a cross, from which not even Jesus had escaped.

The trial which Luke describes here in Acts 4 bears uncanny similarity to a day Jesus had experienced a few months before. Luke describes that day in chapter 20 of his gospel.

LUKE 20	ACTS 4	SIMILARITY
Chief priests, teachers of the law, elders (20:1)	Rulers, elders, teachers of the law, high priest and his family (4:5-6)	The questioners
Jesus	Peter and John	The suspect[s]
"Teaching the people in the temple courts and preaching the gospel" (20:1)	"Teaching the people [in the temple courts] and proclaiming in Jesus the resurrection of the dead" (4:2)	The apparent crime
". . . By what authority . . . ?" (20:2)	"By what power or what name . . . ?" (4:7b)	The question
"The stone the builders rejected has become the capstone" (20:17b)	". . . The stone you builders rejected, which has become the capstone" (4:11)	Quotation of Psalm 118:22
The leaders did not arrest Jesus, because "they were afraid of the people" (20:19b)	The leaders did not punish Peter and John, **. . . because all the people were praising God for what had happened** (4:21b)	The issue of popularity

As the Jews interacted with the apostles, would either group have recognized these similarities? The Jews did take **note that these men had been with Jesus** (Acts 4:13). The apostles may have remembered that within a week of Jesus' encounter with the authorities (see Luke 20), those authorities had crucified Him.

But James and John did not try plea bargaining. If proclaiming Jesus and His resurrection was a crime, they not only pled guilty, but they committed the crime again, right there before the judges! "You killed Jesus; God raised Him. Jesus is the only way to God and salvation" (see 4:11-12). What a display of faith and audacity! When they spoke of Jesus, they were referring not to an ancient figure revered by millions; they were speaking of a man who, just a few months before, had taught, slept, and bled in that very city. The apostles, standing before those who saw themselves as the religious leaders of the nation, in effect said, "We, not you, are on God's side. If that surprises you, look at exhibit A—the man God's Spirit has healed through us. You walked past him every day for years, and could do nothing for him" (a rough paraphrase of 4:8-12).

The Sanhedrin was not used to being treated this way. These Jewish leaders saw themselves as the ones in charge in Jerusalem. But here were common people willing to challenge them. Jerusalem's great men (at least in their own eyes) realized they were facing a force they could not beat and did not want to join. What were the other options? Give the question to a study commission? No. "Let's tell them to keep quiet. Slap their hands and tell them not to do it again, and hope that works. If these men are not afraid of us, or death, then we have no power against them" (see 4:16-17). Power was the real issue that day.

Who had *true* power? The Sadducees had several factors in their favor. Rome had given them control of police action in the area. The captain of the Temple guard could arrest Peter and John and jail them for the night. Money? The Sadducees were known for their wealth. Archaeologists have discovered silver and gold with which the Jewish leaders purchased their meals.[7] Peter and John had nothing of the kind (see 3:6). Members of the high priest's family received the best education Jerusalem offered. The apostles were **unschooled, ordinary men** (4:13). So, the Sadducees won the day, right? Wrong.

Goliath was the weaker force once again. The apostles had healed the man. All the Sadducees had been able to give him were coins. The power that flowed through the apostles astonished the crowds: **... All the people were praising God for what had happened** (4:21). The Sadducees knew it had been a long time since they had amazed anyone. They had acted and were acting "in ignorance" (3:17); the apostles confidently recognized and followed the truth. The list continues. The apostles were able to offer "times of refreshing"—salvation (3:19). The people freely listened to the apostles, and thousands accepted their message (see 4:4). The members of the Sanhedrin found **there was nothing they could say** (4:14b). They acted in fear (see 4:21). Peter and John spoke boldly. The Jewish leaders spoke with all the authority they had, commanding the Christians **not to speak** (4:18). The leaders' commands had no effect. The believers still "spoke the word of God boldly" (4:31).

Based on the evidence already presented here, any objective observer would award the fight to Peter and John, but we have not yet seen their knockout punches. What were the most crucial differences between those who thought they had power and those who actually did have power?

The Sadducees had **crucified** Jesus, God's holy and righteous One (4:10); the apostles followed Jesus (4:13). The Sadducees talked to each other (4:15); the apostles talked to God (4:24-26). The Sadducees stood "against" God (4:27); the apostles were **filled with** God (4:8; see 4:31).

At this point, you may be tempted to cheer for the underdogs. Your team has beaten insurmountable odds. But, before you do that, stop to reconsider which colors you are *really* wearing.

On what did the Sadducees depend for their power? Their roles, money, and education—all things they could see. We all want to picture ourselves with Peter and John. That's not too hard to admit, especially as we sit reading a book in a comfortable home. But, few of us have given much thought to paying the price they paid.

At the time of this writing, my wife and I are currently facing a major ministry transition. As far as we know, our steady income from being missionaries ends in two months. Giving up the current ministry also involves giving our car keys back to the mission. We are living in a borrowed house whose owner returns in three months. After that? We will not starve, but facing this uncertainty is shaking us.

How easy it is for any of us to profess dependence on Christ, and yet live a life where we depend on Jesus *and* supports that we can see. This may sound fine, but those who depend on God and something else do not truly depend on God. It's one thing for us to sing, "I'd rather have Jesus than silver or gold." But what do we really mean? Far too often, it's "I'm glad I have Jesus *and* silver and gold." Peter and John left everything to follow Jesus. Without extra baggage to weigh them down, God found them easier to use.

5. THE SHAKEN CHURCH MEETING 4:23-31

"God is God, and we are not." These words summarize the worship session the Jerusalem church held after Peter and John's return. The Christians obviously could celebrate the events of the previous forty-eight hours. Through the miraculous healing of the crippled man, and Peter's subsequent sermon, their numbers had increased by two thousand and one. Two thousand more believed on the basis of the sermon, while the healed man undoubtedly joined their group as well. Throughout the apostles' arrest, jailing and trial, God had proven himself stronger than the Sadducees. He had safely returned the Christians' leaders to them. The events of those days helped them look back. That perspective gave them faith for the future, even in the face of continuing risk.

They looked back to the beginning of time, celebrating the fact that their God, the One to whom they were speaking, was the Creator and

Lord of the universe (see Acts 4:24). Their God was no tribal god in competition with other celestial beings. He had no rivals.

Despite Jesus' apparent defeat before Herod and Pilate, the two most powerful men in Palestine, God still ruled. The conspiracy against God's **holy servant Jesus** merely formed a part of what God **had decided beforehand should happen** (4:27-28).

The Christians looked forward, celebrating God's trustworthiness. They prayed, including no request for protection; the believers merely asked that God would continue to enlighten and empower them for bold speech and action. God confirmed their faith by filling His faithful followers once again **with the Holy Spirit** (4:31).

Luke's account of this meeting raises at least two significant questions. Neither finds simple answers.

One question is that if God **had decided beforehand** what **should happen** (4:28), how could He hold responsible Herod, Pilate, Judas, or the Sanhedrin for Jesus' death? The question might be a bit simpler if Luke had said (or the early church had prayed) that God merely *knew* what would happen; but Luke wrote that God **decided.** We could take the easy way out and say that Luke was accurately recording what the early church prayed, and that those first Christians had gotten it wrong. That's too easy an escape, however. The Cross was *God's* plan. If so, did Herod or Pilate have any choice in the matter? Where does God's predestination end and human free will begin? This question receives quite different answers from people on both ends of the theological spectrum. People on both sides have a difficult time supporting their answers from Scripture. Who is right—those who lean toward human free will (called Arminians) or those who lean toward the sovereignty of God (called Calvinists)? When a question arises in Bible study, it's of course best to look for answers in Scripture. The best place to start? Right where the question arises. What insight can we find in the account of the praise meeting?

On one hand, the church worshiped God as the Sovereign Lord, the Creator. While they noted that nations and peoples could rebel against God and His plans, the wording of their rhetorical questions (4:25-26; quoted from King David's words in Psalm 2:1-2) implies that rebellion against God is futile. The psalm which they quoted continues, "The One enthroned in heaven laughs; the Lord scoffs at them" (Ps. 2:4). God rules, no matter what others may do.

On the other hand, Luke's account implies just as strongly that people do make real choices. Would it make sense for God to scoff at nations who plot against Him, if God himself had *determined* that they would reject His plan? Or, would the requests that the Christians included in their prayer (for example, **Enable your servants to speak your word with great boldness** [Acts 4:29b]) make sense if God had predetermined all things? Would God predetermine their prayer so He could give them something He had already predetermined to give them?

This broad question of God's sovereignty and human free will appears to be one where the right answer is found not on either extreme nor in some hard-to-discern midpoint between them. The right answer is found by hanging onto both extremes at once, despite the fact that they apparently cancel each other. God is sovereign. He does accomplish whatever He desires. Nothing and no one can stand in His way. At the same time, He leaves all capable human beings, created in His image, with the option to reject His plan. The **nations [can] rage and the peoples plot** all they like (4:25), and they may bear the consequences of their choices, but *God will still accomplish His goals*.

Consider a second interesting question. How many times can believers be filled? At the end of the praise meeting, **the place where [the Christians] were meeting was shaken. And they were all filled with the Holy Spirit . . .** (4:31). Did some of the Spirit "leak out" subsequent to their filling the first time (see 2:4), requiring them to get a "refill"? What does it mean to be filled with the Spirit? When does it happen?

To answer these questions, we need to take a step back and consider a broader picture. In Acts, Luke uses at least three phrases to describe God's giving of the Holy Spirit to believers. These include being "baptized with the Holy Spirit" (1:5, for example); being "filled with the Holy Spirit" (2:4, for example); and "receiving the Holy Spirit" (see 2:38). The meaning of, and relationship among, these phrases has caused and continues to cause much discussion among Christians.

To a large degree, Luke uses these phrases interchangeably. The prophecy Jesus spoke to His disciples—"You will be *baptized* with the Holy Spirit" (1:5b, my emphasis)—was fulfilled on the day of Pentecost when "all of them were *filled* with the Holy Spirit" (2:4a, my emphasis). Later that same day, Peter promised his hearers that those who repented and were baptized would have their sins forgiven and would "receive the gift of the Holy Spirit" (2:38). Peter and the disciples did not greedily keep God's gifts for themselves, but freely promised that God would give His Spirit to all those who would repent and believe. (Remember that Jesus had described being "born again" as being "born of . . . the Spirit"

[John 3:5]. Paul also reminded the Roman church that all Christians had received the Holy Spirit: "If anyone does not have the Spirit of Christ, he does not belong to Christ" [Rom. 8:9b].)

Now, of course, Peter and the others of the 120 believers gathered on Pentecost had believed in Christ *before* that great day. But, because God had not yet freely given the Holy Spirit to His people, they received the Spirit *after* they believed. But, after Pentecost, all was changed. New believers would receive the Holy Spirit at the time they stepped across the line into faith.

You may already be thinking of some exceptions to this rule. What about those early believers who appeared to receive the Spirit at a time *after* they became believers? Several such examples appear in Acts.

On at least one occasion, God appears to have postponed, for special reasons, new believers' reception of the Holy Spirit. The first Samaritans to believe in Christ after Pentecost did not immediately receive the Spirit. Only a few days later, after Peter and John arrived and laid hands on the group, did God give them this gift (see 8:14, 17). Why the delay? (Could the Spirit be given without the apostles' laying on of hands? Certainly. Cornelius and his household believed the good news and received the Spirit while Peter was still preaching to them [see 10:44].) Acts 8 records a crucial occasion where non-Jews, for the first time since Jesus had returned to heaven, received salvation. To help the Jerusalem church leaders accept this unprecedented event, God appears to have withheld the gift of the Spirit until the leaders were there to witness God's approval. Then there could be no doubt as to the Samaritans' authenticity as believers.

The experience of a group of Ephesians (see Acts 19) also raises some questions. This group had believed to the best of their knowledge, but until Paul arrived, they did not know anything close to the full truth about Jesus. After Paul filled in their knowledge gaps and helped them to grasp a more complete understanding of the gospel, they believed in Jesus and "the Holy Spirit came on them" (19:6). This group did receive the Spirit when they truly believed in Jesus.

What about Saul? He appears to have been filled with the Spirit in Damascus, at the home of Ananias, a few days after his encounter with Jesus (see 9:17-19). It could be that God, as in the case of the Samaritans, purposely held Paul's being filled with the Holy Spirit so that Ananias could witness the moment. If so, the scene would have confirmed for Ananias the authenticity of Saul's conversion. Or perhaps Saul did not truly (or fully) believe in Jesus until Ananias gave him a clearer understanding of what that faith involved. If the latter is true, then Saul did receive the Holy Spirit at the time he believed.

In another sense altogether, God sometimes gave fresh outpourings of the Holy Spirit. The group who gathered for prayer after Peter and John's release offers one such example: **After they prayed. . . . they were all filled with the Holy Spirit and spoke the word of God boldly** (4:31). It is possible that Luke includes these words merely to remind his readers that these faithful followers had been previously filled with the Spirit. But it seems much more likely that, along with the shaking of the building, God was giving His Holy Spirit to these believers once again. What did that experience involve?

It appears that this particular filling of the Holy Spirit followed a pattern that God had set in Old Testament days. Before God poured out the Holy Spirit on all believers at Pentecost, He had, for special purposes at special times, filled with the Spirit certain individuals or groups. For example, on one occasion God briefly filled seventy Hebrew elders with the Spirit so that they could prophesy (see Numbers 11:25). National leaders (Moses, for example) or spokespersons (such as Isaiah) received the Spirit so that they could lead the nation of Israel with God's wisdom and speak with God's power. Even early in the New Testament period, God still followed this example of giving His Spirit in short bursts (for examples, see Luke 1:15, 41, 67). Even after Pentecost, after all believers had the Spirit living with and in them, God offered fresh fillings of the Spirit on special occasions. Examples of those who experienced this phenomenon might include Stephen and Saul (see Acts 7:55; 13:9).

What about us today? If you have been born again, then you have been born of the Spirit. If you have repented and believed in Jesus, then you have received the Holy Spirit. Does that mean that you have received all of God that He can give you? Of course not. Does this mean that you have experienced all the spiritual growth you will ever know, or that all of God's sanctification comes to you at salvation? Of course not.

When I became engaged to my wife, I thought I loved her as much as I ever could. When I took the further step of marrying her, I was sure I couldn't love her any more deeply. I was wrong. After eighteen years, I am still growing in my love for her.

God has given you His Spirit. Has He given you half of His Spirit? No. He has given you all of His Spirit. At the same time, God always has more to give you. How can this be? A glass full of water can hold no more. How can one who is already full of the Spirit become even more full? A finite person can never hold *all* of God. God always has more of himself to give. In Ephesians 5:18, Paul wrote (to people who were already believers and who had already received the Spirit), "Do not get drunk on wine. . . . Instead, be filled [keep on being filled] with the Spirit."

ENDNOTES

[1]In the New Testament, Pentecost primarily refers to the event when the Holy Spirit was given to the church; this occurred on the day of Pentecost. The Greek term *Pentecost* comes from means "fiftieth" or "the fiftieth day" and is literally the fiftieth day after the end of the Passover. It is also known as the Jewish Feast of Weeks. This day is part of the Jewish observances, and was the beginning of the offering of first fruits.

[2]Charles Wesley, "O for a Thousand Tongues to Sing," 1739.

[3]William Barclay, *The Acts of the Apostles* (Philadelphia: The Westminster Press, 1976), p. 32. Barclay explains a few background details that illumine our understanding of the story. The Jews had three daily hours of prayer: 9:00 A.M., 12:00 noon, and 3:00 P.M. The disciples showed their ongoing loyalty to the Jewish faith by going to the Temple at the hour of prayer. Beggars sat outside sites of religious importance, hoping that worshipers would be more inclined to give money there. Worshipers' hearts, preparing for prayer, might be softer.

[4]The Gospels include the New Testament books of Matthew, Mark, Luke, and John.

[5]M. Robert Mulholland, Jr., "Acts" in *Asbury Bible Commentary,* Eugene Carpenter and Wayne McCown, eds. (Grand Rapids, Michigan: Zondervan Publishing House, 1992), p. 941.

[6]Law refers to either the Levitical Code (all God's rules and regulations), the Ten Commandments, or the Pentateuch (the first five books of the Old Testament: Genesis, Exodus, Leviticus, Numbers, and Deuteronomy). Often capitalized when it means the Pentateuch or the Ten Commandments.

[7]Philip Yancey, *The Jesus I Never Knew* (Grand Rapids, Michigan: Zondervan Publishing House, 1995), p. 62.

4

TWO TRIALS

Acts 4:32–5:42

In your study of Scripture, remember that chapter and verse divisions were not part of the Holy Spirit's inspiration. They were not part of the original writings, but were added centuries later to help believers locate specific portions of the text. Without them, our interaction with the Bible would be quite complicated. Imagine the difficulty of directing a friend to a particular tree in the middle of an unmarked forest. Without chapter and verse divisions in Scripture, we'd struggle to find our way around in a large book like Acts.

On occasion, however, chapter and verse breaks can hinder the effectiveness of our Bible study. For example, Luke never intended any interruption between chapters 4 and 5. Without asking anyone's permission, I have made a break between verses 31 and 32 of Acts 4, placing the last few verses of Acts 4 with Acts 5.

Why did I do this? The last few verses of chapter 4 neatly set the stage for the events of chapter 5. How? Chapter 4 ends with a description of the church's unity and the generosity of individual members, with Barnabas mentioned as a specific example. Chapter 5 opens with the story of a couple—Ananias and Sapphira—who appear to follow the example set by Barnabas and others. However, they intended to deceive the church. Luke tells their story not to commend them, but to offer a warning. He also, in the process, lets us know that church hypocrisy is not new in our century.

Acts 5 looks at two quite different trials the early church faced. The first—the judgment of Ananias and Sapphira—took place within the church, with God as judge. The verdict? Guilty. The accused had not spoken the truth. In the second case—the Jews' arrest and questioning of the apostles—the church itself was on trial. The apostles were judged guilty, with Jewish authorities as the judge, because they *had* spoken the truth. As you review these two stories, look for other similarities and differences.

1. GOD PUTS A HUSBAND AND WIFE ON TRIAL 4:32–5:11

In the first four chapters of Acts, many new things had already happened. In this section, we see something new that breaks the pattern of good new things that had been happening. **Great fear seized the whole church** (Acts 5:11a). The church had already twice been shaken up by the Spirit. The leading apostles had been arrested and had faced serious punishment. But, to this point, Luke has not described the church as fearful. What happened? The first church funerals. This might have caused some in the church to grieve, but would it have caused them to fear? Grief came because some of the new Christians had died, but the likelihood that God himself had killed Ananias and Sapphira led the entire church to shudder with fear. Could the believers trust God? Whom in the church might He kill next?

Review Luke's story thus far. Literally thousands of Jews had come to accept Jesus as the Messiah and their Lord. As they experienced the new life Jesus gave them, and the teaching and fellowship within the church, their old priorities were turned upside down. Many new Christians found they now cared more for *people* than possessions.

No one claimed that any of his possessions was his own, but they shared everything they had (4:32b). Karl Marx, the pioneer of Communism, did not invent his well-known philosophy: "From each according to his ability. To each according to his need." This spirit of sharing goes back much farther than Marx, an anti-Christian philosopher. It reaches at least as far back as the early church in Jerusalem. The Christians there no longer saw their possessions as belonging to them. Their possessions belonged to God and His people. (This transformation of the new believers' attitude toward money and possessions is surely as great a miracle as the healing of the man born lame [see Acts 3:1-10].)

There was evidently some poverty among the first believers. It is possible that some of the Pentecost[1] converts, from places far away from Palestine, had stayed in the area to enjoy their new faith and learn more. Perhaps some of these immigrants struggled to find work and, thus, could not purchase food or supply their own housing. The apostles themselves, in one sense, were out of work. (Peter and John, for example, would have found it difficult to do much fishing in the city of Jerusalem!) Peter and John had told a beggar that they had no **silver or gold** (3:6); they may have needed financial support. In any case, the Jerusalem church rallied to meet the needs of others.

The first who gave generously felt good. People reached out to thank them. Others followed their example of giving. This spirit of generosity became known around the city, attracted the interest of nonbelievers, and led to further church growth. The successful preaching of the apostles, mentioned in 4:33, might indicate this.

Barnabas, who played a major role in Luke's subsequent account (see 9:27; 11:22-30; 13:1–15:39), made his first appearance here. He was one of many who **sold a field he owned and brought the money and put it at the apostles' feet** (4:37). Perhaps his gift was larger than most. In any case, it served as a contrast to the next gift Luke mentions.

Luke says little about the background of Ananias and Sapphira. It's safe to assume that they were believers, perhaps part of the "Pentecost three thousand," or the two thousand more who believed on the day the lame man was healed (see 2:41; 4:4). Ananias and Sapphira, who owned property, wished to experience the joy of sharing and to receive the praise of others.

But God judged them. Why? Because they did a bad thing? Yes. They lied. But why did they lie? Did they lie because they had done a bad thing? No. They lied to cover the fact that they had done a *good thing* . . . for the *wrong reason*.

When they first thought of giving, they may have had a sincere desire to help others. But, as things ended up, they gave to boost their own reputation as "spiritual" people. They wished others to see them as stronger Christians than they actually were. Their deception proves this fact. If they had truly cared for other people, they either would have given the full amount, or would have been honest about keeping some of the money for themselves. For Ananias and Sapphira, a concern for image was more important than speaking honestly. What others thought of them took priority over what God thought of them, and thus they became willing to lie to the Holy Spirit (see 5:3).

Jesus had reserved His harsh condemnation for those He called "hypocrites." He warned His followers in the Gospel of Matthew, "Be careful not to do your 'acts of righteousness' before men, to be seen by them. If you do, you will have no reward from your Father in heaven" (Matt. 6:1). People who give to impress *others* don't impress *God*.

I know how careful I must be here. For example, I need to ask myself why I am writing this book. Am I merely hoping to add an impressive line to my résumé? If I write the book of the year, but don't have love, "I am nothing" (see 1 Corinthians 13).

God judged Ananias and Sapphira, even though part of their motivation may have been pure. After all, they had given a generous offering to the church. No one had demanded that they give anything at all. But suppose God judged them because on this one occasion their motivation was not entirely pure; where would *we* be if God judged us every time our motives were mixed? There are two questions here.

Why did God judge Ananias and Sapphira so harshly? God could have considered giving them a warning first, promising stronger punishment if they fell into pride again. We don't have the mind of God; we can't be sure of all His reasons. However, it does appear that God acted as He did because He felt an overwhelmingly strong concern for the purity of His church. He seems to have taken more precaution in protecting His church from inner taint than from external harm. Note that He judged Ananias and Sapphira, the deceitful church members, quite severely. Later, however, He did not strike dead the Jewish leaders who wished to kill Stephen and James (see 7:54-60; 12:1-2).

In another situation, Peter similarly offered strong rebuke to a believer who wished to use his money in a manner that would have subverted the church. Simon the sorcerer wished to purchase Holy Spirit power. Peter's response? **"May your money perish with you . . ."** (8:20). Simon did not immediately die, but may have if Peter's prayer had not intervened.

God saw more need to protect the church from prideful believers than from external persecution. Of the Evangelists, Luke alone records Jesus' parable of the rich fool (see Luke 12:13-21). Within that story, the rich man had done nothing obvious to harm anyone else. His sin was selfish, prideful concern for himself. Within the parable, God judged the man, and the man died. "This is how it will be with anyone who stores up things for himself [for example, Ananias, Sapphira, and Simon the sorcerer] but is not rich toward God" (12:21).

There is a second crucial question in God's judgment of Ananias and Sapphira. What about us? Our motives are so rarely pure or unmixed. Don't we continually deserve God's judgment? How do we escape? God's grace. We can never earn God's love and favor. Fortunately, God does not require absolute perfection from anyone. If He did, we would all be in trouble. When we admit our weaknesses, when we depend on God's goodness rather than our own power or worthiness, then God continually offers His grace. But this does not give us permission to abuse God's grace. He wishes to help us, to purify our actions and our motives, so that we love as He loves.

2. THE JEWS AGAIN TRY THE APOSTLES 5:12-42

Let's review Acts 5:12-42—"Round Two" for the apostles—by noting first the similarities to material Luke has already given. We will also note features appearing for the first time. Both the similarities and the differences highlight material Luke wished to emphasize.

Chapter 3 of this commentary offers a chart comparing the events of Acts 2 and Acts 3–4. Many of the features repeated in those two passages appear again here. God enabled the apostles to perform miracles (see 5:12). The people of Jerusalem responded excitedly (see 5:15-16). Peter had opportunity to preach.

Note one key difference here. The authorities had learned a lesson. They decided to arrest Peter and *all* the apostles, at least as Luke offers his summary of these events, before anyone could follow the new assortment of healings with fresh preaching to the crowds (see 5:17-18). The Jewish strategy did not work. God released His servants. Before the authorities could re-arrest them, the apostles took opportunity publicly **to teach the people** (5:19-21).

As Peter spoke to the Jewish leaders, he offered the same strong message they had heard before. "You killed Jesus. God raised Him. **We are witnesses.** If people repent, God offers **forgiveness of sins"** (see 5:30-32).

These events and words seem to be the core of the "Jerusalem gospel" repeated three times, each time Peter and the church moved into battle. Note the key truths included in this message.

First, God led His army. God initiated each battle as He enabled His people to perform miracles that were beyond their own means.

Second, the enemy—the ones who killed the last leader God sent— was present.

Third, God would not be defeated. He who has power over death itself could face no enemy stronger than himself. The enemy was still present and trying to fight, but had to either surrender or face inevitable defeat. (As I write, I see snow on the ground outside the house. The snow appears strong. It covers the ground for miles around. The war is not over, but it is a defeated enemy. The days are getting longer. The sun is moving higher in the sky. Nothing can hinder the forward movement of spring.)

Fourth, God's actions were essential to the forward movement of His kingdom, but He chose to use a human army. The primary qualification of the soldiers? They were witnesses to God's power. They had yielded themselves to His command.

Fifth, God wished not so much to punish the enemy, as to love it into submission. God wished to **give repentance and forgiveness of sins to Israel** (5:31).

These five points summarize God's strategy in Peter's message to Jerusalem and to today's world.

What new features appear in this section of Scripture (5:12-42)?

All of the apostles were arrested (see 5:18). The Jewish leaders must have felt fearful. The miracles were increasing in number or, at minimum, continuing without decrease. The popularity of the Christians was growing; **crowds gathered . . . from the towns around Jerusalem . . .** to interact with the apostles (5:16). The miracle power was not limited to one or two; all the apostles were a threat to the Jews.

God took supernatural action, not so much to protect the apostles, as to insure that the proclamation of the gospel would continue uninterrupted. At their last recorded praise meeting (see 4:23-31), the church had stridently quoted Psalm 2:1-2. In effect, David had written, "Why do the rulers in this world try to obstruct God? God laughs at their puny efforts." God must have had a good belly laugh as He opened the jail doors, instructing the apostles to set up in the Temple, the city's public forum, to preach Jesus (see Acts 5:20). The Jews had arrested the apostles specifically to prevent that proclamation. God likely chuckled as the **high priest . . . sent to the jail for the apostles.** Of course, **. . . the officers did not find them there . . .** (5:21-22). Luke invites all of his readers to join in God's laughter. If only the Jewish leaders could have laughed at themselves! If only they had realized that they were attempting the impossible. No one can fight God. If only the Jews had given in to Him—but no. They clenched their position, despite God's demonstration of support for the new group.

The authorities had already given Peter and John a warning: Don't "speak or teach at all in the name of Jesus" (4:18). The Jews had hoped their threats would be adequate to suppress the Jesus movement. Had the apostles obeyed? Yes and no. They had chosen to **obey God rather than men** (5:29). In the process, they had **filled Jerusalem with [God's] teaching** (5:28). Luke emphasizes their courage. Perhaps, as he wrote, some of his readers were facing persecution. The apostles' example could give them, and us, strength.

Luke may have intended the stubbornness of the apostles to impress his readers. It did not impress the Sanhedrin. (Its members saw themselves as God's representatives. Imagine how they reacted when the apostles accused them of being God's enemies!) The Jews **were furious and wanted to put them to death** (5:33). The fear of the Jewish leaders was increasing. Authoritarian governments rule by forcing others into fear. But when their subjects refuse to cower, it is time for the rulers to shudder. The apostles were not about to give in. Despite the fury of the Jews, the apostles had resolved *not* to stop **teaching and proclaiming the good news that Jesus is the Christ** (5:42).

Only one person from the Jewish Council realized that its threats were accomplishing little. Gamaliel looked at the apostles a bit more objectively, questioning within himself the source of their astounding strength. At least the thought crossed one Sanhedrin mind that he and his colleagues could be fighting an unwinnable battle. He suggested a new strategy: "If we can't beat this thing, let's try waiting it out. If we can't kill these men's spirits with our threats to kill their bodies, maybe if we wait long enough, the movement will die on its own. Other such movements have. [Gamaliel here mentioned two examples of revolutionary movements that had died prematurely. These earlier movements had been led by Theudas and Judas the Galilean, figures who do not appear otherwise in Scripture (see 5:36-37).] But, if this is of God, then nothing will stop it" (see 5:35-39). Gamaliel was a wise man.

The rest of the Council heard Gamaliel. They released the apostles, again attempting the futile warning, "Don't **speak in the name of Jesus**" (5:40). This time, the Council added more bite to their words. The apostles each received a flogging, a beating severe enough to *kill*. Turning around the values of the world, the apostles rejoiced **because they had been counted worthy of suffering disgrace for the Name** (5:41). They could thank God (and Gamaliel) that they were able to continue proclaiming that Name.

Perhaps Gamaliel was not far from the Kingdom. There is certainly great wisdom in his words. Perhaps Luke hoped his non-Christian readers would take a hint from Gamaliel.[2] Occasions still arise when the church could benefit from his patience. We often choose our battles and want to win them too quickly. Sometimes Christians can find themselves fighting, with wrong methods and motivation, those who could help them forward, if permitted. We need discernment. Rather than rushing in where any hotheads could pick a fight, we would do better if we allowed God to show us the true enemy. Nothing will stop God from winning the war and the battles in which He chooses to engage.

Endnotes

[1]In the New Testament, Pentecost primarily refers to the event when the Holy Spirit was given to the church; this occurred on the day of Pentecost. The Greek term *Pentecost* comes from means "fiftieth" or "the fiftieth day" and is literally the fiftieth day after the end of the Passover. It is also known as the Jewish Feast of Weeks. This day is part of the Jewish observances, and was the beginning of the offering of first fruits.

[2]William H. Willimon, *Acts* (Atlanta: John Knox Press, 1988), p. 57.

5

STEPHEN, THE FIRST MARTYR

Acts 6:1–8:1a

C hapter 6 of Acts follows a pattern set in chapter 5. Both chapters begin with a description of a problem *within* the church. After each problem was resolved, God enabled church leaders to perform "many miraculous signs and wonders among the people" (5:12; see also 6:8). In time, people outside the church became jealous and arrested the miracle workers. The first trial resulted in the apostles' being flogged. The second resulted in the first Christian martyrdom.

What were the internal situations with which Acts 5 and 6 begin? In one sense, they were problems every church would like to have; in another sense, they were potential disasters.

How can problems be good problems? Wouldn't every church like to have its members trying to mimic the generosity of others, as Ananias and Sapphira did (see Acts 5)? The problem that opens Acts 6 was a direct result of the church's growing faster than its leadership could handle.

But these "good" problems were also potential disasters. God severely judged Ananias and his wife. They were bringing a deadly spirit of deceit and pride into the young church. And in Acts 6, Luke portrays a move toward grumbling within the church. Money was again the culprit. This time the problem arose not in how the money was *given* to the church, but in how the church *spent* the money it received.

1. THE WIDOWS' CONTROVERSY 6:1-7

The problem Luke describes in Acts 6 involved Christian widows from different cultural groups. Some historical information enriches our understanding of this conflict.

Within almost all ancient cultures, widows were particularly vulnerable. Occupational and financial power belonged to men. Parents prayed to have *sons,* who would better be able to care for them in their old age. Female children were cherished in Jewish homes, and yet, in reality, were thought of more as an economic burden. As a daughter matured, her father sought out a suitable husband who would welcome her into his home, providing for all her needs.

If a husband died young or without wealth, his widow was left to fend for herself in a male-dominated world. A fortunate widow had an extended family upon whom she could depend. Others had no one. They often had little choice but to depend on charity. The traditional Jewish community had taken care of its widows (see Exodus 22:22; Deuteronomy 14:28-29; 24:17-21).[1] The Christians, from the beginning, followed the same loving pattern. Certainly, a portion of the money the church received from the generosity described in Acts 2:44-45 and 4:32-35 helped to supply the needs of widows. (Later in the New Testament period, Paul would detail guidelines for the appropriate administration of a "widows fund" [see 1 Timothy 5]).

Another component of the Acts 6 story is a cultural division within Judaism,[2] a division which the early church inherited. The origins of this division dated back a few centuries. During the centuries preceding Christ, various countries "took turns" controlling the area around the Mediterranean Sea. Back into Old Testament times, the Assyrians and then the Babylonians dominated the biblical "world." You may remember them as the empires which conquered the Northern and Southern Kingdoms of Israel.

The Assyrians and Babylonians took pockets of people from the lands they conquered and spread them around the whole region. Daniel and his friends, taken to Babylon, typify this forced migration. The writers of Psalm 137 offer another example. After these empires declined, many Jews chose to remain in their new homes, even though they were far from Jerusalem. By the first century, there may have been more Jews living outside Palestine than within its bounds. These scattered pockets of Jews became known as the Diaspora—the "dispersed ones." They play an important role later in Acts. When Paul and his companions traveled the Roman Empire, they began their preaching ministry in each city by visiting the synagogue, the meeting place for each community of Jews. By visiting these people with a ready-made understanding of the Old Testament and its God, Paul needed to offer less pre-evangelism.

During the period of time between the two Testaments, a number of other countries dominated the region. In the fourth century before Christ, the

Persians had their moment at the top. After the fall of the Persian Empire, Alexander the Great and the Greek nation took preeminence. While previous empires had made no systematic attempts to unify the Mediterranean in terms of culture or language, Greece did. (Persia had influenced many areas east of the Mediterranean—Palestine included—by introduction of its language, Aramaic. Aramaic became the common language of Palestine. Jesus and His companions, for example, would have spoken Aramaic.) Greece attempted and, to a great degree, succeeded at Hellenizing (Greek-izing) the whole area. Greek, for example, became (and remained for centuries) the common language for nearly all people groups which Alexander conquered. (This was another factor which contributed to the spread of Christianity during the period which Luke describes in Acts. Christian missionaries did not need to learn hundreds of languages, because so many people knew Greek. The New Testament books were all written first in Greek.)

In contrast to the Diaspora (the Jews scattered around the Mediterranean Sea), the Jews who remained in Palestine resisted Hellenization. They wished to retain their own worship, language, and traditions. During the century or two immediately preceding Christ, some Hellenistic Jews (those from the Diaspora who had been more strongly influenced by Greek language and culture) returned to their ancestral homeland. The Jews who had lived away from their national home found it a bit awkward to fit into traditional Jewish patterns. (Compare this to the tensions when a student who has been away at college for several years returns home to live with Mom and Dad!) It was not easy for the two groups—"Jewish Jews" and Greek-influenced Jews (the New International Version calls them **Grecian Jews** [Acts 6:1])—to live side by side. Within the Christian community, a conflict arose between these two groups.

The eleven apostles, those remaining from Jesus' original Twelve, were definitely Jewish Jews. They had all had grown up in Galilee. Aramaic was their language. Among the converts at Pentecost (remember all the nations that were represented at that festival; see 2:9-11) were **Grecian Jews.** The apostles likely did their best to be fair in distribution of food to all the needy. Despite their best efforts, a problem of attitude, if not of unfair treatment, arose. Spirit-filled believers still felt cultural prejudices coming with them from their pre-Christian days. The division between the two groups of Jews still looked large to them.

Here in Acts 6, we see that the Grecian Jewish widows felt they were being discriminated against. Were they? Luke does not address this question. But the Grecian widows were convinced that the Aramaic-speaking apostles were not treating them fairly. The women complained. (The Greek verb used here documents the intensity of the complaint. Greek translators of the Old Testament used the same word to describe the murmurings or "grumbling" of the ancient Israelites against Moses [see Exodus 16:7; Numbers 14:27]. God severely judged the Israelites' complaining.[3]) The apostles took the widows' complaint seriously and called a church conference. As they thought about their ministries, the apostles must have realized that they were trying to do too much. They suggested the appointment of a new committee. Its seven members would give full attention to the church food cupboard. This new group has become known as the "deacons." This English word relates closely to the Greek verb meaning "to serve" *(diakoneo),* which Luke uses in Acts 6:2. The New International Version translates that word as **wait on.** There were two traits which all the deacons shared.

First, all seven of the "servers" had names with Greek, not Old Testament Hebrew, origins. By appointing men to the committee of deacons who were from the group allegedly receiving neglect, the church bent over backward to suppress the complaints and restore unity to the body. They took a risk of alienating Aramaic-speaking members of the community. Would the Grecian committee discriminate against the Palestinian widows? The apostles risked this problem because they wished to speak strongly against any cultural division within the church.

Second, note the high standards set for membership on the food committee. The "servers" needed **to be full of the Spirit and wisdom** (6:3). Their qualifications were slightly different, but were just as high as the qualifications for the apostles' committee (see 1:21-22). The apostles must not have seen food distribution as a secondary task. They saw the need to maintain their ministry **of prayer and . . . of the word** (6:4), but there's no indication that anyone saw the servers as less spiritual.

The apostles **prayed and laid their hands on** the seven (6:6). The ancient ritual of laying hands on another person indicated, among other things, that the recipient went forth as a representative. The seven deacons did not become apostles, but served with equal honor and responsibility. (Luke uses the same Greek word, *diakonia,* to describe both the ministries of food and the Word [see 6:1, 4].) And, in fact, the ministries of two deacons receive primary attention in the next two chapters of Luke's account in Acts.

The apostles' plan (the committee) succeeded in solving the immediate problem. More importantly, the church, in unity and the power of the Spirit, continued to move forward in rapid growth.

Ironically, the move to appease the Grecian Jews led, indirectly at least, to the conversion of some of the most Jewish of the Jews: **. . . A large number of priests became obedient to the faith** (6:7).

Luke's record of the "grumbling widows story" offers key insights into leadership and ministry.[4]

First, true leaders lead by serving. Whether preachers or table waiters, God's people lead for the benefit of others. Whether offering spiritual or physical food, leaders serve so that others may serve more effectively.

Second, taking care of church members is an essential part of Christian ministry. Meeting the spiritual needs of those who do not know Jesus is crucial, but so is ministry to those within the church. Likewise, the church cannot ignore physical needs. Evangelism and discipleship are central to the forward movement of the church, but the healthy church ministers to whole persons. It insures that even the more mundane needs of its members are cared for.

2. THE MINISTRY AND DEATH OF STEPHEN 6:8–8:1a

This passage contains sixty-nine verses. Luke devotes fifty-two of these verses to Stephen's sermon. No other sermon in the book of Acts is recorded at such length. Luke evidently viewed Stephen's sermon as crucial to the whole story of the early church. What is its place in the narrative?

The Stephen story closes out the first major block of the book, the Jerusalem section of Acts. In the first five chapters, Luke portrays a gradually increasing level of resistance to the early church. The first arrest of Christians involved only Peter and John, who received a verbal warning and were later released unharmed (see 4:3, 21). A bit later, the Jewish leaders arrested *all* the apostles. On this occasion, the apostles received a painful flogging, but were able to continue their ministries (5:18, 40-42).[5] The third stage of persecution, in which Stephen served as a prime catalyst, led to the first Christian martyrdom and an attack on the Jerusalem church as a whole. This great persecution broke up the tight new Christian community and sent most of its members fleeing for their lives.

What did Stephen do that aroused such antagonism? What did he say or do that was worse than the apostles' previous words and actions? After all, the apostles had blatantly accused the Jews of murdering Jesus. And the apostles had reminded the Jews that their crucifixion of Jesus had accomplished *nothing*. Crucifixion had given God the opportunity to raise Jesus from the dead. The apostles' unstoppable courage, combined with God's astounding displays of power through them, had already revealed the Jewish leaders' powerlessness. So what could Stephen say to anger them any more than that?

From a Jewish perspective, the ideas Stephen included in his sermon did move miles beyond the apostles' words. The apostles preached that Jesus came to *fulfill* the Old Testament faith. Stephen announced that Jesus came to *replace* the current Jewish system (see 6:11-14). Let's see how Stephen's argument developed. First, take a look at Stephen himself.

Luke tells us surprisingly little about Stephen. Stephen appears quite suddenly in the story of the widows' complaint (see 6:1-7). Within what appears to be no more than days, he was dead. What can we learn about him? He seems to have been a Grecian Jew, maybe a newcomer to Jerusalem. He likely came to faith in Jesus at Pentecost or some time soon after. Stephen did not follow Jesus halfheartedly; Luke describes him as "a man full of faith and of the Holy Spirit" (6:5). Perhaps Stephen had been a member of **the Synagogue of the Freedmen,** a relatively cosmopolitan Jewish group (6:9).

In any case, members of this synagogue first heard Stephen's "heresy." They tried to argue with Stephen, but failed (see 6:9-10). Desiring help in their attempts to quell Stephen, they recruited agents who would publicize his "treasonous" ideas. Their summaries of Stephen's theology were not accurate, but neither were they total lies. Just as accusers had twisted Jesus' words (see Luke 23:2), these Jews placed Stephen's statements in the worst possible light.

Their scheme succeeded. Soon, **the elders and the teachers of the law,**[6] men who had opposed the church on previous occasions (see 4:5-7; 5:17-21), became **stirred up** (6:12). False witnesses (the agents of the Freedmen again?) came forward. Luke summarizes the charges they stated against Stephen: **This fellow never stops speaking against the holy place and against the law. For we have heard him say that this Jesus of Nazareth will destroy this place and change the customs Moses handed down to us** (6:13-14).

The Sanhedrin waited **intently** for a response (6:15). They may have felt a bit surprised as Stephen began what appeared to be a harmless summary of Old Testament history. But if that were all Stephen offered, why would the Jews have battered him to death? Merely for the last three verses of his sermon where he moved into attack mode (see 7:51-53)? No. The conclusion to Stephen's sermon did not appear out of the blue. It contained the final summary of Stephen's defense, a defense which he turned into an accusation. Notice three particular statements Stephen made in his last minutes of speaking: (1) **You are just like your fathers:**

You always resist the Holy Spirit! (7:51b); (2) **You . . . have received the law . . . but have not obeyed it** (7:53); (3) **The Most High does not live in houses made by men** (7:48a). Let's take these one at a time.

You are just like your fathers . . . (7:51b). Throughout his defense, Stephen frequently referred to the "fathers" of the Jewish nation. Whom did he include in this group? **Abraham** (7:2); **the patriarchs** (the sons of Jacob; 7:9; see 7:11-12, 15); **our people** (the entire nation of Israel — those who had been mistreated in Egypt and whom Moses led to freedom; 7:19; see 7:38-39, 44); and the next generation whom **Joshua** led into the land of Palestine (7:45).

The Jewish leaders Stephen addressed proudly saw themselves as the children of these respected "fathers." Also, they probably wanted to see themselves as the *current* "fathers of the nation." Within his "sermon," Stephen noted how God had interacted favorably with the leaders He had chosen for His people (Abraham — 7:2-8; Joseph — 7:9-10; Moses — 7:30-38; Joshua — 7:45; David — 7:46). At least as Stephen summarized the accounts, God did nothing but help the leaders. God was continually faithful to them. Through those leaders, God showed His goodness to all the people.

As the Jewish leaders listened to Stephen that day, they might have been congratulating themselves for following in such a great, God-ordained, divinely blessed tradition. But Stephen was not intending to praise them. In his sermon, he not only gave attention to the ancient fathers of the people, but he described the people surrounding God's chosen leaders, particularly Moses and Joseph. Joseph? **The patriarchs** became **jealous of** him and **sold him as a slave** (7:9). Moses? When all God's people became slaves in Egypt, they did not understand **that God was using him** [Moses] **to rescue them** (7:25). They rejected Moses as leader and forced him to flee (see 7:27, 29). On their way to Palestine, the nation **rejected** Moses and **refused to obey him** (7:35, 39). The nation forsook Moses and his God for other gods (see 7:40-41).

God was faithful to both Joseph and Moses. Through these chosen leaders, God ministered to His people. But, the people did not recognize God's choice, and they abused His chosen ones.

In Stephen's summary, he described two groups of "fathers." The members of the Sanhedrin certainly thought they were children of their father Moses. Stephen had other ideas. **You are just like your fathers. . . . Was there ever a prophet your fathers did not persecute? They even killed those who predicted the coming of the Righteous One. And now you have betrayed and murdered him** (7:51b-52).

What was Stephen saying? "You may claim Moses as your father. If you do, you are wrong. You have followed another set of fathers—those who rejected Moses. As your fathers refused to obey Moses, you have refused to heed the one God sent to you. You killed God's chosen one." These words would not have helped Stephen to "win friends and influence people."[7] (Note the similarities between Stephen's tactic and one Jesus employed, as John describes it in John 8:42-44.) Perhaps to drive his point home, Stephen drew several other parallels between Moses and Jesus, a **prophet** whom Moses predicted (Acts 7:37): (1) Stephen called Moses the people's **ruler** and **deliverer** (7:35); (2) Moses was one who performed **wonders and miraculous signs** (7:36); (3) Moses spoke God's **living words** (7:38); (4) Despite Moses' divine call, the people repudiated him (7:39-41).

Consider also Stephen's other sword thrusts at the Jewish leaders. He hit them again as he directly responded to the charges against him: **This fellow never stops speaking against this holy place and against the law** (6:13). How did Stephen answer these accusations?

He subtly pointed out the origin of both the Temple and the Law. Both came from God himself. God had given the Law and the plans for the Tabernacle (the portable house of worship that set the model for the permanent Temple) to Moses at Mount Sinai (see 7:38, 44).[8] But the national leaders to whom Stephen spoke had worshiped God's gifts (of the Law and Temple) instead of God himself. Attempting to protect God's gifts, they had killed God himself.

The Law? Jesus had not kept the Law, at least to the Jews' specifications. For example, He did not fast as the Pharisees fasted (see Mark 2:18). He did not keep the Sabbath as they thought He should (see 2:24; 3:2). These "transgressions of the Law" led them, quite early in Jesus' ministry, to decide that He must die (see 3:6).

The Temple? Jesus' action in clearing the Temple aggravated the leaders (see Matthew 21:12-16, 23). At Jesus' trial, "the chief priests and the whole Sanhedrin" put forth false witnesses who testified that Jesus planned to destroy the Temple (Mark 14:55-59).

The Jewish leaders perceived Jesus as a threat to both the Law and the Temple. Their grasp on these divine gifts made it impossible for them to accept Jesus as a divine messenger. Thus, they killed God to preserve God's gifts.

The Jews thought they were prosecuting Stephen. Like the apostles before him, Stephen turned the tables. He put the Sanhedrin on trial. The Jews accused Stephen of abusing the Law and the Temple. Stephen accused them of abusing God himself (see Acts 7:48-53). Stephen highlighted their opposition to all three members of the Trinity: (1) You have tried to tie God to the Jerusalem Temple (7:48-50); (2) You have killed Jesus (7:52); (3) You have resisted the Holy Spirit (7:51).

The apostles had previously shown how their faith in Christ offered a necessary supplement and reform to first-century Judaism.[9] From the nonbelieving Jews' perspective, that had been bad enough. But Stephen went further, showing how God was seeking to replace the system the Jews held so dear.

Where do you see yourself in this story? Readers of this commentary know how dearly we sometimes hold on to our church traditions. (Often these traditions are the innovations we fought for just a short while ago.) When others suggest changes to the practices or ideas we cherish, we often attempt to defend our values. Church traditions all have value, but we must continually examine ourselves to see when our habits of practice or thought have moved into prejudice. We, like the Sanhedrin, can find ourselves fighting God in order to defend our ideas about God and how He works. To protect the style of worship we prefer, we can destroy worship altogether. We wish nonbelievers to see us as a community living in obedience to God. Yet, our disagreements over interpretation of God's commands can hinder our witness. In humility, we must admit that our pictures of God are not God himself.

Along another line of thinking, we, like the Jewish leaders, need to consider which set of fathers we are imitating. As we look at this story, none of us wants to be like the elders and teachers of the Law. We all want to be like the apostles, right? If so, then we need to resist the temptation to move toward criticizing or attacking others. We may feel a need to stand firm in the cause of right, just as the apostles did. Wonderful! (We would not mind a few miracles now and then, to confirm our favored position.) But if we idolize the *strength* of the early church, wanting a similar position of spiritual power *for ourselves,* we may end up imitating the Sanhedrin.

The first Christians did proclaim the truth, not from a position of obvious strength, but at great risk to themselves. They bore on their backs the scars left by jagged metal at the end of a whip. Stephen was willing to speak strongly, but from a position of vulnerability that cost him his life. And even then, he was willing to forgive those who abused him.

Which set of fathers do we imitate? What kind of power do we seek?

ENDNOTES

[1]William Barclay, *The Acts of the Apostles* (Philadelphia: The Westminster Press, 1976), p. 51. Barclay details the synagogue system for taking care of the poor. Two men went door-to-door among the Jews each week, collecting money. This money purchased food for those who had no other supply.

[2]Judaism is the life and belief system of the Jewish people and involves a covenant relationship with God. Though there are various branches of Judaism, the underlying theme among them has been monotheism and a recognition of the Law, or the Torah. The Hebrew word from which *Torah* comes is translated *law* and refers to divine instruction and guidance. The Torah is comprised of the instructions and directions given to Israel by God. Torah is another name for the Pentateuch (the first five books of the Old Testament: Genesis, Exodus, Leviticus, Numbers, and Deuteronomy), also known as the Law of Moses. It is considered the most important division in the Jewish Scriptures, with highest authority, since it was traditionally thought to have been written by Moses, the only biblical hero to have spoken with God face-to-face.

[3]John R. W. Stott, *The Spirit, the Church, and the World* (Downers Grove, Illinois: InterVarsity Press, 1990), p. 120.

[4]These two ideas are similar to thoughts expressed by William Willimon in *Acts* (Atlanta: John Knox Press, 1988), pp. 59–60.

[5]F. F. Bruce, *The Book of the Acts* (Grand Rapids, Michigan: Wm. B. Eerdmans Publishing Co., 1988), p. 420. Exactly what did this flogging involve? We can't be sure, but Roman floggings usually involved a scourge, made of leather strips attached to a large wooden rod. At the end of each of the strips was a jagged piece of metal or bone. Such floggings often killed weaker men.

[6]Law refers to either the Levitical Code (all God's rules and regulations), the Ten Commandments, or the Pentateuch (the first five books of the Old Testament: Genesis, Exodus, Leviticus, Numbers, and Deuteronomy); it is often capitalized when it means the Pentateuch or the Ten Commandments.

[7]Dale Carnegie, *How to Win Friends and Influence People* (Livermore, California: Pocket Books, 1994).

[8]At least in a negative sense, Stephen hinted at the purpose of the Law and the Temple. Neither could hope to contain God. God had been able to interact freely with Abraham and the next few generations, long before God gave the Law to His people (see Acts 7:2-36). Was God limited to the Tabernacle or the Temple? No. God had met His people in Mesopotamia, Egypt, and the desert/wilderness (7:2, 9, 30) long before the Law was given or the Temple built.

[9]See endnote 2.

Part Two

GOD PREPARES THE CHURCH TO TAKE THE GOSPEL TO THE GENTILES

Acts 8:1b–12:25

I n the first part of Acts, Luke has shown how God established the church in Jerusalem and took preliminary steps to strengthen it for its future ministry. In the second part of Acts, we see how God lifted the church into a new stage of preparation. During that time, God helped the church to overcome significant barriers of prejudice. Each step took the Jewish church a bit further from its comfort zone and a bit closer to the world full of needy Gentiles. What were the hurdles for the church?

- Ministering for the first time to Samaritans (8:5-25)
- Ministering for the first time to Gentiles who had become proselytes (8:26-39)
- Ministering for the first time to God-fearing Gentiles (10:1–11:18)
- Ministering for the first time to pagan Gentiles (11:20-26)[1]

In the process of helping the church to overcome these ethnic hurdles, God also helped the believers to forgive and receive the ministry of one of their archenemies (see 9:1-31).

ENDNOTE
[1]These terms are more fully described in the commentary that follows.

SETTING
THE STAGE

Acts 8:1b-4

In the last half of the book of Acts, we have a new central figure, Saul. Luke introduces Saul at the end of the passages about Stephen. At this point, Saul sneaks into the narrative, a mere spectator at the stoning of Stephen, "giving approval to his death" (Acts 8:1). What would Saul have witnessed? A man dying with childlike faith in God—a scene that Saul never forgot (see 22:20).[1] Saul had been proud of his own righteousness, but likely was afraid to trust God for grace.

(This morning, I read Galatians 6, in which Paul describes the attitudes of Jewish legalists. I felt I was reading not only what Paul had observed in others, but his memories of his own hardheartedness. "These people who are attempting to force the ways of circumcision on you have only one motive: They want an easy way to look good before others, lacking the courage to live by a faith that shares Christ's suffering and death. . . . They only want you to be circumcised so they can boast of their success in recruiting you to their side. . . . I have been . . . set free from the stifling atmosphere of pleasing others and fitting into the little patterns that they dictate" [Gal. 6:12-14 THE MESSAGE].)

Perhaps Saul envied Stephen's angel-like face (see Acts 6:15), his vision of God in heaven (7:56), and his ability to forgive others and relax even in death (7:59-60). Saul felt no such peace. Certainly Stephen's theology made Saul and others like him angry, but perhaps Saul's own personal anxiety and anger also motivated him to destroy others who had what he wanted.

A great persecution broke out against the church at Jerusalem . . . (8:1). The persecution scattered most of the Christians. But Luke mentions one exception: the apostles. What was going on? Were the apostles the strongest ones, the only ones brave enough to remain in Jerusalem to resist the new persecution? Possibly. It seems more likely, however, that the apostles and perhaps some of the newly converted priests, mentioned in 6:7 (see also 15:5), may have remained more conservative than other Christians with Grecian backgrounds. It may have taken men like Peter and James, Jesus' brother, a bit longer to move away from their strong loyalty to Jewish traditions (see 10:14; Galatians 2:12). (Years later, a conservative Jewish church remained in Jerusalem [see Acts 20:20-24].) The Jewish leaders targeted those like Stephen, who viewed discipleship to Jesus as a brand-new life and, thus, saw less need for the traditional Jewish lifestyle. (The only people scattered from Jerusalem that Luke specifically identifies were others who likely held the broader outlook: Philip, one of the seven deacons [8:5], and some men from Cyprus and Cyrene [11:20].)

Why belabor this point? We don't want to sling mud at the early church. But, even in the power of the Spirit, its members experienced some disagreement. There were varying opinions on how far the new faith should venture from its traditional basis in Judaism.[2] (For instance, notice that when the Jerusalem church heard that Samaritans had received the gospel, the leaders acted with great caution: "How can this be? Samaritans?" They sent a high-ranking delegation to check out the situation [see 8:14]. This pattern repeated itself several times, as witnesses took the gospel to groups culturally and religiously farther from the home church.) The Jerusalem Council may have been the high watermark for this intrachurch debate.

In time, the early Christians reached some agreement. The destruction of Jerusalem in A.D. 70 and the subsequent dispersion of the Jewish "power base" sealed the matter. What is important for us is that the church *did* experience such controversy. When we're caught in some church disagreement today, we may be dismayed. We need to work toward consensus lovingly. But disagreement in itself is not sin. Even the earliest church did not escape all dissension at heated "church board" meetings.

Despite the church's potential for internal disagreement, its grief at Stephen's death, and its concern over ongoing big-time persecution (see 8:1-3), the church continued to grow. Again, at the risk of becoming too critical of the Jerusalem church, we must admit that it is possible the church grew not *despite* persecution, but *because of* persecution.

Jesus had told the apostles to be His "witnesses in Jerusalem" and then move out in ever larger circles (1:8). Perhaps in time the Jerusalem church would have purposefully sent witnesses out to the world. But the first evangelistic travel, at least the first that Luke describes, came not through church planning, but through persecution. God may not have engineered the persecution, but He certainly used it for His purposes.

During the next stage of evangelism, the church took the gospel to a variety of people. Saul was certainly a Jew, but the other converts mentioned in Acts 8 through 11 came from outside the Jewish family: Samaritans ("half brothers" of the Jews); the Ethiopian eunuch, who was, at minimum, a God-fearer (an "associate member" of the Jewish faith) and, more likely, a proselyte (a full convert to Judaism); Cornelius, a Roman army officer, a devout God-fearer (a "close neighbor"); Gentiles in Antioch, people with no previous allegiance to the Old Testament faith ("total strangers").

Luke begins his description of this evangelistic expansion with 8:4, one of the most glorious verses in all of Scripture. Those who left Jerusalem, fearing for their lives, did not move into secret caves to guard their lives. They continued to risk their lives, as they **preached the word wherever they went.** If Saul and his colleagues hoped this persecution would squash this growing "heresy," they underestimated the believers' zeal! They might as well have tried to kill a seed by burying it. The seed sprouted and reproduced itself many times.

ENDNOTES

[1]Augustine said that "the Church owes Paul to the prayer of Stephen." Quoted in William Barclay, *The Acts of the Apostles* (Philadelphia: The Westminster Press, 1976), p. 62.

[2]Judaism is the life and belief system of the Jewish people and involves a covenant relationship with God. Though there are various branches of Judaism, the underlying theme among them has been monotheism and a recognition of the Law, or the Torah. The Hebrew word from which *Torah* comes is translated *law* and refers to divine instruction and guidance. The Torah is comprised of the instructions and directions given to Israel by God. Torah is another name for the Pentateuch (the first five books of the Old Testament: Genesis, Exodus, Leviticus, Numbers, and Deuteronomy), also known as the Law of Moses. It is considered the most important division in the Jewish Scriptures, with highest authority, since it was traditionally thought to have been written by Moses, the only biblical hero to have spoken with God face-to-face.

7

THE MINISTRY OF PHILIP

Acts 8:5-40

The first great persecution scattered many believers. They left Jerusalem and headed in many directions, proclaiming the good news as they traveled. Luke could have told exciting stories involving many of them. He chose, however, to include only a few stories. The first two involved Philip. Like Stephen, this Philip had been chosen to help manage church financial matters (see Acts 6:1-6). Also like Stephen, Philip moved outside that narrow role to preach powerfully.

1. THE GOSPEL TO THE SAMARITANS 8:5-25

Philip, like the other deacon, Stephen, preached and acted with power (see Acts 8:5-6). Among the Samaritans, many **believed** and were **baptized** (8:12). Many healings, **signs** that the Kingdom had come, accompanied the preaching (8:6-7, 13).

Who were the Samaritans? They were a people of mixed blood, descendants of Jews (those who had lived there since the days of Joshua) and people of other nationalities. When the Assyrians had ruled the region, they had purposely moved groups of people far from their homes in an attempt to break down ethnic loyalties. Groups which the Assyrians moved into Samaria intermarried with Jews from the area. The Samaritans were the result.

It might have been expected that the pagans moving into the area would bring change to the theology and religious practices in Samaria. However, to a large degree the Samaritans retained their Jewish faith.

Disputes between Jews and Samaritans went back as far as Nehemiah's time. The Samaritans had chosen to worship on Mount Gerizim, rather than in Jerusalem. Noting passages such as Deuteronomy 27:12-13, they believed that Joshua had established Mount Gerizim as a national worship center. Wanting to maintain the priority of their worship site, the Samaritans fought the construction of the new Jerusalem Temple.

The gap between Jews and Samaritans widened during the intertestamental period. During that time, the Samaritans had built their own temple. They had also been more open to the process of Hellenization (see commentary on Acts 6:1-7). Thus, by the time of Jesus, common thought said, "Jews do not associate with Samaritans" (John 4:9c).

During His ministry, Jesus told His disciples not to go to the Samaritans, and yet He opened the door, by His last words, for evangelization of the Samaritans (see Matthew 10:5; Acts 1:8). Note also that Luke, in his gospel, includes at least two stories where Samaritans appear as heroes: Jesus' parable of the Good Samaritan (Luke 10:25-35), and the healing of the ten lepers (Luke 17:11-19). The Samaritan woman fruitfully proclaimed Jesus (John 4:39, 42).

Philip likely had heard others quote Jesus' Great Commission (see Acts 1:8). But none of the other believers had yet ventured across this centuries-old barrier of distrust and hatred. Luke mentions many miracles that Philip performed in Samaria (see 8:6, 13). Perhaps none of them were greater than a Jew's offering of the good news to the Samaritans, or the Samaritans' acceptance of such a gift.

Philip's preaching of the Christ did catch attention in Samaria. The Samaritans were anticipating the coming of the Messiah (see John 4:25). Philip announced that the Messiah had come. As the common people in Jerusalem had received this good news, many in Samaria received it as well.

In his account of salvation's coming to the Samaritans, Luke focuses his attention not so much on the Samaritan group as a whole, as on the Christians' encounter with a sorcerer named Simon. This man had, through magic, set himself up as something of a Messiah figure. He had deceived great numbers of Samaritans into viewing him as **the divine power known as the Great Power** (Acts 8:10). Magicians were quite common in ancient days. God saw that magic would tempt His people, so He specifically forbade in Old Testament Law[1] (see Leviticus) their involvement in "divination or sorcery" (Lev. 19:26).

Luke describes in Acts two more such encounters between Christians and sorcerers (another individual in Acts 13:6-11, and large groups in 19:13-19). What distinguished magic from the power which the early Christians exercised? Magicians attempted to control God by using word formulas or enchanted objects. Magicians *may* have helped people, but they primarily sought money from others. Christians also sought miracles, but did so in submission to God. They found it unnecessary to use any specific words or magic tokens. They offered God's gifts freely and sought to draw attention *to God,* the source of their power.

Centuries before, magicians had done their best to mimic the miracles Moses performed. Simon the magician probably did the same. After observing **the miraculous signs [Philip] did** (8:6), Simon may have gone home to study his manuals. How could he keep up with this new competition? When Simon the magician saw Peter and John giving the Holy Spirit through the laying on of their hands, manifesting a power that healed people's bodies and their inner selves, Simon knew he had met his match. "I can't beat them; I will join them" (see 8:13).

Ananias and Sapphira had been more subtle in their attempts to purchase a spiritual reputation (see 5:1-11). Simon hid nothing. He offered to bribe the apostles if they would share their power with him (8:18-19). ("How hard it is for the rich"—those accustomed to depending on their money—"to enter the kingdom of God!" [Luke 18:24]). As Peter had rebuked the deceptive couple, on this occasion he again responded with strong words: "May your money die with you!" (see Acts 8:20-23). There's little chance that Simon had heard what had happened to Ananias and Sapphira, but he recognized the danger he faced: "Help! I am not ready to die!" (see 8:24).

William Barclay summarizes Simon's two faults. People in the church still struggle with these same weaknesses. First, Simon "was not interested in bringing the Holy Spirit to others so much as in the power and prestige it would bring to himself." Even in our Christian service, we can be tempted to seek satisfaction and power for self, rather than seeking glory for God and help for others. Second, Simon "forgot that certain gifts are dependent on character; money cannot buy them."[2] Jesus himself pointed out that wealth can hinder one's entrance into the Kingdom (see Matthew 19:23). Once a person has come to faith, he needs to remember that wealth offers no aid to spiritual power.

Luke does not tell us the end of the Simon story. Evidently, he did not die on the spot. Did he truly repent? Early church tradition says he did not. Ancient sources describe how Simon became a leader in a Christian cult group that competed with the true church.

Philip's venture into Samaritan evangelism helped many people to believe. Some received physical healing (see Acts 8:7). Others experienced deeper change as they **accepted the word of God** (8:14), and subsequently **received the Holy Spirit** (8:17). Philip and John—who undoubtedly had questions about crossing the cultural gap between Jews and Samaritans—experienced change, too. As they touched the Samaritans (a taboo within the Jewish system), they could not deny God's approval of these people whom they might otherwise have rejected. God gave the same Spirit to Jews *and* Samaritans!

Jesus was continuing to transform His apostles. Note that as **Peter and John returned to Jerusalem,** they preached **the gospel in** *many* **Samaritan villages** (8:25, my emphasis). In their minds, God had broken down significant barriers between the two groups of "brothers" who for so long had despised each other. (Who are those people you have been taught to dislike? Be honest. God wants you to see that He loves them, too.)

The Samaritan encounter raises one other theological question. Some within our holiness tradition have used this passage of scripture (along with Pentecost of Acts 2[3] and the "Ephesian Pentecost" of Acts 19:1-7) as scriptural support for the doctrine of entire sanctification. Since, on these three occasions, Christians received the Holy Spirit in a dramatic manner *after* their first encounter with God, this is seen as the norm for all believers. I do not want to deny the validity of the entire sanctification experience. I merely wish to point out that these three passages are not its best supports.

What is happening in these three passages? Why is the Holy Spirit dramatically given in some kind of "second experience"? The apostles could not receive the Spirit until Jesus had returned to heaven; therefore their reception of the Spirit at Pentecost came after they had known Jesus for some time. The Ephesian twelve had not, prior to their encounter with Paul, heard the complete gospel. They, therefore, could not believe and receive what they had not heard. The "Samaritan Pentecost" offers a bit more of a puzzle. It appears that God purposely withheld His Spirit on this occasion; He delayed the descent of the Spirit on the Samaritans to give Peter and John a lesson. As described above, they benefited from this visible proof that God did not distinguish between Jews and Samaritans.

God does remain God, free to act as He chooses. When Gentiles first heard the gospel, God poured out His Spirit on them even as Peter was still preaching (see 10:44). This proved that there need be no lapse between conversion and reception of the Spirit. Must an apostle (a church official) lay hands on people before they can receive the Spirit? "No" to both questions. When Gentiles first heard the gospel, "the Holy Spirit came on all" of them "while Peter was still speaking" (10:44).[4]

2. THE GOSPEL MOVES TOWARD AFRICA 8:26-40

I like neat packages. I like to think that Luke, in his selection of the evangelism stories of chapters 8, 10 and 11, chose four representative incidents displaying a tidy sequence, as a door gradually opening.

At first the Jewish believers had offered Jesus only to Jews, but God helped them to see that His grace included others. The door opened just a crack as the gospel went from Jewish Christians to Samaritans (who were something like "half brothers" to the Jews; see 8:5-25). The door gradually opened wider and wider as the church offered the good news to the Ethiopian, likely a proselyte (a person not born a Jew, but who had converted to Judaism[5]—even before his belief in Jesus, perhaps the Jews would have considered him an "adopted brother"; see 8:26-40); to Cornelius and company, God-fearing Gentiles (persons who had been attracted to Judaism and kept many, but not all, of its ways—the Jews might have considered them "cousins"; see 10:1–11:18); and then to the Gentiles of Antioch (people who had no previous allegiance to Judaism and its God—at best, the Jews would have considered them "neighbors," but more likely would have seen them as "total strangers" or even as enemies; see 11:20-26). God was helping the church to cross barriers of ever increasing size, moving it out of its comfort zone.

The Ethiopian convert whom Luke describes in 8:26-39 likely was born a Gentile. (The term "Ethiopian" implied black, non-Jewish skin.) If so, he was, at least in Luke's account, the first such person to hear and receive the gospel.

What was his story? Through one of the Jewish communities scattered around the Mediterranean, he had heard of the true God. Without having yet heard of Jesus, the Son of God, the Ethiopian eunuch[6] had pledged his allegiance to this God of the Jews. The man took his faith seriously. He had traveled hundreds of miles to Jerusalem to participate in the Temple rituals of worship and sacrifice. As he was a chief officer in his nation's government, his trip to Jerusalem also might have had some business purpose, but Luke does not mention this. Luke says the **man had gone to Jerusalem to worship,** perhaps for one of the annual festivals (8:27). This man wanted to know God more fully. God saw his heart hunger and found a way to satisfy it. Notice the variety of means that God used to enable the conversion of this Ethiopian eunuch.

God used the means of divine miracle and human effort. At least twice, God gave Philip supernatural instructions toward the chariot (see 8:26, 29). At the end of the story, God miraculously whisked Philip away (8:39). There's no doubt that God was at work in this situation. God, not Philip nor the Ethiopian, initiated this encounter. Yet, Philip needed to use his own power to walk from Jerusalem toward Gaza (8:26-27). He even needed to run to approach the chariot (8:30). God reached out to the Ethiopian, but gave Philip the opportunity to participate in the miracle. Philip could have refused. He could have reasoned that there was little purpose in traveling an abandoned **desert road** (8:26). He could have rejected the risk of approaching a person of higher social rank than himself. (The use of proper protocol in inter-class encounters was much more important in ancient societies, but picture what might happen to you even today if you attempted to run alongside a government motorcade.)

Note another paired strategy God employed: both His written word (the Isaiah scroll that the Ethiopian was reading) and the spoken word of His appointed messenger (see Acts 8:32-33, 35). The Ethiopian benefited from both the old covenant[7] (worship in Jerusalem and the writings of the ancient prophet Isaiah; see Acts 8:27, 32-33) and that which was quite new (**the good news about Jesus** [8:35]).

While riding in his chariot, the official was reading from chapter 53 of the book of Isaiah. You may recognize this passage, for the Christian church has often associated it with Good Friday or other commemorations of Jesus' sufferings on the cross. More vividly than any other Old Testament text, this chapter describes Jesus' sacrificial death.

To this day, many Jews debate the meaning of Isaiah 53 and the surrounding chapters, known as the "Servant Songs." Some feel that Isaiah was describing the entire nation of Israel as God's suffering servant. Others feel Isaiah may have been describing himself or some other individual. Philip knew that Jesus had interpreted His own crucifixion in light of this chapter (see, for example, Luke 22:37). Philip could not have asked for a better Old Testament text or a better lead-in question—**Who is the prophet talking about . . . ?** (Acts 8:34)—from which to present Jesus to the traveler. Luke proclaimed the gospel, and the official believed.

It may be difficult "for the rich to enter the kingdom of God," but all things are "possible with God" (Luke 18:24, 27). In the story of the Ethiopian, we see an apparently rich man (certainly one with power) who remained humble. He saw no problem in admitting his ignorance and need for help (see Acts 8:31). As the chariot approached a place with suitable water, the man did not demand baptism, but graciously requested this privilege (see 8:36). As the story ended, he **went on his way rejoicing,** not in his own power, but in the help he had received (8:39). At least two ancient Christian writers describe how this man returned home as an evangelist to his people. These writers may have had no more information than we do, but their conclusion fits with what Luke tells us.

Some have felt that this story solves all questions about the "proper" form of baptism. The man **went down into the water** (8:38). Does that not argue for total immersion? Unfortunately not. Ancient tradition also supports the (now infrequent) possibility of pouring as a means of baptism. In this scenario, people descend into water that might be only waist deep. The officiant, with hands cupped together or a container of some sort, picks up water which is then poured over the head of the recipient. The baptism debate goes on!

John Stott compares Philip's two evangelistic encounters (with the Samaritans and the Ethiopian) and points out lessons that are not debatable.[8] Stott first contrasts details in the stories: "The people with whom Philip shared the good news were different in race, rank and religion." Note also that in the first situation, Philip was ministering to a large group, while in the second, he was speaking to a single person. Because of all these factors, the two situations called for different methodologies. In Samaria, Philip performed miracles and publicly preached. With the eunuch, Philip quietly explained the meaning of Scripture.

As we offer the gospel today, we face a similar wide variety of situations. As Philip did, we must be ready to shape our methodologies to reach specific people. Yet, as Philip did in both cases (see 8:12, 35), we must offer all people the same message: Jesus.

ENDNOTES

[1]Law refers to either the Levitical Code (all God's rules and regulations), the Ten Commandments, or the Pentateuch (the first five books of the Old Testament: Genesis, Exodus, Leviticus, Numbers, and Deuteronomy); it is often capitalized when it means the Pentateuch or the Ten Commandments.

[2]William Barclay, *The Acts of the Apostles* (Philadelphia: The Westminster Press, 1976), p. 67.

[3]In the New Testament, Pentecost primarily refers to the event when the Holy Spirit was given to the church; this occurred on the day of Pentecost. The Greek term *Pentecost* comes from means "fiftieth" or "the fiftieth day" and is literally the fiftieth day after the end of the Passover. It is also known as the Jewish Feast of Weeks. This day is part of the Jewish observances, and was the beginning of the offering of first fruits.

[4]Of course, other New Testament passages do support the desirability, or even the need for, "a second work of grace" (see 1 Thessalonians 5:23; Romans 12:1-2; Ephesians 5:18—all written to believers in whom the Spirit dwelled).

[5]Judaism is the life and belief system of the Jewish people and involves a covenant relationship with God. Though there are various branches of Judaism, the underlying theme among them has been monotheism and a recognition of the Law, or the Torah. The Hebrew word from which *Torah* comes is translated *law* and refers to divine instruction and guidance. The Torah is comprised of the instructions and directions given to Israel by God. Torah is another name for the Pentateuch (the first five books of the Old Testament: Genesis, Exodus, Leviticus, Numbers, and Deuteronomy), also known as the Law of Moses. It is considered the most important division in the Jewish Scriptures, with highest authority, since it was traditionally thought to have been written by Moses, the only biblical hero to have spoken with God face-to-face.

[6]Ancient Eastern governments so frequently employed castrated men in leadership roles that the term "eunuch" often took the place of "government official." The word was thus used in two ways: narrowly to describe men who were physically eunuchs, or more broadly to describe any man who served in the upper levels of government. If the man of Acts 8 were a true eunuch, he might not have been able to participate fully in Jewish worship (see Deuteronomy 23:1). Isaiah 56:3-8, a passage just a few pages from where the Ethiopian was reading, however, does offer more hope to such men.

[7]A covenant is a solemn promise made binding by a pledge or vow, which may be either a verbal formula or a symbolic action. Covenant often referred to a legal obligation in ancient times. In Old Testament terms, the word was often used in describing the relationship between God and His chosen people, in which their sacrifices of blood afforded them His atonement for sin, and in which their fulfillment of a promise to live in obedience to God was rewarded by His blessings. In New Testament terms, this relationship (the new covenant) was now made possible on a personal basis through Jesus Christ and His sacrifice of His own blood.

[8]John Stott, *The Spirit, the Church, and the World* (Downers Grove, Illinois: InterVarsity Press, 1990), pp. 163–64.

8

THE CONVERSION OF SAUL

Acts 9:1-31

In the section we are about to study, Luke finishes on a high note: **Then the church throughout Judea, Galilee and Samaria enjoyed a time of peace. It was strengthened; and encouraged by the Holy Spirit, it grew in numbers, living in the fear of the Lord** (Acts 9:31). Contrast this verse with the words that open Acts 9: **. . . Saul was still breathing out murderous threats against the Lord's disciples** (9:1a). What caused this dramatic reversal? The conversion of one significant man. (We know that Luke saw the story of Saul's conversion as a crucial turning point. How do we know? Luke includes this same story *three* times in Acts [see the other accounts—22:5-16; 26:12-19; see also commentary covering these scriptures for notes on differences among the three accounts].)

Most of us can easily explain the events which caused this amazing reversal. We have heard the story many times. As you review it one more time, try to put yourself back into the story as it occurred.

Join the Christians in feeling fear toward Saul. If you think the early church was too strong to be afraid, review Luke's account. The disciples in Jerusalem remained afraid of Saul even *after* his conversion (see 9:26), not to mention the earlier days when he was still "breathing murder." Move with the Christians as they shift their fear from Saul toward **living in the fear of the Lord** (9:31). You cannot feel their awe before the Rescuer until you feel their terror before the danger.

We need first to establish the scene. Saul was on his way to arrest Christians in Damascus.[1] On what charges? In Acts 9, Luke does not describe the "crimes" which the Christians had committed—crimes that were, according to Saul and the Jews, worthy of death! We can assume that believers outside Jerusalem were following patterns set by their Jerusalem brothers and sisters. What charges had been laid against believers in Jerusalem? "Proclaiming *in Jesus* the resurrection of the dead" (4:2, my emphasis; see 4:17-18), acting and speaking in power adequate to make the Jews jealous (see 5:17), and changing "the customs Moses handed down to us" (6:14). Were the Christians guilty of any true crime? No, for Jesus subsequently reminded Saul that he was persecuting not merely the believers, but ultimately Jesus himself (see 9:4-5), even though Saul thought he was doing God's will (see Philippians 3:5-6).

How had the gospel reached Damascus, a city outside Palestine and 150 miles to the northeast? That's another question Luke leaves unanswered. Many believers whose names were never recorded played key roles in the spread of the Kingdom. Some of these anonymous Christians must have been the first to witness for Jesus in Damascus. There they shared the good news with Jews such as Ananias who, like each of them, became an effective servant of God.

Sermons on Acts 9 usually focus on Saul, and perhaps rightfully so. But Ananias is the quiet figure without whom Saul might have remained blind and confused. Who was this man Ananias? Luke tells us so little. About all we can say is that Ananias must have been a mature leader in the Damascus church.

Picture yourself as Ananias quite early in this story. You **have heard many reports about . . . all the harm** Saul **has done to** God's **saints in Jerusalem,** raising **havoc** there (9:13, 21). (It appears likely that others in Jerusalem followed Stephen to martyrdom.) You know that Saul is now on his way toward you **with authority from the chief priests to arrest** you and your fellow Christians (9:14). He plans to take your group **as prisoners to Jerusalem** to face trial and potential execution there (9:2; see 9:21).

How do you feel? If you manage to escape fear for yourself, you will feel a dreadful weight for those left behind. You ask yourself, "Who will lead the church if its shepherds are removed? Who will care for the orphaned children left alone?" You reflect on the psalms you have known since childhood: "This poor man called, and the LORD heard him; he saved him out of all his troubles. The angel of the LORD encamps around those who fear him, and he delivers them" (Ps. 34:6-7). You have hope, but you realize that God sometimes delivers His children only through death. Even in the months just prior to Saul's travel to Damascus, God had rescued Peter and John, but permitted Stephen to die.

God answers your unspoken prayer rather dramatically. He calls you by name: **Ananias!** (Acts 9:10). Does God want you to take the community into hiding? Does God want you to go and fight this Jew? No. To your surprise, you hear God telling you to welcome the enemy Saul into your house.

We don't know the tone of voice in which Ananias responded (see Acts 9:13-14). Disbelief? Fear? Anger? In any case, God reassured Ananias. Everything would be okay. The Christians of Damascus would escape separation and death. But there was even better news: God would not only defuse the threat, but use the persecutor of the church as a proclaimer of the truth.

(You can see God's words to Ananias [see 9:15-16] as a summary of the second half of Acts, just as 1:8 summarized the first half. Acts 1 through 12 focus on the church's spread through **Jerusalem, . . . Judea and Samaria, and to the ends of the earth** [1:8]. [Some ancient thinkers considered Ethiopia (see 8:26-39) one of the places where the world ended.] Acts 13 through 28 focus on Saul/Paul, the **chosen instrument,** as he carried Jesus' name **before the Gentiles and their kings,** as well as the scattered Jews. In that process, Paul would **suffer for** Christ's name [9:15-16].)

Ananias may have had his questions, but he obeyed. As God directed him, Ananias went **to the house of Judas on Straight Street** (9:11). (A funny picture of God consulting a street map comes to my mind.) Luke skips over some details here. In his account, it appears that Ananias walked into the house, walked straight to Saul, and began praying. I picture Ananias sliding into the house rather cautiously, not knowing what to expect. His picture of Saul, the stallion-riding battler, is shattered as he sees a small, broken man, helplessly staring off into darkness. Overcoming his qualms, Ananias pulls up a chair beside the blind man and asks Saul to tell him his story.

"I was not far outside your city. I was planning how to gather the people on my hit list. A flash of light was the last thing I saw. The experience shocked me right off my horse. I was grappling around for some sense of what was happening, when I heard a voice: **Saul, Saul, why do you persecute me?** [9:4b]. In my darkness, I began to see the light. I was told to come here. Yet, I sensed that I was completely turned around. Here I am waiting, as I was told, for further information. Can you give it to me, sir?"

Ananias begins to realize the magnitude of the miracle before him. In faith, he begins to speak: **Brother Saul . . .** (9:17). No longer an enemy,

Saul is now a member of the family. Ananias touches Saul and feels the healing power of the Holy Spirit remove Saul's physical blindness and begin the process of spiritual healing. Saul receives baptism as well as food. His strength returns.

The story raises many questions. Note some of these questions and the answers Luke offers in the text.

Why did God choose Saul (see 9:15)? First, God wished to rescue His church from pressing danger (9:1-2). Second, God hoped to recruit one who could be a qualified ambassador to Gentiles, kings, and Jews (9:15). Saul's qualifications included his Jewish heritage, his strong education within his faith, and the secular training he certainly had received in Tarsus, one of the educational centers of the Roman Empire.[2] Third, Saul had several personality traits that would serve the Kingdom well. Saul did nothing halfheartedly. The same determination that led him to fight *against* the church moved him into battle *for* the church (9:20-22). From the beginning, Luke describes Paul's preaching as fearless and bold (9:27-28). Fourth, Saul was a fighter, but he had the wisdom to give up when he knew he was beaten. He recognized that he had been grasped by a power greater than himself. Recognizing his helplessness, he was willing to accept assistance from others.

What actually happened in Saul's Damascus road experience? Was it a vision, or a series of events that one could have picked up through the five senses? Perhaps both. Consider the evidence. Luke describes spectacular phenomena: **a light from heaven** bright enough that it blinded Paul, but did not damage his companions' sight (9:3; see 9:8); and a voice that only Paul could understand (see 9:4; 22:9).

Was it a vision that transformed Saul? Had God chosen to do so, He certainly could have spoken through a vision or dream. He often spoke through these means. He spoke to Joseph, Jesus' earthly father, through dreams (see Matthew 1:20; 2:19). In Acts 10:9-16, Luke describes how God revealed His will to Peter through a vision. If, on the Damascus road, God disclosed himself to Saul only through a vision, it's unusual that Saul's companions sensed anything at all. In this case, those traveling with Saul did hear the voice (of God), although they could not understand what it said (see 9:7; 22:9). They could see the light (22:9), but saw no divine figure (9:7). The fact that they experienced any of the special phenomena argues that God revealed himself to Saul in a way that went beyond a merely internal vision.

So, what actually happened? There's one fact of which we can be absolutely sure: Saul never doubted the reality of what he experienced.

On that day, God turned Saul's life upside down (see 1 Corinthians 9:1; 15:7-10; Galatians 1:12-16; 1 Timothy 1:12-16).

How did the Damascus road experience change Saul? Note three stages: He was a man with direction—he traveled from Damascus to Jerusalem to persecute the Christians (9:1-2); he lost his direction—he became physically blind (9:8; in a much broader sense, he became one needing direction [see 9:6]); he regained his direction—he traveled from Damascus back to Jerusalem to join the Christians (9:26). To put Saul's transformation in other words, Saul changed roles completely, from persecutor to proclaimer to persecuted. Consider these last two roles as Luke describes them in 9:20-30.

Saul began preaching Jesus immediately. He began this proclamation, as became his practice in subsequent ministry, in the Jewish synagogues. He stated his new realization plainly: **Jesus is the Son of God** (9:20). Some Jews there tried to convince him otherwise. Saul was not about to give in that easily. In power, he **baffled the Jews** with strong argument (9:22). He was already fulfilling the commission he had received from God via Ananias (see 9:15). Then Saul experienced a taste of what he had come to give: **The Jews** of Damascus **conspired to kill him** (9:23). God had predicted that Saul would **suffer** much for the name of Jesus (see 9:15), but Saul's ministry was not yet finished; it had only begun. The Jews there were *not allowed* to kill him. He sneaked out of town and headed home for Jerusalem (see 9:25-26).

It seemed Saul had no friends in Jerusalem. The Christians, at first, still saw him as a persecutor (see 9:26). The Jews, however, quickly saw his transformation. **They tried to kill him** (9:29b). Barnabas intervened to protect Saul from the Christians (see 9:27). Then all the Christians rallied to protect him from the Jews **and sent him off to** a safe haven in **Tarsus** (9:30).

Saul's ministry in these first two cities, Damascus and Jerusalem, was effective. Otherwise it might not have attracted the attention of the Jews. Saul himself was courageous. He continued to preach, despite threats on his life.[3]

Two other primary lessons for today's church stand out.

First, don't give up hope for *anyone's* salvation. Before Stephen died, he prayed that God would forgive those responsible for his death. Perhaps others, like Stephen, believed that God could change even Saul. It is good to pray that God will save you and other Christians from the harmful words and acts of nonbelievers around you. It is better to pray that God will save the nonbelievers and bring them to himself. The best way to get rid of enemies is to make them (let *God* make them) your friends.

Second, we often see God using "up front" people like Saul. God and Saul wasted no time. Saul became a central figure from the beginning. Bold, extroverted leaders, such as Saul, receive most of the contemporary "press coverage." But, in this story, where would Saul have been without Ananias's and Barnabas's work behind the scenes to disciple him and to assist his entrance into the community? Today's church, Christ's body, requires mouths and knees, feet and hearts.

ENDNOTES

[1]Luke, in Acts 9:2, describes Christianity as "the Way." Early Christians (or those around them) may have used this phrase to describe their new faith. For them, a relationship with Christ was much more than a system; it was a lifestyle. For other occurrences of this phrase, "the Way," in Acts, see 19:9, 23; 22:4; 24:14, 22.

[2]For one biblical summary of Paul's background, see Philippians 3:4-6. For further details, see a book focusing on Paul, such as *Paul: Apostle of the Heart Set Free* by F. F. Bruce (Grand Rapids, Michigan: Wm. B. Eerdmans Publishing Co., 1977).

[3]William Barclay, *The Acts of the Apostles* (Philadelphia: The Westminster Press, 1976), p. 74.

9

THE MINISTRY
OF PETER

Acts 9:32–11:18

For the last several chapters, Luke has turned his attention away from the apostles to describe the food controversy and the subsequent appointment of the deacons. Two of these deacons, Stephen and Philip, and then the persecutor Saul, have received Luke's attention.

Neither Luke nor, of course, God was yet done with the original apostles. God still had work to do *on* them and, subsequently, *with* them. In Luke's account, Peter becomes God's next target, and tool, for ministry.

1. PETER HEALS TWO IN JUDEA 9:32-43

To this point in the book of Acts, Luke has given only one detailed description of a healing, involving the lame man of chapter 2. That incident led immediately to a crucial event: the apostles' being arrested for the first time. In contrast, there are two healings in Acts 9 which appear as somewhat isolated incidents. One wonders why Luke records these two stories. They do not directly lead into new experiences for the church. Neither do they introduce characters who play any role in the remaining accounts. The stories of Aeneas and Dorcas could be seen merely as "fillers" between the conversion of Saul and a conversion for Peter (Peter's vision and his first evangelism among Gentiles).

Why does Luke include these stories? The events were, of course, quite significant for Aeneas and Dorcas, but the early Christians healed many other people whose stories Luke has passed over quickly (see, for example, 6:8; 8:6). Why are these stories here? There are at least four possible reasons.

First, Luke may have included the Dorcas story because it was so spectacular. Perhaps this was Peter's greatest feat, being used by God to raise someone from the dead. Just as Jesus, during His earthly life, performed miracles which astounded witnesses, He was still at work, after His ascension, enabling His apostles to manifest divine power. (Luke gives the names of those Peter healed and their hometowns, thus opening the possibility for his first readers to verify the accuracy of his accounts.)

Second, Luke certainly wished to show God's continual guidance and empowerment for the church. The enemies of persecution (Saul), illness (Aeneas), or even death (Dorcas) could not threaten God and His sovereign plan for His people.

Third, Luke may have seen the need to explain how Peter ended up in Joppa, outside Jerusalem, where he last appeared. For it was in Joppa, after the raising of Dorcas, that Peter received his significant vision of the unclean animals (see 10:5, 9-16).

Fourth, it may be that Luke felt it important to mention Judea, the region surrounding Jerusalem. (A Bible atlas or the maps in the back of a study Bible can help you better understand the next paragraphs.) Jesus' words (see 1:8) may have guided Luke's writing: ". . . You will be my witnesses in Jerusalem . . ." (Luke covers the church's growing ministry in the capital city quite well in the first seven chapters of Acts), "and in all Judea" (hardly mentioned to this point) "and Samaria" (given some attention in Philip's ministry there; see 8:5-25), "and to the ends of the earth" (the major focus of Acts 13 through 28).

What about Judea? Was God at work there? Acts 8:40 offers the only substantial hint that Luke has dropped so far: Philip preached "the gospel in all the towns" from "Azotus . . . until he reached Caesarea" (at several Judean locations along the Mediterranean coast). Philip (or likely others before him) had planted the seed. Had it grown? Was it bearing fruit? Yes! The church was present in Judea before Peter's arrival (see 9:32, 36). And, strengthened by Peter's ministry, the church continued to grow: **All those who lived in Lydda and Sharon saw him** [Aeneas, after his healing] **and turned to the Lord. . . . This** [the raising of Dorcas] **became known all over Joppa, and many people believed in the Lord** (9:35, 42). Let's now consider the two stories separately.

The Aeneas story does not receive much attention. Apparently Aeneas was one of **the saints**[1] **in Lydda** before Peter arrived (9:32), although we cannot be sure. Luke merely tells us that Aeneas had been **a paralytic . . . bedridden for eight years** (9:33). As Peter saw Aeneas, he may have remembered the time several people brought a paralyzed man to Jesus (see Luke 5:17-26). Jesus had healed that man, commanding him to pick up his mat and head home. Jesus could perform this miracle again. Thus, Peter spoke boldly: **. . . Jesus Christ heals you. Get up and take care of your mat** (Acts 9:34). Aeneas believed and obeyed. This miracle served as a sign that helped many turn to the Lord.

Luke gives more detail in the Dorcas story. Who was she? A disciple (a believer) who used her gift to help the community. She was always doing good and helping the poor. She imitated her Master, who also "went around doing good" (10:38), and lived among the poor. She demonstrated the fact that the early Christian church gave itself not only to evangelism, but also took care of the needy (remember 2:44-45; 4:32-35; 6:1).

Later in Luke's account, he tells more specifically about Dorcas's kindness to others. It appears that when Peter arrived, all the widows of the village may have been participating in an unplanned "Dorcas fashion show." They showed Peter the clothing Dorcas had made for them. They probably did not have to go to much trouble to pull out her sewing; they were probably wearing her handiwork. If Dorcas was the humble person I picture, she probably wouldn't have wanted all the praise she was receiving!

As the Aeneas incident had a solid parallel in Jesus' ministry, so did the raising of Dorcas. Compare Peter's raising of Dorcas with Jesus' raising of the daughter of the Capernaum synagogue ruler (see Luke 8:40-42, 49-56). In both cases, the death was fairly recent. (In most ancient cases, burial followed death without much delay.) In both cases, the body was laid within a house. Outside, there was much mourning. Jesus had asked that He be left nearly alone with the body; Peter followed this model. Both Jesus and Peter spoke the words, **Get up** (Acts 9:40; see Luke 8:54), grasping a hand and assisting the one just returned to life. Both resuscitations, of course, astonished the family and friends. God continued to display His power.

For His glory, God used an assortment of ordinary people in typical, small Judean villages. These people can be examples to you and me. Aeneas and Dorcas—an invalid and a seamstress—these ordinary people are the stars in this section of Acts. Who would have anticipated this? Aeneas did not get himself to Peter. Either others carried him to Peter or he asked Peter to visit. Dorcas could have sewn her garments for decades in total anonymity, an enduring example of servanthood. People around Dorcas had faith to believe that something could happen despite her death. They sent for Peter, hoping for a miracle.

You may feel like an ordinary person. Like Aeneas, you struggle with some physical (or emotional or mental) challenge that keeps you from doing all you would like. Perhaps like Dorcas, you have been working away for years, and only a few people know or care. Continue to be faithful. Your moment for glory will come, perhaps in this life.

Recently, a Rochester, New York, newspaper featured three pastors who, like Peter, have used fishing as part of their ministry. You may never end up on the front page. But if you continue giving your best, you have the satisfaction of serving God and helping people, and you have the hope of receiving your reward on that day when the last shall be first (see Luke 13:30).

Do you find it hard to keep on? Do you wish your life were more spectacular? Do you find the tasks, the life to which God has called you, too routine? In the two miracles of Acts 9:32-43, God helped Peter to do that which was otherwise impossible. Perhaps God wishes to perform a miracle through you, not a spectacular miracle that everyone will immediately recognize, but the miracle of enabling you to carry on with His quiet plan for this day, this week, this year.

During both of the miracles described in this section, Peter must have sensed the power of God flowing through him. He was able to help individuals in crisis and, through those interventions, see many people come to God. God likely was preparing Peter for the next situation, where he would find himself in crisis. It's as if God were saying, "Peter, I am with you. The last two men who came looking for you [see 9:38] were agents of good; I will show you that the next men coming for you [see 10:19] are also part of My plan." We, too, must pay close attention to each person we meet. Who knows whether God is engineering "a chance meeting" for His purposes.

2. GOD PREPARES CORNELIUS AND PETER 10:1-23a

Acts 9 records the great vision that God gave Saul, a vision that turned Saul's life around. It seems that Peter, however, needed more than one miraculous vision. He had already seen the Transfiguration and the Resurrection, not to mention many more mind-boggling events. Peter had preached to thousands, pioneering the Christian church of Jerusalem. He not only had seen miracles but, with God's help, had performed them—two big miracles not long before this next vision in Acts 10. God had freed Peter from prison unbelievably. You'd think that Peter would have "had it together" by this time.

Recently, I listened as a godly friend shared his spiritual struggles with me. He felt so disappointed in himself. He felt that God could potentially give up on him. "Shouldn't I be closer to perfection by now?" he asked.

God *is able* to come and fill a person with perfect love. God *can* enable us to love Him with all our being, and to love our neighbors as we love ourselves. But that does not mean that any of us reaches absolute perfection in this life. I know how much help I still need. If we would admit our needs to each other, we would be better able to help each other toward our goal of becoming all that God wants us to be.

Despite all that God had done in Peter's life, Peter still needed more divine help. To help Peter forward, God needed to give him yet another special vision. To paraphrase Jesus, "Blessed are those who do not see special visions, and yet are always open to receiving new insight, new strength from God" (see John 20:29). Let us join the hymnwriter in praying,

> I ask no dream, no prophet ecstasies
> No sudden rending of the veil of clay
> No angel visitant, no opening skies,
> But take the dimness of my soul away
> ("Spirit of God Descend Upon My Heart,"
> George Croly).

Let's pick up Peter's story as it unfolded. Again, as in Acts 9, God offered a double vision. In chapter 9, you remember that God spoke both to Saul and to Ananias, preparing them to meet each other. Now in chapter 10, within two consecutive days, God spoke both to Cornelius and to Peter, preparing them for their encounter. At first, Peter resisted God's direction. Cornelius, after overcoming his initial fear of the angel, must have been overjoyed to hear from God. God promised that Cornelius and his household were about to hear a message that would bring them salvation (see 11:14).

Who was Cornelius? He was a Roman centurion, an officer in command of one hundred men (note the similarities between the English words *centurion* and *century*). **Cornelius,** the **centurion,** was **devout and God-fearing** (10:1-2). He demonstrated his love for God by kindness **to those in need** and by devotion to prayer (10:2). The Jews **respected** him (10:22).

Throughout his writings, Luke describes four different centurions. He portrays all four positively. Luke 7:1-10 pictures a God-fearing centurion in Capernaum who built a synagogue for his village. Next, the centurion supervising Jesus' crucifixion was sensitive enough to observe the character of the man on the central cross (see Luke 23:47). Cornelius the centurion was, of course, worthy of praise. The last in Luke's catalog is Julius, a centurion who treated Paul well while supervising his transport from Caesarea to Rome (see Acts 27:1, 3, 43). Either the Romans chose their centurions well, or Luke hoped to impress his Roman readers by praising their countrymen. Perhaps both.

God, through an angel, spoke to Cornelius, calling him by name. In each vision Luke records in Acts 9 and 10, God called people by their names (see 9:4, 10; 10:3, 13). The Shepherd knows His sheep (see John 10:3).

The angel spoke: **Your prayers and gifts to the poor have come up as a memorial offering before God** (Acts 10:4b). The picture is similar to the Old Testament idea of prayer rising to God as a sweet fragrance. Did Cornelius's good acts make him worthy of God's love? No, but God is faithful and will reveal himself to those who seek Him.

Again, as with Saul, when God spoke to Cornelius, He could have told him everything he needed to know. Or God could have found a thousand other ways to reveal himself to this seeker. But God wanted to reveal the breadth of His love, not only to Cornelius, but also to Peter. (God does not *need* us to minister for Him. He is self-sufficient. He chooses to use us, in order to give us the benefit of serving Him.)

God told Cornelius exactly how to find Peter: **Send men to Joppa to bring back . . . Simon who is called Peter. He is staying with Simon the tanner, whose house is by the sea** (10:5-6). Cornelius would have received and obeyed orders frequently from his human superiors. He recognized the angel as a *true* superior and wasted no time in obeying him.

The following day, as Cornelius's messengers **were approaching** Joppa, **Peter went** to God in prayer (10:9). It might have been interesting to listen to his words. Was he reflecting back over the miracles of recent days? Was he experiencing the letdown that follows overwhelming experiences? Was he discerning God's next plan? In any case, even while praying, Peter the apostle became hungry. It's comforting to know that even apostles face distractions to prayer. The early Christians did not walk on some cloud above the human needs you and I experience.

If nothing else, Peter's vision shows God's creativity and sense of humor. Rather than a bland command—"Peter, I love Gentiles. I want you to love Gentiles, too"—God picks on Peter's hunger and his strict Jewish upbringing.[2] God spreads out a feast for Peter, but it is a collection of tasty treats long forbidden to Peter and other Jews (see

Leviticus 11). It's almost as if God walked up to a hungry man faithfully dieting to lose weight, and offered a table full of ice cream, cheesecake, and chocolate. In one sense, such an offer is torture. On the other hand, it could be "heaven." "Eat! Today, I have changed the rules. You can get away with anything you want."

Surely not, Lord! Peter replied (Acts 10:14). You would think that Peter would have learned by now. Several years earlier, when Jesus had told the disciples that He would be killed, Peter had responded, "Surely not, Lord!" (see Matthew 16:22). When Jesus had come to wash Peter's feet, Peter had refused: "Surely not, Lord!" (see John 13:8). On those occasions, Jesus had gently shown Peter that His way was best. And Jesus did it again. Here in Acts we see that He gave Peter the identical vision **three times** (Acts 10:16). Did the threefold repetition take Peter's thoughts back to the Sea of Galilee? There Jesus had told him three times to feed the Lord's sheep (see John 21:15-17). Peter had previously grasped the need to care for the lambs; God at this moment wanted to teach Peter that God's flock was much bigger than Peter had thought.

Peter was still up on the roof of the house. Several voices brought him back to earth. First, he heard voices in the street (in a foreign accent?) mentioning his name. At the same time, the Spirit instructed Peter to go with the foreigners. Interestingly, Luke, at this point, does not describe the messengers as being sent by Cornelius, but as being sent by God (see Acts 10:20). Cornelius and Peter were not ultimately in control.

Introductions took place. Peter asked the men their purpose in coming. They offered Peter an invitation any preacher would desire: "Our master wants you to come with us, so that he can **hear what you have to say**" (10:22). Knowing his potential congregation was a Gentile crowd and, to make matters worse, led by one of the Roman officers holding his country captive, Peter might have been tempted to say, "Surely not, Lord!" But he had learned another crucial lesson. And this would not be the last. Peter broke his old habits by inviting the Gentiles in as his guests. Together with them, he finally got his lunch.

3. GOD WELCOMES GENTILES 10:23b-48

Meanwhile, back in Caesarea, Cornelius could hardly wait for Peter's arrival. He had spoken to a large collection of **his relatives and close friends** (Acts 10:24). When Peter arrived, they were all waiting. Cornelius, not knowing any better, confused Peter with the Savior whom

Peter had come to proclaim. Peter worked out that problem and entered Cornelius's house—no small step for a strict Jew.

Peter reminded the **gathering** (10:27) of the gulf that had previously separated Jews from Gentiles. He then proclaimed to the people that God had bridged that gulf. There can be little doubt as to why Luke included the Cornelius series of events in his account. Not only was this interaction between the early (so far, exclusively Jewish) church and Gentile outsiders a historical first, but it set a theological precedent for all subsequent Christian-Gentile relationships.

Remember that Luke himself was a Gentile. Remember also that the first readers of Acts were largely Gentiles living in Rome. Had the church not reached across the ethnic barrier, Luke (and most of Acts' ancient and contemporary readers) would have been excluded. With that thought in mind, listen to Luke's quoting of Peter's words: **God has shown me that I should not call any man impure. . . . God does not show favoritism but accepts men from every nation** (10:28b, 34b-35a).

As Luke retells this story, he goes beyond describing the visions God gave to Cornelius and Peter (see 10:1-16). Luke gives them both an opportunity to tell their stories in their own words (see 10:30-33; 11:4-17). With this repetition, no one should miss the divine origin or the great significance of these events.

With an eager congregation before him, Peter proclaimed **the good news of peace through Jesus Christ** (10:36). He confirmed and supplemented reports of Jesus that the group had already heard, events that he himself had witnessed. What were the key elements of that good news? **John preached** and offered **baptism** (10:37). Jesus began His ministry as God gave Him **the Holy Spirit and power** (10:38). Jesus traveled **the country of the Jews and in Jerusalem . . . doing good and healing** (10:38-39). The Jews **killed** Jesus (10:39).[3] **God raised** Jesus and revealed Him to selected **witnesses** (10:40-41). Jesus **commanded** His followers **to preach** Him **to the people** (10:42). God has **appointed** Jesus **as judge** of all people (10:42). All who believe in Jesus receive **forgiveness of sins** (10:43).

We recognize this list both as the core of nearly all sermons Luke included in Acts, and as a summary of the Gospels[4] (which themselves should be read as early-church preaching). We believers accept these statements as easily as we do the life histories of our spouses or parents. But try to put yourself in Cornelius's place.

Which elements of Peter's gospel summary would have most surprised Cornelius, a practically minded Roman army officer? How would *you* respond to such a story? In the last ten years, a man who lived within one hundred miles of your home had survived death, not merely in soul form, but in a bodily form people could see. Stand with Cornelius as he hears that this man, whom God appointed as judge, **is Lord of all** (10:36). Today, we don't know whether to laugh or cry when cult leaders proclaim themselves as "messiahs." We find their claims too ridiculous to believe. How would you have reacted if you had been Cornelius, hearing a message that was equally "impossible"?

Yet, all of those gathered in Cornelius's house moved quickly toward belief. How do we know? **While Peter was still speaking . . . , the Holy Spirit came on all who heard . . .** (10:44). God does not give His Spirit randomly. He gives himself to those who freely open themselves to Him.

God also enabled these new believers to speak in tongues (see 10:46). Interpretation of this particular New Testament phenomenon (see Acts 2:4; 19:6; 1 Corinthians 12:10, 28; 13:1; 14:1-40) has caused disagreement in the twentieth-century church. Two questions have provoked the most debate.

Do all New Testament references to tongues denote an ability to speak in human languages not naturally learned (as was apparently the case in Acts 2)? Or do at least some of the passages describe a nonhuman ecstatic "prayer language" (as many argue that the Corinthian correspondence does)? On this question, the churchwide jury is still out. Which side of the debate you choose may not be as important as your willingness to submit to Paul's instructions on the use of tongues (and on broader church interaction) in 1 Corinthians 12 through 14. Love should always be central (see 1 Corinthians 13:13). Within a context of love, Paul encouraged both orderliness and freedom in worship (see 14:39-40).

The second question is this: Is the gift of tongues *the* manifestation of the Spirit's presence in a believer's life? In Acts 2, 10 and 19, tongues were given as *an* evidence, but other Spirit outpourings do not mention tongues (see, for example, 2:38; 8:17; 9:17-19). Neither do the Epistles[5] cite tongues as *the* evidence. The primary New Testament evidence of the Spirit's presence seems to be the fruit of love, joy, and peace (see Galatians 5:22-23).

On this particular occasion with Cornelius and the others in Acts 10, God may have given the Gentile group the gift of tongues primarily for the sake of Peter and the other Jews present. Peter had been wise enough to take witnesses with him (see Acts 10:23; 11:12). If anything unexpected turned up, he wanted others to observe the experience with him. Peter, with all the extra warning God had given him, probably wasn't surprised by God's seal of approval on the Gentiles. But his companions were shocked! However, they could not dispute the reality of what they saw and heard. Peter gave them the chance to speak before he baptized the Gentiles, but there was nothing they could say. God had given himself to *all* who believed (see 10:35, 43). Jesus was not merely the Messiah of the Jews; He was the Savior, the Lord of all.

Some readers have been upset by what they call Luke's anti-Semitism. Acts 10:39 might offer some support for their claims. In this verse, Luke quotes Peter as he seemingly laid all blame for Jesus' death on the Jews. A review of the gospel record shows clearly that the Roman governor sentenced Jesus to death. Romans soldiers fulfilled that sentence. Should not these Gentiles also bear responsibility for their actions? Did Peter (or Luke) shade the truth, hoping to soften that truth for his Roman hearers (readers)? Possibly.

The Romans did contribute to Jesus' death. But the Gospels offer no evidence that the Romans would have seen Jesus as a threat if the Jews had not instigated His arrest. Matthew even quoted these strong words from the Jews of Jerusalem: "Let his blood be on us and on our children" (Matt. 27:25).

Who was responsible for Jesus' death? The Jews? Yes. The Romans? Yes. But also any person whose sin has broken his or her relationship with God, a relationship Jesus lived and died to restore. Today's Jews have no more responsibility for Jesus' death than do today's Christians. Jesus died for Jews just as He died for Gentiles. Any form of racial prejudice, anti-Semitism included, has no place in the Christian's life.

4. THE HOME CHURCH SETTLES SOME QUESTIONS 11:1-18

I currently live in a small town where news (if you wanted to be less generous, you might call it "gossip") travels quickly. This is not a new phenomenon. There evidently was a good grapevine between Caesarea and Jerusalem: **The apostles [in Jerusalem] and the brothers throughout Judea heard that the Gentiles also had received the word of God** (Acts 11:1). At minimum, the Jewish Christians had serious questions about bringing Gentiles into the family. Luke honestly describes how some of them not only had doubts, but were convinced that Peter had gone beyond proper bounds. Some **circumcised believers criticized** Peter (11:2). In effect, they said, "You have defiled yourself (and thus alienated God) by eating with Gentiles."

You have heard similar words in your church, too. "We've never done it that way before. (And, of course, the way we have done it all these years is God's way.)" How do we respond in such situations? How do we best cooperate with more conservative, tradition-bound brothers and sisters? Most Christians are usually sincere in looking for that which is best for their churches. (Never forget, the day will come, if it has not already, when *you* will be the one defending some tradition you hold dear.) On one hand, Christians cannot throw out all traditions without losing ideas and practices central to the faith. On the other hand, some traditions require modification if the church is to remain faithful to its divine calling.

In this situation in Acts 10 and 11, perhaps the critics remembered the tragedies God's people had faced in past centuries. Many of their ancestors' problems came when they too freely associated with those outside God's flock. The people of Israel had lost their homelands and faced decades as refugees in exile for adopting the philosophies and lifestyles of Gentiles around them. Peter's critics accurately recognized that God's people needed to remain separate. Even the example and teaching of Jesus (see, for instance, Matthew 10:5) argued for maintaining strong relationships only "within the family."

How did Peter respond to the criticism? He could have returned the criticism he was receiving. But he did not attempt to argue. He merely **explained everything to them precisely as it had happened** (Acts 11:4).

How far can we go in setting up as an example Peter's action in the Cornelius story? Some might want to point out that Peter did not ask permission for Gentile evangelism before visiting Caesarea. He could be seen as providing support for the old saying, "It's easier to ask forgiveness after the fact than to receive permission first." You and I might need to be careful before adopting that philosophy. Ananias and Sapphira took that gamble, and we know how they ended up (see 5:1-11). But Peter had lived with Jesus for a number of years. Peter had been filled with the Spirit and interacted with other Spirit-led church leaders for a subsequent period of time. When he had moved toward Gentile evangelism, he had not jumped at changing church tradition, but had been moved only reluctantly in that direction. When Peter had preached to Cornelius, he had had no doubt that he was following God's plan. He had not asked Jerusalem's permission, because he had felt no need to do so.

Even after the "church board" criticized Peter's interaction with Gentiles, Peter did not criticize in return. He merely laid out the facts. He did not color the truth; he retold the story exactly as it had occurred. In some cases, he used different words (for example, compare the angel's words as recorded in 10:4-6 with those of 11:13-14), but the facts were the same.

Peter also emphasized that he had not acted totally alone—another good lesson for today's Christians. He had taken **six brothers** with him (11:12). Together, the seven of them had witnessed the Holy Spirit's coming to the Gentiles, just **as he had come on** the 120 Jews **at the beginning** (11:15).

Someone listening to Peter that day might have chuckled a bit as he spoke: **. . . Who was I to think that I could oppose God?** (11:17). Peter told the group how he had at first resisted God's direction (see 11:8). By resisting, Peter had merely followed a pattern he had already established in his interaction with Jesus (see Matthew 16:22; John 13:8). Despite that, God had used him powerfully.

After Peter finished, the conservative Jerusalem group **had no further objections** (11:18). They **praised God, saying,** "Truly, God is in this." In these words, those who frequently find themselves defending traditions can hear a lesson. The Jerusalem leaders quietly listened as Peter told his story. There is no sign that they interrupted him or distrusted his words. As they listened, they realized that they had been wrong. They proved that they were more eager to grasp truth than to defend their own positions. When Peter clearly showed that God was bigger than their opinions, they let their prejudices go. They rejoiced in the results of Peter's action, which previously they had criticized: "Even to those to whom we would not have reached out and in a manner we never would have approved, **God has granted even the Gentiles repentance unto life** (11:18b)."

ENDNOTES

[1] William Barclay, *The Acts of the Apostles* (Philadelphia: The Westminster Press, 1976), pp. 77–78. Luke's use of the word "saints" here (also in 9:13, 41; although in the last reference, the editors of the New International Version translate the Greek word as "believers") helpfully reminds us that all God's people, not just the most spiritual, are special people, separated for God's use.

[2] Ibid., pp. 80–81. Peter had already made some progress toward ministry to people outside the inner circle of proper Jews. He was staying in the house of a tanner. Such a person, who worked continually with dead animal skins, would have been continually unclean in the Jewish ceremonial sense. (He thus would have been unable to participate, for example, in Temple worship.) Peter would himself have become unclean when he stayed in the house of an unclean person.

Why was Peter praying on the roof? House roofs were flat. They offered a quiet place away from the people that often filled small houses.

[3] Leon Morris, *New Testament Theology* (Grand Rapids, Michigan: Zondervan Publishing House, 1986), p. 189. The phrase, "You **killed [Jesus] by**

hanging him on a tree (Acts 10:39; see also 5:30; 13:29), is an Old Testament phrase. In its original context, it speaks of the curse borne by one killed in this manner. Acts contains relatively little explanation of how Jesus' death effects human salvation. Luke's use of this phrase may indicate his belief that Christ had borne a curse in the place of all humanity (see Galatians 3:13; 1 Peter 2:24).

⁴The Gospels include the New Testament books of Matthew, Mark, Luke, and John.

⁵The Epistles are comprised of the New Testament books of Romans; 1 and 2 Corinthians; Galatians; Ephesians; Philippians; Colossians; 1 and 2 Thessalonians; 1 and 2 Timothy; Titus; Philemon; Hebrews; James; 1 and 2 Peter; 1, 2 and 3 John; and Jude. The books of James; 1 and 2 Peter; 1, 2, and 3 John; and Jude are called General Epistles because they are books or letters written to broad groups of people, rather than being addressed to specific individuals or churches the way that, say, Paul's letters to the Corinthians were.

10

A NEW CHURCH IN ANTIOCH

Acts 11:19-30

The first seven chapters of Luke's account in Acts describe how the first Christian church remained firmly Jewish and based in Jerusalem. As that block of writing ends, Luke introduces Saul, the one who drove many Christians, and thus a large segment of the church, out of Jerusalem (see Acts 8:1-4). As Luke thought out the book he intended to write, he knew he wanted to describe in detail how Saul, who would become known as Paul, took the good news to what is now Turkey, Greece, and Italy (see Acts 13–21). Acts 8 through 12 serve as a necessary transition between the Jewish, Jerusalem-based church and the more ethnically diverse group which had Antioch as its headquarters.

How do chapters 8 through 12 accomplish their purpose? First, Luke tells his readers how God intervened to bring Saul, the persecutor, into the church (see Acts 9). Chapters 8, 10 and 11 show how God helped the church gradually open its arms to embrace increasingly diverse people: Samaritans—people committed to the God of the Old Testament, although they worshiped in a manner different than that of the orthodox Jews; the Ethiopian eunuch—perhaps a proselyte (a full convert to Judaism[1]), at minimum, a God-fearer (a Gentile strongly attracted to Judaism, even if not a full convert); a collection of Gentiles, led by Cornelius (who was certainly a God-fearer)—this first evangelistic outreach to Gentiles had been specifically engineered by God himself.

Before Luke could portray Saul's/Paul's movement from Antioch in order to evangelize the entire Mediterranean region, Luke needed to add a few more pieces to his puzzle. In other words, he needed to answer a few more questions. How did the church become open to more *free* evangelism among Gentiles? How did Antioch become the great missionary-sending church? How did Saul/Paul end up in Antioch? Acts 11:19-30 fills the gaps in the picture and answers these last questions.

Another anonymous group of evangelists (like those who first proclaimed Jesus in places such as Lydda and Joppa; see 9:32, 36) took the gospel to Antioch. In this city, the church faced a totally new situation. First, Antioch was outside Judea, Samaria, and Galilee, where Jesus had ministered. Second, Antioch was, even by modern standards, an urban center. Joppa may have had a few hundred or maybe a thousand residents; Jerusalem had perhaps fifty thousand,[2] while Antioch was home to as many as five hundred thousand people! Antioch was the third largest city in the Roman Empire, ranking only behind Rome and Alexandria (in Egypt). Antioch was a city known for its love of pleasure and luxury. Its temple to the goddess Daphne involved ritual prostitution.[3]

How did a small-town Jewish church end up in urban, Gentile Antioch? The story here goes back to the martyrdom of Stephen. Luke again refers to the story of those **scattered by the persecution** that followed Stephen's death (11:19). The **scattered** Christians took the gospel in various directions. Luke mentions evangelists traveling southeast to Phoenicia, west to the Mediterranean island of Cyprus, and north to Antioch (see 11:19). At first, these evangelists offered the news of the Messiah only to those who were expecting His arrival—the Jews. Antioch had its large pocket of Jews, part of the dispersion (see chapter 6 of the commentary). The first Christians in Antioch came from its Jewish community.

Some of them, however, men from Cyprus and Cyrene, went to Antioch and began to speak to Greeks [Gentiles] **also, telling them the good news about the Lord Jesus** (11:20). This move toward Gentiles was overwhelmingly significant. This was the church's first deliberate move toward Gentiles. In its previous ministry among non-Jews, Cornelius the Gentile had made the first move (at God's instigation).[4] (There may have been a large time gap between the establishment of "Antioch First Church" [see 11:19] and "Antioch Second," which included Gentiles; see the additional notes at the end of this chapter of the commentary.) Although God had not specifically instructed this move, He showed His approval by the fruit it bore: **A great number of people [from the Gentiles] believed and turned to the Lord** (11:21b).

Once again, word of new and different converts traveled. Even without telephones and e-mail, the word of a Gentile church in Antioch **reached the ears of the church at Jerusalem** (11:22). The leaders there had perhaps learned a lesson, after criticizing Peter's work among Gentiles. They were not so quick to condemn, but they still acted cautiously. They decided to send one of their own to check out this situation and verify its validity.

The Jerusalem church could not have chosen a better representative than Barnabas. He had already shown his worth by his generosity (see 4:36-37) and open-mindedness (helping Saul to enter the fearful Christian leadership group; see 9:27). Barnabas sized up the Antioch situation, noting its present value and potential for the future. He discipled the new believers. (When Jews of the first century became Christians, they had a head start. They already knew God the Father and Old Testament history, and they lived by God's strong ethical teaching. But Gentiles, coming from a pagan background, had so much to learn, starting from Genesis 1!) Under Barnabas's leadership, the church continued to grow.

Barnabas soon realized that he needed help. As the Jerusalem church had chosen well in nominating him for his pastoral role, he did equally well in recruiting his assistant. Who was it? None other than Saul. As an educated Jew, who had been raised in a Gentile city, but who was now fiercely loyal to Jesus, Saul was especially well suited. In the Barnabas-Saul partnership, they could accomplish two goals. Of course, Saul could help disciple the Gentiles. But at the same time, Barnabas could mentor Saul, as Saul developed his own rich potential. **. . . So for a whole year Barnabas and Saul met with the church and taught great numbers of people . . .** (Acts 11:26).

Did they do a good job? Yes. The other residents of the city noticed a real difference among the believers. This group of "Jesus people" became so distinct that those around them coined a new name for the believers. The pagans of Antioch first called those who had joined Barnabas and Saul the "Christ-ones" or, as we say today, **Christians** (11:26).

The Antioch church received all that Barnabas and Saul could give them. But as they received, they became givers, too. When the new believers heard that their "spiritual grandparents" in Jerusalem would be facing financial need, they responded generously; **each according to his ability** gave an offering (11:29). The believers sent this to Jerusalem via their pastors, Barnabas and Saul. The two men must have celebrated all through that journey, knowing that they carried not only cash, but the wonderful news of God's work among the Gentiles.

As you consider this passage again, note the wonderful balance manifested in Antioch: evangelism *and* discipleship; ministry to spiritual *and* physical needs; listening, speaking, *and* doing; and a *variety* of ministries shared among many people who both gave *and* received. Such balance does not come easily. It is a sign that God is truly at work.

ADDITIONAL NOTES ON THE CHRONOLOGY OF ACTS

The chronology of Acts is one of the questions arising as scholars investigate ways to coordinate the book of Acts and Galatians 1–2. This is not an easy task. In Galatians, Paul mentions a gap of three years between his conversion and his first visit to Jerusalem (see 1:18), and a further span of fourteen years before his next such visit (2:1). Could there be seventeen years between the conversion of Saul/Paul (sometime after the death of Stephen; see Acts 9) and Paul's second trip to Jerusalem (likely the one described in 11:30)?

Coordinating the dates of these events is further complicated when we consider other dates outside this specific time period. Scholars tell us that Jesus' death, resurrection, and ascension (see 1:9) took place in roughly A.D. 30. Likewise, the end of Paul's first visit to Corinth, on his second missionary journey, can be dated at about A.D. 50 (see 18:18; extrabiblical information about Gallio, the proconsul, helps to fix this date). That's a period of twenty years in which to fit all the events of Acts 1 through 18. But Paul's chronology in Galatians apparently gives seventeen of these years to the events of Acts 9 through 11—from Paul's conversion to His second trip to Jerusalem. We do seem to have a problem here.

What help can we find? It is possible that Paul intended his mention of fourteen years (see Galatians 2:1) to include the three years (1:18). Also, ancient counting of days and years (and other denominations of time) included both the first and the last. For example, Christ's time in the tomb is counted as three days, even though he was dead for less than forty-eight hours. So, possibly Paul intended us to see only a thirteen-year gap between his conversion (see Acts 9) and the "famine visit" from Antioch to Jerusalem (11:27-30). This hypothesis seems to coordinate more easily with Luke's account in Acts.

A tentative overall chronology of Acts might look like this:[5]

Pentecost[6]	A.D. 30	Acts 2
Stephen's death	A.D. 33–34	Acts 7
Paul's Damascus road experience	A.D. 34–35	Acts 9
Paul's first missionary journey	A.D. 46–48	Acts 13–14
The Jerusalem Council	A.D. 48–49	Acts 15:1-35
Paul's second missionary journey	A.D. 49–53	Acts 15:36–18:22

Paul's third missionary journey	A.D. 54–58	Acts 18:23–21:17
Paul's Caesarea imprisonment	A.D. 58–60	Acts 21:27–26:32
Paul's travels to Rome	A.D. 60–61	Acts 27
Paul's house arrest in Rome	A.D. 61–63	Acts 28

ENDNOTES

[1]Judaism is the life and belief system of the Jewish people and involves a covenant relationship with God. Though there are various branches of Judaism, the underlying theme among them has been monotheism and a recognition of the Law, or the Torah. The Hebrew word from which *Torah* comes is translated *law* and refers to divine instruction and guidance. The Torah is comprised of the instructions and directions given to Israel by God. Torah is another name for the Pentateuch (the first five books of the Old Testament: Genesis, Exodus, Leviticus, Numbers, and Deuteronomy), also known as the Law of Moses. It is considered the most important division in the Jewish Scriptures, with highest authority, since it was traditionally thought to have been written by Moses, the only biblical hero to have spoken with God face-to-face.

[2]Joachim Jeremias, *Jerusalem in the Time of Jesus* (Philadelphia: Fortress Press, 1969), p. 83. Scholars debate the first-century population of Jerusalem. Joachim Jeremias, a respected New Testament scholar, after much research, feels that fifty-five thousand may be a good estimate.

[3]William Barclay, *The Acts of the Apostles* (Philadelphia: The Westminster Press, 1976), p. 89.

[4]Ibid., p. 88.

[5]This chronology is taken from Bruce Metzger, *The New Testament: Its Background, Growth, and Content* (Nashville, Tennessee: Abingdon Press, 1983), pp. 179–80.

[6]In the New Testament, Pentecost primarily refers to the event when the Holy Spirit was given to the church; this occurred on the day of Pentecost. The Greek term *Pentecost* comes from means "fiftieth" or "the fiftieth day" and is literally the fiftieth day after the end of the Passover. It is also known as the Jewish Feast of Weeks. This day is part of the Jewish observances, and was the beginning of the offering of first fruits.

11

PETER'S ARREST AND MIRACULOUS RELEASE

Acts 12:1-25

B y the end of chapter 11 of Acts, Luke must have felt ready to move on. His next goal? To take his readers along with Saul/Paul as he evangelized areas north of the Mediterranean Sea. Before Luke did so, he stayed with Saul and Barnabas in Jerusalem for a short while longer (see 11:30; 12:25). Those days in Jerusalem offer yet another conflict between those who should have recognized Jesus' appearance and those who did recognize it.

The Jews of Jerusalem were those closest to the Temple, the main location where God's presence could be said to dwell. Herod, the ruler of Palestine in this time, was himself the descendent of Jewish kings. (This was Herod Agrippa I, the nephew of the Herod involved in the deaths of John the Baptist and Jesus.) Herod had free access to the history of God's people. He and others living around Jerusalem should have been most open to God's revealing himself once again. But they missed their opportunity. Rather than believing that God had revealed himself, they attacked those who did believe.

While the good news of Jesus spread in many directions (see 8:4–11:30), God was still at work among the believers in Jerusalem, although no one could blame them for feeling a bit of doubt. The reality was that, although God remained in control, Satan was not ready to roll over and die. Satan had lost Saul, but he led King Herod and the Jews to continue the persecution Saul had started.

Herod **had James, the brother of John, put to death with the sword** (12:2). Why did God allow this to happen? God could have miraculously freed James, as he was about to free Peter. The church undoubtedly prayed for James as fervently as it prayed for Peter (see 12:5). But God allowed James to die.

How would you have felt if you had been a member of James's family? Perhaps they rejoiced in the miracle God had worked on Peter's behalf. Perhaps they felt honored that James had been able to follow his Master to death (see Mark 10:39) near the anniversary of Jesus' death (Acts 12:3-4). Yet, they must have asked all kinds of questions.

Was God able to use James's death for good (see Romans 8:28)? Yes, but Luke does not tell us how. And if James's death somehow produced good for the church, why did God not double that good by allowing Peter to be killed? We, too, have many questions and not many answers. Then, as now, God works in mysterious ways.

In Luke's retelling of the story, James's death served primarily to indicate the seriousness of Peter's situation. Humanly speaking, Peter had little hope. The execution of his apostolic colleague **pleased the [Jerusalem] Jews** (Acts 12:3). The squad of guards around Peter appeared solid (12:4). Herod was ready to bring Peter to trial. The Jews were hoping for more blood (12:11).

What were the charges laid against the apostles? Luke gives no hint. Disturbing the peace? Upsetting the status quo? Nowhere in Acts do we read that the enemies of the church were able to show the Christians to have truly broken any law. Envy appeared the primary cause for arrest.

What would happen if we asked God today to powerfully manifest His power in our lives or our churches? What if He worked so strongly among us that those around us viewed us with envy? Are you willing to take that risk? Remember, however, that the Jews never had any reason to envy the material wealth or the physical comfort of the Christians.

What possessions *did* the Christians have that the Jews wanted? Perhaps the Jews envied the Christians' joy. Despite the early believers' circumstances, joy seemed often to characterize them. Confidence in God? These Christians rarely, if ever, lost their faith. Strength to withstand difficult circumstances? The church never let its trials tear it from its belief in Jesus. Be careful, however, not to worship the early church. **The night before Herod was to bring [Peter] to trial** (12:6), God worked a miracle that no one—not even the early Christians—could believe.

As mentioned above, **the church was earnestly praying to God for [Peter]** (12:5). Peter probably prayed before going to sleep for what might have been the last time. But the early church (so often idolized today) and the great Apostle Peter evidently had little faith for a miracle. Perhaps the church's "unanswered" prayer for James had dampened their spirits. In any case, when the angel woke him up, Peter **thought he was seeing a vision** (12:9). Also, when Rhoda, the servant girl, told the still-praying church that its prayers had been answered, the Christians told her that she was **out of [her] mind** (12:15).[1]

Why could no one believe what had happened? Why weren't they expecting a miracle? The soldiers were certainly surprised (see 12:18), but that was to be expected, for they weren't believers. But Peter and the church? Peter had participated in "impossible" miracles before: for example, the healing of the man lame from birth (Acts 3); the raising of dead Dorcas (9:36-41); and even one similar angelic release from jail (5:19).

The church was earnestly praying, but perhaps, as time passed, the focus of their prayers shifted. Maybe they had moved to asking God to help Peter face death. (If so, that prayer was answered, though many years later. Despite the fact that Peter seems to have taken the safe route by leaving Jerusalem after this event [see 12:17], early church historians tell us that he remained faithful to Jesus, ultimately to the point of death.) Maybe those at the church prayer meeting were asking God to provide leadership to replace Peter. (God answered that prayer in the person of James, the brother of Jesus. It is in this story in Acts that James first appears as a church leader [see 12:17; also 15:13-21; 21:18; Galatians 2:9]). The believers' faith was not large, but at least they were praying. They continued to see God as the One who could help them. God apparently passed over the fact that their faith was small, and gave Peter back to them. We can find assurance there. God gives himself to those who *seek*.

Luke finishes this Jerusalem chapter with an ironic twist. The chapter begins with Herod in power, ready to kill. Peter was in prison, ready to be killed. By the end of this account, Herod had died, and Peter was free to serve God in power.

How did Herod's death come about? A group of his subjects flattered him with blasphemous adulation. They called him a god. Herod accepted this worship, the worship that Christians had refused to give him. The miracle of Peter's release should have adequately reminded Herod that he was *not* in control. It did not. After the miraculous release of Peter, Herod did not admit his powerlessness. He still clung to what power he had, ruthlessly ordering the death of the soldiers who had done everything they could to obey his commands (see Acts 12:19a). God had given Herod opportunity to recognize Him as the true God. Herod, however, showed his true loyalties—to himself. God chose to remove Herod from the scene.[2]

God displayed His sovereignty. No prison, no chains, no king—not even the death of an apostle close to Jesus—was going to prevent **the word of God** from continuing **to increase and spread** (12:24). Luke, in Acts 12, portrays one last Jerusalem conflict between the Jews and the Christians. He leaves no doubt as to who won.

Despite any possible appearances to the contrary, *God governs*. Those who follow Him join in His victory, although some, like James, experience that victory through suffering and death. Before we today celebrate *our* victory prematurely, we need to verify that we are, to the best of our knowledge and ability, following God, even at a cost to ourselves. Satan can attack the church from outside in an obvious manner. He can also work from within. That's what he did in the centuries preceding Christ, pulling the Jerusalem Jews away from their relationship with the true God. In the church today, we should seek to recognize all the attacks of the Evil One.

ENDNOTES

[1]It is possible that the house of John Mark's mother was the same upper room to which Mary Magdalene and others had first taken the good news of Jesus' resurrection. On that occasion, too, the infant church had rejected the apparently unbelievable miracle.

[2]See I. Howard Marshall, *Acts* (Grand Rapids, Michigan: Wm. B. Eerdmans Publishing Co., 1980), pp. 211–13. The first-century Jewish historian, Josephus, describes Herod Agrippa's death in similar terms.

Part Three

PAUL: GOD'S MESSENGER TO THE GENTILES

Acts 13:1–21:16

et's review what Luke has done in the first twelve chapters of Acts. He has opened the book by describing the last days before Jesus' ascension. Jesus interacted with the disciples, further unfolding the meaning of the past, as well as the disciples' hope and task for the future. After His return to the Father, Jesus sent the Holy Spirit to empower them for the work that lay ahead (see Acts 1:1–2:4).

Luke then portrays the amazing growth of the church in Jerusalem. Several supernatural acts attracted crowds to the believers. Peter and others seized these opportunities and preached Jesus to the Jews in the city. Great numbers believed. The religious leadership in the city grew jealous of the church and attempted to frighten the apostles into conformity. The apostles refused, and God confirmed their faith with further church growth (see 2:5–6:7).

The Jewish persecution of the church climaxed with the first Christian martyrdom and the resulting scattering of believers (see 6:8–8:4; also 9:32-43). This scattering of believers, however, backfired on the Jews. It merely gave believers the opportunity to proclaim Jesus wherever they went. Nothing could stop the church's growth, not even continued persecution (see 12:1-25). As the church grew, it spread not only over geographical borders, but also beyond previously uncrossed ethnic ones. One by one, the barriers fell. Samaritans, an Ethiopian proselyte, a God-fearing Roman officer, and then finally totally pagan Gentiles in the huge city of Antioch—all entered the community of Jesus Christ (see 8:5-40; 10:1–11:30).

Along the way, Luke has paused to tell how God brought one key individual onto the team: Saul of Tarsus (see 9:1-31). In a brilliant, unbelievable move, God turned one of the church's great threats into one of its most gifted proclaimers.

Luke has skillfully set the stage for the next step forward: several *planned* tours focusing on evangelism and discipleship. Luke enables us to ride along with Saul/Paul and his companions on these three trips. During their travels, they preached Jesus and discipled new believers in what is now western Turkey and Greece. Luke shows Saul, who now begins to be called Paul, gradually moving closer to Rome, the capital of the entire Roman Empire.

THE FIRST
MISSIONARY TRIP

Acts 13:1–14:28

cts 13 and 14 portray Saul's/Paul's first missionary journey.
Now in Acts 13, we will see Saul begin to be called Paul, a name
that will be used for him through the remainder of the book of
Acts.[1] Paul and Barnabas reached out to the island of Cyprus and also
a mainland region known as Galatia, now part of central Turkey.
Throughout the Acts account, Luke continues to highlight many
missions firsts.

1. THE ANTIOCH CHURCH SENDS MISSIONARIES[2] 13:1-3

Even the beginning of this trip was a crucial moment in church history.
For the first time, a local church took the initiative to send representatives
out on a Christian mission. Before observing the particular details of Paul
and Barnabas's adventures, note how and among whom God instigated
this venture. What do we know about the Antioch church? What features
made it uniquely fit to be the missionary-sending church? (You may wish
to review the beginnings of the Antioch church, described in the
commentary on 11:19-30.)

The Antioch church was made up of *new* Christians. Its members
could still easily remember their days before Christ. They still reveled in
the novelty of grace. When first-century Jews came to faith in Jesus, they
came to know their God more fully. In contrast, the Gentiles in Antioch
were coming to know the true God for the first time. This astonishing
realization that they, too, were included in God's family would have
motivated them to share this news with others in their city (see Acts
11:26) "and to the ends of the earth" (1:8).

The Antioch church was made up of *Gentile* Christians. Because their faith was still fresh, it had not yet had opportunity to solidify into rigid forms. Would the new Antioch Christians have felt any discomfort in taking the gospel to people whom some Jews might have rejected? No. It's likely that the new Antioch believers could hardly believe that God had truly accepted *them.* If anyone ever has, certainly they would have felt like the proverbial beggars who had found bread; they realized there was more than enough bread for beggars of all kinds everywhere.

The Antioch church was made up of *world-conscious* Christians. It had been founded by missionaries (see 11:20); these early witnesses helped to shape the outward-looking vision of the Antioch group. **Barnabas,** assisted by **Saul** [Paul], certainly would have encouraged this inclination (13:1). The breadth of the leadership team they gathered around them demonstrated their open-mindedness. It was quite a group: **Simeon called Niger,** perhaps an African person of color, indicated by his second name (there is a slim chance that this is none other than Simon of Cyrene, who carried Jesus' cross[3]); **Lucius of Cyrene,** perhaps one of the "men from Cyprus and Cyrene" who had first offered Jesus to Antiochene Gentiles (see 11:20); and **Manaen (who had been brought up with Herod the tetrarch),** likely an aristocrat of some wealth (13:1). Barnabas himself was originally from Cyprus. Although a "second-generation Christian"—not an apostle who had interacted with Jesus in the flesh— Barnabas had become a trusted member of the Jerusalem team (see 4:36-37; 9:27; 11:22). Paul combined his strongly Jewish heritage with his Roman citizenship and experience in his hometown of Tarsus, a center of Greek education. Apparently, none of the five leaders came originally from Antioch. The leadership team likely gave the Antioch church a greater world-consciousness.

The Antioch church was made up of *generous* Christians. They had manifested this by sending a love offering to those in Jerusalem who were potentially facing famine (see 11:27-30).

New Christians, Gentile Christians, world-conscious Christians, generous Christians—they combined all those traits with a *true dedication* to God. Luke picks up their story on a day when the Christians of Antioch were **worshiping** (the original Greek word used here might indicate "serving") **the Lord and fasting** (13:2). Luke gives no indication that this was a special event; it appears that this church regularly worshiped and fasted. (The church fasted again as it farewelled its leaders [see 13:3]). Fasting had been a regular component of Jewish worship, but many of the Antiochene believers had not come from this background. Their willingness to forfeit food shows the seriousness of their faith. A group such as this would have been more sensitive to the Holy Spirit's speaking.

The Antioch church was also made up of *obedient* Christians. When God spoke, they heard and obeyed.

What did the Spirit say? He asked for Barnabas and Paul (Saul). The young Antioch believers might have felt as if the Spirit were asking them to give up two key members of their leadership team. In one sense, He was. Barnabas and Paul never returned to Antioch in the same roles they had previously held. In another sense, the Spirit did not ask the Antioch church to give up Barnabas and Paul. He merely asked this group to extend its ministry beyond the confines of Antioch and the immediately surrounding area. To quote John Wesley, the Spirit asked the Antioch believers to "see the world as their parish."

How did the Spirit speak?[4] With an audible voice the entire group could hear? Perhaps. At least some of the leadership team possessed the gift of prophecy—a discernment of God's voice that compelled one to speak God's word. Perhaps the Spirit spoke through one or more of them. The Antioch church had experienced such ministry previously, when the prophet Agabus "through the Spirit predicted . . . a severe famine" (11:28). The group may have felt a God-given consensus. Possibly, in one meeting or in a series of meetings, they realized that it would be "right" to send Barnabas and Paul.

Does the Spirit still speak to people today? Of course. Should we listen to every person who claims that the Spirit has spoken to him or her? Probably not. We certainly need to be careful. The ancient Antioch situation, described here in Acts 13, offers two significant hints to recognizing the truth of such claims. First, the Spirit spoke simultaneously to several individuals. The Antioch church might have had, and believers today still have, more reason to doubt the validity of "a word from God" if only one person heard it. Second, among those who heard this message were at least some of the church leaders. Those who have known God for longer periods of time are more likely to recognize when He is speaking.

Why were Barnabas and Paul sent? Because they were the ones selected by the Spirit. One need not be a genius to see why the Spirit chose them. Note their traits mentioned above. Note the perfect matching of Barnabas, an experienced "pastor" with the gift of encouragement (see 4:36), and Paul, the bold action-taker. Also, both men had roots in the areas targeted for ministry: Barnabas on the island of Cyprus; and Paul in Tarsus, near Galatia.

Members of the Antioch church could have balked when God called away gifted members of the leadership team: "How can we get along without Barnabas? He has been our faithful pastor for so long!" But, in actuality, there was no sign of resisting the Spirit. Further fasting (perhaps to confirm God's will) and prayer (for the success of the venture, as well as, perhaps, for the continued health of the Antioch church) preceded the farewell.

Picture the church members' grief as they **sent them** [Barnabas and Paul] **off** that day (13:3). Remember, first-century travel involved more risk taking than we are used to. Daily e-mails from Barnabas to the home church? No chance. Would they see or even hear from Barnabas and Paul again? No one knew.

Picture the joy as the church members watched the ship sail away. They had been obedient to God. They had **placed their hands on** the two missionaries (13:3), indicating that Barnabas and Paul would be their representatives. At least in symbolic form, the entire church was going out on that ship. God was going to use not only Barnabas and Paul, but the entire church. As the home folks continued to worship, fast, and pray, they were helping others to sense the grace they had experienced. With joy, the church committed its representatives to their gracious God (see 14:26).

Who sent the two men off on their travels? The church did. Luke says this in the last words of 13:3. The Holy Spirit did. Luke says this in the first words of 13:4. John Stott helpfully observes the model given here. Any decision made by a church, apart from the Holy Spirit, would move too far toward institutionalism. On the other hand, it could be dangerous if a church were forced into action every time someone said, "The Holy Spirit told me . . ." without appropriate confirmation from the whole body. When the church as a whole can work in cooperation with the Spirit, we find the best balance.[5]

During this first journey, Paul and Barnabas[6] would visit a number of sites. Their ministry in each location would involve unique situations and events. But we can see a pattern of events repeated in nearly every city and village they entered. Before reviewing the one-time events of the first journey sequentially, let's examine the repeated pattern. This overview helps to reveal both the missionaries' original strategy and their hearers' typical responses:

- Paul and Barnabas entered a population center.
- There they preached the good news, first to Jews and then to Gentiles.
- Some people responded positively and became the core of new Christian churches.
- Others responded negatively. Those who rejected the message usually rejected the messengers.
- Persecution arose.
- Paul and Barnabas moved on to another site.

Let's "unpack" that list, item by item.

What can we say, collectively, about the places Paul and Barnabas visited? These places were all population centers. The missionaries gave priority to places where they would find crowds of people. Of the places they visited, Paphos, Pisidian Antioch,[7] and Lystra were all major centers of Roman life and government. The other four targeted sites may not have been as significant politically, but they still provided large audiences. Salamis was the main city on the eastern side of the island of Cyprus.[8] Perga was a major port city, while Iconium and Derbe were at least market towns.

Why would Paul and Barnabas have targeted population centers? Obviously, the more people who heard, the more potential believers in Christ there would be. Also, if Christian communities could be planted in major centers, then the door for evangelism in surrounding areas would be opened. When "suburbanites" went to "the city," they might rub shoulders with believers. Or when city Christians traveled outside their neighborhoods, they could share their faith with friends and business contacts. Evangelical churches today still follow this strategy. In attempts to evangelize unreached peoples, leaders target key groups that serve as entry points for reaching other groups which are even less accessible.

As Paul and Barnabas visited these centers, what message did they preach? Luke employs several phrases to describe the content of their preaching: "the word of God" (13:5, 7, 46); "the teaching about the Lord" (13:12); "the word of the Lord" (13:44, 48); "the message of his [the Lord's] grace" (14:3); "the good news" (14:21); "the word" (14:25).

Luke describes two of Paul's sermons in greater detail (see below). But one-phrase summaries of the preaching (listed above) disclose some key facts: the source of the missionaries' message—God; and the content of their message—grace, good news, the Lord (Jesus). Paul, on this first journey, was foreshadowing words he later wrote to the Corinthians: "We do not preach ourselves, but Jesus Christ as Lord . . ." (2 Cor. 4:5).

It also appears that, at minimum, words were one of the missionaries' primary means of communication. This conclusion may seem obvious, but it is worth noting. While loving actions are a wonderfully helpful (and necessary) aid in evangelism, Christians must use *words* if they wish to communicate the content of the gospel effectively. The gospel cannot be smelled, tasted, felt with the hands, or grasped by intuition. In order to receive the gospel, inquirers must hear it proclaimed via written or spoken words. From experience, Paul knew the only answers to the questions he later asked the Roman church: "How can they believe what they have not heard? How can they hear without a preacher ["preacher" meaning, in the broadest sense of the word, one who verbally communicates the good news from God, about God]?" (Rom. 10:14, paraphrase).

So, what groups heard Paul and Barnabas's message, and where did they hear it? If Luke mentions a specific location for preaching, it is always a local synagogue (see Acts 13:5, 14; 14:1). Acts 14:1 describes the missionaries' going *"as usual* into the Jewish synagogue" (my emphasis). Why did they search out the Jewish centers of worship? Hadn't it been the Jews, at least the ones in Jerusalem, who persecuted Jesus and the church? Of course! Yet, despite the Jews' failure to respond appropriately, God had retained a special love for His chosen people, the descendants of Abraham. Paul would later state the principle that the gospel is the good news of salvation for "everyone who believes: *first for the Jew,* then for the Gentile" (Rom. 1:16, my emphasis). So, Paul and Barnabas sensed theological support for taking God's message to the Jews (". . . We had to speak the word of God to you [Jews] first . . ." [Acts 13:46]).

Another reason for going to the synagogues was quite practical: The synagogue was the place to find people who were best prepared for the gospel. Those who knew God and were looking for His Messiah might be most open to the news of that Messiah's coming. Again, Paul's example instructs us today. We, too, can target receptive peoples (without neglecting those who may only appear closed).

Did Jews, in fact, believe? Not to the degree for which Paul and Barnabas hoped. In Pisidian Antioch, some Jews did ask to hear Paul preach a second time (see 13:43). But there is no record that any of them believed. (In fact, the Jews there seemed to lead the mob which abused the Christian visitors; see comments below.) Only in the account of the visit to Iconium does Luke mention Jews who accepted the good news of Jesus (see 14:1).

What other groups heard and received the message? God-fearers (see commentary on 8:26-40 for a definition of this term)—another group associated with the synagogue—are mentioned at Pisidian Antioch, but

Luke does not specifically describe their response (see 13:43). Gentiles heard and believed both at Antioch and Iconium (see 13:48; 14:1). At Lystra and Derbe, Luke mentions "disciples"—new believers—but does not further identify them (14:20-22).

What about those who rejected the gospel? Again, both Jews and Gentiles are mentioned as disbelieving. Both groups subsequently became involved in persecution. For what it's worth, on this missionary trip it was always the Jews who initiated the persecution. Why? Perhaps the Gentiles saw little threat in a new religion. The Jews, however, felt they had more to lose. First, their own theology was being questioned. They knew that God was one being; they saw no way that one of their own contemporaries could be declared "Lord." They also may have felt that they, as God's chosen people already, needed no call to repentance and fresh belief in God. Second, they may have feared that attendance at the synagogue could drop, should some from their congregations defect to the new sect.

When Paul and Barnabas sensed that they had lost their welcome, they took that as a hint to move on. Apparently they were willing to risk and even experience suffering for the gospel (see, for example, 14:19), but sensed that martyrdom was not yet God's plan for them.

Now, let's look at Barnabas and Paul's journey in greater detail.

2. SALAMIS 13:4-5

Barnabas and Paul first headed toward Cyprus. This was a logical choice. Barnabas had grown up on this island (see Acts 4:36). He would have been familiar with its terrain and people. Cyprus was an island province in the Mediterranean Sea. It was known for its copper mines, its shipbuilding industry, and its perfect weather. It was also an island full of pagan people. Its goddess was Venus, the goddess of love.[9]

Luke does not give much information about the missionaries' visit to the city of Salamis on the eastern side of Cyprus. All he says is that **...** **they proclaimed the word of God in the Jewish synagogues** (13:5a). Why doesn't Luke tell us more? Or, on the other hand, if that is all he wished to say, why does he even write that much? As we move through the accounts of Paul's journeys, we often face puzzles like this. Why does Luke include or omit particular details? (In some instances, we can guess at his reasoning. In others, we have only questions. Luke, as all historians, chose what was crucial for his purposes. We must do the best we can to piece together the stories from the information we have).

Returning to the original question, how might one explain the brevity of Luke's account of the visit to Salamis? Perhaps an already active Christian community there motivated Paul and Barnabas to make only a quick stop. (Were Paul and Barnabas under some time pressure? Not that we know of. Except in rare cases, time pressure does not seem to be a biblical phenomenon.) There were at least some believers on Cyprus, for Christians from that island had helped to found the church in Antioch (see 11:19). As already mentioned, Barnabas himself had roots on the island (see 4:36).

3. PAPHOS 13:6-12

Between Salamis and Paphos, also on the island of Cyprus, Paul and Barnabas **traveled through the whole island** (Acts 13:6). Did they move nonstop (a distance of about ninety miles), or did they pause en route to preach? Perhaps Luke wanted to avoid the possibility of boring his readers with too much detail. It's possible that Luke himself had never heard the details of those particular days. In any case, he took his account quickly to **Paphos** (13:6). There, in the Roman provincial capital, Barnabas and Paul met the Roman **proconsul** (governor), **Sergius Paulus** (13:7). (If Luke's first readers lived in Rome and potentially were needing reliable information about Paul, then this early positive encounter with a Roman official could prove helpful to Paul's cause. It did not hurt matters that Luke called the governor **an intelligent man.**)

Barnabas and Paul not only met the local leader, but they met a member of his staff: **a Jewish sorcerer and false prophet named Bar-Jesus** (13:6). (A local government official, living in a more superstitious age, often kept a fortune-teller on his staff.[10]) Since this **sorcerer,** also known as **Elymas** (13:8), was a Jew, he was "in trouble" on at least two counts. First, he was breaking the Old Testament Law.[11] Leviticus 19:26b forbade Jews to practice magic. Second, and more crucial for the moment, Elymas faced a man with greater power than any he himself possessed. When Elymas tried to oppose the missionaries (in a manner which Luke, again, does not describe), Paul identified the magician for who he was: **You are a child of the devil and an enemy of everything that is right!** (Acts 13:10). I. Howard Marshall insightfully offers the contrast between the man's name ("Bar-Jesus" meant "son of Jesus") and what Paul called him—a **child of the devil.**[12] After pointing out the magician's true allegiance, Paul called blindness down upon him. Perhaps Paul chose blindness as an appropriate temporary handicap, remembering how his own temporary blindness had helped bring him to eternal sight (see 9:9, 18). (You may notice similarities between this story and Peter's encounter with a magician—Simon of Samaria; see 8:9-24.)

The proconsul quickly sized up the situation and allied himself with the missionaries and their God. Their teaching had already appealed to him (see 13:8). Their sign confirmed the teaching. A powerful Roman joined the Christian team.

You can guess what Barnabas might have written in an e-mail that evening to the home church in Antioch: "You will never believe what happened—a Roman governor has believed in Jesus!" In the course of his correspondence, Barnabas would have broken some other news to his prayer partners. He and the man whom the church knew as "Saul" had chosen to make some changes. First, from then on "Saul" would drop the use of his Jewish name and be known by his Latin name **Paul** (as evidenced by 13:9; it appears no more than coincidence that the local proconsul held the same surname). Second, Barnabas evidently realized that Paul had shown his gifts as a natural leader. Luke has already pointed out what a model Barnabas was; here was Barnabas's greatest moment. Although his thoughts are not mentioned in the text, Barnabas may have thought along these lines: "In order for Paul to develop fully, I must let him take charge. For the good of the Kingdom, I will stand aside." From here on in Acts, **Barnabas and Saul** (13:7) became known as "Paul and his companions" (13:13). While previously Luke has always referred to Barnabas and Saul/Paul in this particular order, in most subsequent cases where Luke mentions them, he lists Paul's name first, thus indicating that Paul took priority at that point (see 13:42-43, 46, 50; 15:2, 22, 35; exceptions are 14:12, 14; 15:12, 25).

Paphos witnessed two power displays that day. Only one was obvious to everyone, the one that undoubtedly occupied local conversation that evening. A visitor had blinded a well-known local! The proconsul had sworn allegiance to a new god! These events may have changed the atmosphere on the island. But the less obvious event—Barnabas's quietly yielding to the power of Paul's leadership—may have changed the history of the world.

4. PISIDIAN ANTIOCH 13:14-52

Luke next moves quickly over the missionaries' sea and land travel in order to talk about Pisidian Antioch, in Galatia. The group passed through **Perga,** a major seaport (Acts 13:14). Why did they not stop to preach there? Paul's subsequent letter to the Galatian churches that he was about to visit offers a hint. In Galatians 4:13, he describes how he went to them "because of an illness." It is possible that Paul became ill on the sea journey, or while first in Perga. For his health, he may have felt the need to bypass ministry in Perga and head for the drier interior highlands, specifically Pisidian Antioch.[13]

It was while the team was in Perga that John Mark left for home (see commentary below on 14:21b-28 for a discussion of this event).

Luke's account of Paul's time in Antioch is longer than his record of the remainder of the trip put together![14] Was this city or the events that took place there more important than the others? No. It's more likely that Luke chose this spot to give a record of what Paul typically preached to Jews who were unfamiliar with the "Jesus events." Note that Paul addressed his words to the **men of Israel and you Gentiles** [God-fearers] **who worship God** (Acts 13:16; see also 13:26). Paul spoke in a manner he hoped would bridge the barriers that lay between Christians and Jews.

To do this, he focused first on God's interaction with His people under the old covenant.[15] Christians shared this history with the Jews. But then Paul pointed out how Jesus had come to fulfill God's covenant.

If we wanted to outline Paul's sermon in a contemporary sense, we might do so focusing on the term "promise." Key information from only three verses shows the thrust of the sermon:

a. We preach the promise made to **our fathers** (13:32).
b. God promised our fathers to send a **Savior,** through the line of David (13:23).
c. This **Savior** is **Jesus** (13:23).
d. Jesus' resurrection documents the fact that He is the fulfillment of the promise (13:33).

Or, here is another outline, giving more attention to the full content of each sermon segment:

a. 13:17-22—God gave the promises to **our fathers.**
   i. 13:17-19—These fathers include descendants **of Israel . . . in Egypt,** freed in the Exodus, whom Moses **endured** during their wilderness wanderings, and whom God miraculously brought into the land of **Canaan.**
   ii. 13:20-22—These fathers also include the nation of Israel in the Promised Land, including the **judges . . . Samuel the prophet . . . Saul,** and **David . . . a man after God's own heart.**

(To this point, all the Jewish listeners would have listened politely, even enthusiastically. But then Paul moved onto *new* ground which provoked a strong negative response.)

b. 13:23-31—God fulfilled His promises in the life of Jesus, in whom we hear the **message of salvation.**
  i. 13:24-25—**John preached repentance and baptism,** and the imminent coming of the Messiah.
  ii. 13:27, 29—**The people of Jerusalem . . . fulfilled the words of the prophets that are read every Sabbath. . . . They . . . carried out all that was written [in the Old Testament] about [Jesus],** as they had him killed.
  iii. 13:30—**God raised him** [Jesus] **from the dead.**

(The Jews of Antioch might have known of John the Baptist and even have respected him. But, as Paul began describing Jesus and the treatment He received from the Jews of Jerusalem, Paul began taking more risks. To cover himself, Paul doubly emphasized that Jesus' death had been foretold by the Old Testament prophets whom all Jews revered. Paul then clinched his argument, citing the fact of Jesus' resurrection.)

c. 13:32-37—Here is a series of ancient promises which Jesus, in His resurrection, has fulfilled.
  i. 13:33—God spoke of one who was His **Son** (see Psalm 2:7).
  ii. 13:34—God promised to **give** that One the **blessings promised to David** (see Isaiah 55:3).
  iii. 13:35—A blessing God promised through David was a body that would **not . . . decay** (see Psalm 16:10).

(If I had been Paul, I would have finished right there: "Therefore you should believe in **Jesus** and receive **forgiveness of sins."** He did mention forgiveness [13:38], but then concluded with an unexpected twist.)

d. 13:38-41—The promise is now for you and for **everyone who believes!**

To this point in his sermon, Paul has addressed everything to the Jews and to those Gentiles who have allied themselves with Jewish worship: **"It is to *us*** that God has sent salvation" (13:26); **"We tell *you*** [those gathered in the synagogue] **the good news"** (13:32); "We proclaim forgiveness **to *you***" (13:38, my emphasis). But, as he concluded, Paul opened the gates wide! ***Everyone* who believes is justified from everything you could not be justified from by the law of Moses**[16] (13:39, my emphasis).

What was Paul doing? Through the first part of the sermon, he had seemingly done so well at helping the Jews to move toward acceptance. Here, he appears to have blown it. He bluntly announced that the Jewish law was inadequate. If that wasn't enough, he slammed them with the word that God's new promise extended far beyond their favored circle. Then, without giving his hearers a chance to respond, he came close to calling them **scoffers,** warning them not to reject the unbelievable truth he had just proclaimed (13:41).

Did they stone Paul? Not yet. This group politely invited Paul to speak again the next week. But we can imagine the furor such a message aroused in the Jewish synagogues.[17]

This story sounds quite like an account earlier in Luke's history. Paul's master (Jesus) had once had a synagogue congregation applauding Him and His message, until He mentioned God's concern for *Gentiles*. On that day, the Jews of Nazareth had nearly killed Jesus (see Luke 4:16-30).

The next Sabbath, after Paul's sermon in Antioch, many Jews did turn on him: **They were filled with jealousy and talked abusively against what Paul was saying** (Acts 13:45). It appears likely that the Jews were reviling not only the missionaries, but also Jesus himself. In any case, Paul on several occasions saw such abusive talk as a signal. Once the Jews began blaspheming his message, he realized that he had fulfilled his duty to the Jews. It was then appropriate to offer the message to local Gentiles (see, for example, 18:6; 19:9).

Paul, on this occasion, reminded his hearers that God's (Old Testament) plan had been for them, the Jews, to serve as **a light for the Gentiles** (13:47). Despite the fact that the Jews had failed in this task, God still loved them and continued to offer light to them. But the Jews' choice to stay in darkness could not prevent Paul from taking the gospel to those who would welcome it. At this, many Gentiles rejoiced and believed (see 13:48).

The word of the Lord spread through the whole region (13:49). It appears that the Gentiles who felt accepted by God could not keep this fresh, wonderful news to themselves. As they spread the Word, they attracted others to the faith. This growth process would have taken some time. Evidently, Paul and Barnabas had opportunity to begin discipling the new believers. As the local church strengthened, the Jews were losing patience. They saw both their theology and their position in the community being threatened. They could not stand passively and watch this happen. They attacked—indirectly.

The Jews used their influence over **God-fearing** [Gentile] **women of high standing** who had been sympathetic to the synagogue and the Jewish faith, perhaps hoping that these women would sway their husbands, some of **the leading men of the city** (13:50). In any case, persecution arose. Paul and Barnabas left the city—either being physically removed from Antioch, or following their common sense which dictated a hasty departure. **They shook the dust from their feet in protest** as Jesus had instructed His disciples to do (13:51; see Matthew 10:14).

The Jews of Antioch, like those of Jerusalem, had rejected their Messiah. But their foolishness did not hinder the truth from reaching many Gentiles, who were also among those **appointed for eternal life** (13:48; on the question of predestination, see commentary on 4:23-31). God's salvation was for **everyone who believes** (13:39).

Today, the great majority of Christians are from non-Jewish backgrounds. How easily we take for granted the *universal* offer of fellowship with God. It would help us to remember that first-century Jews considered this generosity unbelievable (see 13:41). Sensing God's grace afresh should affect us as it did the Gentiles of Antioch: They were **filled with joy** (13:52).

5. ICONIUM 14:1-6a

Paul and Barnabas chose next to head ninety miles across land to **Iconium,** also in Galatia (Acts 14:1). During their days there, they must have felt a sense of déjà vu. They **went as usual into the Jewish synagogue. There they spoke . . . effectively** (14:1). Paul likely preached a message quite similar to his Antioch synagogue sermon, quoted at length in Acts 13. The Iconium response was more bipartisan; the believers included both **Jews and Gentiles** (14:1). The belief of some Jews, however, did not prevent (and may have strengthened) the resistance of others. Once again, Jews led the opposition, but they enlisted the aid of leading Gentiles who **poisoned their** [the many listeners'] **minds against the brothers** [Paul and Barnabas] (14:2).

Fortunately, the missionaries were not forced to leave the area immediately; they **spent considerable time there** (14:3). As at Antioch, this gave opportunity both for further evangelism and for discipleship among the new believers. God gave Paul and Barnabas opportunity to speak boldly and to perform miracles (**miraculous signs and wonders;** see Galatians 3:5 for an allusion to these miracles). Soon everyone in the area knew of Paul and Barnabas. Some residents supported the team, others opposed, but all took an opinion. Eventually the strength of the "nays" forced the issue. To escape **a plot . . . [to] stone them** (Acts 14:5), Paul and Barnabas chose once again to leave town. Once again, however, the "yeas" could not be totally silenced. The missionaries had ministered long enough to establish a group of Christian believers.

The amazing fact is not that Paul and Barnabas moved *away* from Iconium; it's that they continued to move *forward*. They had to leave their new disciples, but they headed on to the next communities, **where they continued to preach the good news** (14:7). Missionaries with weaker dedication might have given up. Paul and Barnabas had escaped Antioch and Iconium with their lives, but they did not know what lay ahead.[18] At Lystra, things first looked a whole lot better, but then turned drastically worse.

6. LYSTRA 14:6b-20a

Paul and Barnabas next preached in the Galatian city of **Lystra** (Acts 14:6). Evidently the town had no synagogue, for the missionaries appear to have preached outdoors. After they preached there for a time of unknown length, an incident arose which served as the highlight of their time there. Do you remember how Peter and John passed, on their way into the Jerusalem Temple, a man lame from birth (see 3:1-2)? In Lystra, Paul and Barnabas encountered a similar man. Once again, the Spirit enabled this lame man to stand and walk for the first time. In both situations, the people marveled. But the first healing had occurred in the capital of Judaism[19]; this one took place in a pagan village. In Jerusalem, the miracle had prepared its witnesses to listen to the wonder-workers' message. Here in Lystra, no one waited for Paul and Barnabas to speak *about* God. The gathered crowds immediately decided that Paul and Barnabas *were* gods.[20]

The crowds made moves to prepare sacrifices to Paul and Barnabas (see 14:13). A strong reaction? Perhaps. A legend that was old even in the first century helps to explain the adulation of the crowds. The people believed that the gods had once come to visit their area, disguised as old beggars. Nearly all the townsfolk had ignored or even mistreated the gods. Only one poor, elderly couple had offered them food and shelter. The gods had rewarded this old couple by giving them "eternal life," transforming them into a pair of great trees. Subsequent Galatians had resolved that they would never again mistreat visiting gods. When Paul and Barnabas showed up with miracle power, the locals quickly concluded that the gods had given the people a second chance. They would not miss this opportunity to offer appropriate worship.

For Paul and Barnabas, this situation would have been hilarious, if it had not been so serious. Had they chosen to, they could have played along with a role they had inherited—a role akin to that of the Wizard of Oz—fooling people into thinking they had magical power. But that would have totally contradicted their God-given purpose. How could they promote worship of the true God, if the people worshiped them as false gods?

Attempting to lead the people toward the truth, Paul began preaching. Luke's account of this "sermon" is much briefer than the Antioch message, but it offers an adequate picture of Paul's strategy for reaching uneducated pagans. Paul did not even mention God's (Old Testament) contact with His chosen people. When Paul evangelized Jewish nonbelievers, a description of God's interaction with the Old Testament Jews would have been most appropriate, but that information would have meant little to pagan people, who did not share a Jewish heritage.

In this situation, Paul chose to proclaim the God of creation who is the God of *all* nations. This God is the one who gives rain and harvests to all people (see 14:15-17). Paul wanted his Lystran hearers to recognize that the God he preached was the One True God, in contrast to the many gods most pagans worshiped. This God was the one who had created all, had created *them*. The one who supplied the needs of the world had given them the rain and food they needed. Paul hoped his approach would help the group relate to God the Father, so they then could appreciate the gospel of God's Son, Jesus Christ.

Did Paul's presentation convince his hearers? No, but Paul and Barnabas were still doing well in the local popularity polls. Many from the crowds still wanted to worship the "gods" they could see, rather than the unseen God whom Paul proclaimed.

The script here was already confusing, and then more players came on stage. The Jews **from Antioch and Iconium** had not been content to get Paul and Barnabas out of their own cities. They now arrived wanting to push Paul and Barnabas out of the province. To do this, they **won the crowd** over to their side (14:19). Somehow these visiting Jews convinced the residents of Lystra that Paul and Barnabas were not gods, but false prophets.

Paul and Barnabas couldn't win. They didn't want to be worshiped *as gods,* but neither did they want to be abused because they *weren't gods.* Their goal was neither worship nor abuse; they merely wanted to be heard. But the situation moved outside their control. The crowds, led on by antagonistic Jews, **stoned Paul** until they were sure he was dead, and then **dragged him outside the city** (14:19). Fortunately, God remained in control, and Paul remained alive.

The result? Even in Lystra, some had heard and believed the message. Despite the upheaval, Paul and Barnabas did not leave as total failures. The new Christians ministered to Paul and helped him up, and this unusual man headed right **back into the city** (14:20). But, he and Barnabas did take the hint; they left town the next morning and headed for **Derbe.**

What lessons are here for us? We, too, must remember that a strongly *positive* response to a *false* gospel can, in the long run, be more dangerous than a *negative* response to the *true* gospel.[21] It was not Paul and Barnabas's fault that the residents of Lystra accepted false beliefs. Paul and Barnabas were doing the best they could to correct this incorrect thinking. Today, however, many well-meaning Christians modify the gospel to make it appealing. They feel that the numbers responding justify their actions. (By no means are all rapidly growing churches offering a false gospel.) But, if it comes to a choice, proclamation of *truth* must always take precedence over the goal of seeking *response.*

7. DERBE 14:20b-21a

Their harrowing adventures in Pisidian Antioch, Iconium, and Lystra must have left Paul and Barnabas feeling a bit stressed. In contrast, their relatively uneventful time in **Derbe** (Acts 14:20) must have filled them with joy. Their ministry to the Galatians in Derbe may have been uneventful, and yet it was quite fruitful. After Paul and Barnabas **preached the good news in that city,** they **won a large number of disciples** (14:21). Miracles? Sermon content? Response from Jews? Response from Gentiles? Luke offers no details. Evidently Luke felt that he had already described adequately the outward leg of this missionary trip.

What had happened? Paul and Barnabas had accomplished most of their goals. In several locations, they preached the gospel. The work did not go smoothly, for many people rejected both message and messengers. But, despite rejection culminating in persecution, when Paul and Barnabas left each city, a new church was in place. Their home church, back in Antioch of Syria, would soon have heard the news with great joy, but Paul and Barnabas were not finished yet.

8. THE RETURN JOURNEY AND ARRIVAL HOME 14:21b-28

From Derbe, Paul and Barnabas could have taken a land route back to Antioch of Syria. Why would they want to return to cities from which they had been evicted by violent mobs throwing stones? But, despite the risks involved, Paul and Barnabas felt it best to revisit each of the newly planted churches.

Their ministry on the return leg of the journey serves as a model for the church today. Helping people into the Christian life is wonderful, but leaving infant believers to care for themselves may be counterproductive. What did Paul and Barnabas do? In each of the Galatian cities, they followed the same discipling methods that they had employed with success back in Syrian Antioch. That church had grown to the point where it wished to reproduce itself, which had been a prime motivation in its sending out of pastors on this missionary journey. Paul and Barnabas wanted to see all of their churches reach the point where they could mother still more churches. How did Paul and Barnabas move toward this goal?

First, Paul and Barnabas **strengthen[ed] the disciples** (Acts 14:22). The new believers needed additional teaching. Earlier, Barnabas and Paul had taught the new church back in Syrian Antioch "for a whole year" (11:26). They could not spend twelve months in any of the Galatian churches, but they certainly gave each group a crash course in "Christian Faith and Life 101."

Second, Paul and Barnabas **encourage[d] them to remain true to the faith,** no matter what the cost (14:22). Back in Syrian Antioch, Paul and Barnabas had "encouraged [the church] to remain true to the Lord with all their hearts" (11:23). In the Galatian churches, Paul and Barnabas specifically warned of the **many hardships** the new believers would face **to enter the kingdom of God** (14:22). The Jews who had sent Paul and Barnabas packing the first time around would not give up easily. These Jews would attempt to drive the new churches out of existence either by persecution or by false teaching. (Paul's letter to the Galatians shows how close the Jews came to succeeding.)

Third, Paul and Barnabas **appointed elders . . . in each church** (14:23). During the interval between church planting and the apostles' return, people with leadership gifts had become visible in each church. The missionaries recognized these people and appointed them as elders.

What was the elders' job description? The other members of the leadership team back in Syrian Antioch had acted, along with Barnabas and Paul, as "prophets and teachers" (13:1). Perhaps these people were those best able to read and interpret the Scriptures, thus enabling them to continue the task of offering God's truth to the others. Paul's words for the elders of the Ephesian church (see Acts 20:28-31) give further insight into the responsibility Paul and Barnabas would have given to the elders in each Galatian city.

Fourth, Paul and Barnabas fasted and prayed for each group (see 14:23). They had fasted and prayed with the leaders back in Syrian Antioch. It was while they were spending such time with God that He directed them to initiate this mission venture. The God who had, through prayer and fasting, enabled them to undertake and successfully complete this journey, would continue, through further **prayer and fasting,** to strengthen and protect the new Christians in Galatia. With confidence, Paul and Barnabas could commit these new believers **to the Lord in whom they had put their trust** (14:23). Paul and Barnabas would leave; God would not.

On the return trip, Paul and Barnabas did preach **the word in Perga** (14:25). Luke doesn't mention the missionaries' preaching there on the outward journey. Perhaps this lends support to the theory that Paul fell ill there the first time around.

Paul and Barnabas did not, at this time, return to the new Christians in Cyprus. Barnabas, however, did visit them again before too long (see 15:39), most likely further discipling them as he and Paul had discipled the Galatian churches.

As Luke's account brings the travelers home to Syrian Antioch, he neatly summarizes the trip. Its beginning? The home church had **committed** Paul and Barnabas **to the grace of God for the work** of evangelism and discipleship. That work **they had now completed** (14:26). Had Paul and Barnabas done that work alone? By no means! They **reported all that** *God* **had done through them** (14:27, my emphasis). Done through whom? Paul and Barnabas? Yes, but also through the home church which had sent Paul and Barnabas off with fasting and prayer. The work of the Kingdom is never one person's task. Paul and Barnabas knew that one may plant and another may water, but God "makes things grow" (see 1 Corinthians 3:6). Not Paul, not Barnabas, not the Antioch church, but *God* **had opened the door of faith to the Gentiles** (Acts 14:27). The path "to the ends of the earth" (1:8) was now open. God joined in the Antioch celebration that day, rejoicing in the faithfulness of all members of the missionary team.

Today, God continually calls His church to faithfulness. He invites us to the ministries, modeled in Acts 13 and 14, of prayer and fasting, evangelism and discipleship. God promises to bless faithful churches with fruitful ministry, but such fruitfulness comes via the way of **many hardships** (14:22).

ENDNOTES

[1] Acts 13:9 refers to "Saul, who was also called Paul." In Saul/Paul's day, people customarily held a given name and a second name. "Saul" was, in this case, the given Hebrew/Jewish name, while "Paul" was the Roman/Hellenistic name. The change in reference from Saul to Paul "may be due to Saul's success in preaching to Paulus or to the fact that [Saul] is now entering the Gentile phase of his ministry" (see comments on Acts 13:9 in *The NIV Study Bible,* Kenneth Barker, ed. [Grand Rapids, Michigan: The Zondervan Corporation]).

[2] For years, the church has described the contents of Acts 13 and 14, and 16 through 21 as Paul's first, second, and third missionary journeys. There are at least two problems with this terminology. First, it may not be appropriate to call the trip with Barnabas (Acts 13–14) Paul's *first* missionary journey. At minimum, there is evidence that he may have planted churches in Cilicia long before his "first" missionary journey (compare all the information in 9:30; 15:36, 41; 26:20; Galatians 1:1-24). Also, the first portion of the second missionary journey and nearly all the third are given to discipleship, and not to evangelism and church planting. While discipleship of people who are already believers is certainly missionary work, the connotation of the phrase "missionary journey" often leads people to think that the primary, if not exclusive, focus of these trips was evangelism. But, not wanting to buck (or hope to change) centuries of church practice, I will use the traditional language in my descriptions of the next chapters.

[3] There is further evidence for this possibility in that Simon's sons evidently became Christians of some renown. Mark mentions Alexander and Rufus in 15:21. Paul greets a Roman Christian named Rufus in Romans 16:13. All this makes interesting speculation, but little more.

[4] The Spirit spoke to the church in Antioch. Was the Spirit's speaking to people a new feature of the period following Pentecost? (In the New Testament, Pentecost primarily refers to the event when the Holy Spirit was given to the church; this occurred on the day of Pentecost.) Not really. The Spirit had filled and spoken to and through select individuals throughout Old Testament history. It was through the Spirit that God inspired the prophets to speak and the Old Testament writers to write (see 2 Peter 1:21). What was new? The Spirit had become available to *all* God's people *all* the time.

[5] John R. W. Stott, *The Spirit, the Church and the World* (Downers Grove, Illinois: InterVarsity Press, 1990), p. 218.

[6] It is during this trip that "Barnabas and Saul" become "Paul and Barnabas." To prevent confusion, I will, from this point on, refer to "Saul" as "Paul."

[7]It would seem that God could have made life simpler for Bible students by telling the ancients that they could not give the same name to two different cities. But God did not do so. The ancients in several places honored a Syrian ruler, Antiochus, by naming many cities after him. In your study of Acts, do your best to distinguish Antioch of Syria (the city *from* which Paul and Barnabas traveled) from Antioch of Pisidia (one of the cities *to* which they traveled).

[8]Hopefully, you have already found and used a set of Bible maps (in the back of a study Bible or in a Bible atlas). To this point in Acts, it would have been helpful. From this point on in Acts, it will be *essential*.

[9]William Barclay, *The Acts of the Apostles* (Philadelphia: The Westminster Press, 1976), pp. 99–100.

[10]Ibid., p. 100.

[11]Law refers to either the Levitical Code (all God's rules and regulations), the Ten Commandments, or the Pentateuch (the first five books of the Old Testament: Genesis, Exodus, Leviticus, Numbers, and Deuteronomy); it is often capitalized when it means the Pentateuch or the Ten Commandments.

[12]I. Howard Marshall, *Acts* (Grand Rapids, Michigan: Wm. B. Eerdmans Publishing Co., 1980), p. 219.

[13]F. F. Bruce, *The Book of the Acts* (Grand Rapids, Michigan: Wm. B. Eerdmans Publishing Co., 1988), p. 251. Bruce points out the difficulty of the journey from Perga to Pisidian Antioch. Pisidian Antioch stood on a plateau 3600 feet above sea level. The road between the two traversed dangerous hilly country, often frequented by robbers.

[14]M. Robert Mulholland, Jr., "Acts" in *Asbury Bible Commentary,* Eugene Carpenter and Wayne McCown, eds. (Grand Rapids, Michigan: Zondervan Publishing House, 1992), p. 953. The account in Pisidian Antioch is also the longest description of Paul's stay in any single missionary location.

[15]A covenant is a solemn promise made binding by a pledge or vow, which may be either a verbal formula or a symbolic action. Covenant often referred to a legal obligation in ancient times. In Old Testament terms, the word was often used in describing the relationship between God and His chosen people, in which their sacrifices of blood afforded them His atonement for sin, and in which their fulfillment of a promise to live in obedience to God was rewarded by His blessings. In New Testament terms, this relationship (the new covenant) was now made possible on a personal basis through Jesus Christ and His sacrifice of His own blood.

[16]See endnote 11.

[17]Mulholland, p. 954.

[18]Barclay, p. 108. The missionary's need for courage not only related to their past experiences, but to the danger of moving into rural centers, farther from Roman control.

[19]Judaism is the life and belief system of the Jewish people and involves a covenant relationship with God. Though there are various branches of Judaism, the underlying theme among them has been monotheism and a recognition of the Law, or the Torah. The Hebrew word from which *Torah* comes is translated *law* and refers to divine instruction and guidance. The Torah is comprised of the instructions and directions given to Israel by God. Torah is another name for the

Pentateuch (see endnote 11), also known as the Law of Moses. It is considered the most important division in the Jewish Scriptures, with highest authority, since it was traditionally thought to have been written by Moses, the only biblical hero to have spoken with God face-to-face.

[20]Many contemporary skeptics scoff at the reality of miracles appearing in ancient historical records. "The ancients," they say, "were much more gullible than we are. They saw miracles under every tree. We know such things do not happen." A story like this one belies that simplistic reasoning. This miracle in Lystra was by no means an everyday occurrence for this group of ancients. It drew even from them a response of great wonder.

[21]Not only the idolatrous worship of the Lystrans described here, but also their subsequent giving in to Jewish legalism, as described in Paul's letter to the Galatians (see 1:6-8; 3:1-5), underlines this fact.

13

THE JERUSALEM COUNCIL

Acts 15:1-35

A cts 15 is roughly the midpoint of Luke's account. It describes a major turning point for the early church. The church faced a conflict of large proportion. The resolution of this issue, like so many others in the book of Acts, significantly impacted the subsequent history of the church.

What was the problem? Some Jewish believers from the Jerusalem church had taken it upon themselves to set straight the new Gentile Christians. Without any authorization from the church leaders, these Jewish believers traveled to **Antioch in Syria** (Antioch is the largest city in the province of Syria, north of Palestine), and likely Galatia.[1] These men **were teaching the brothers: "Unless you are circumcised, according to the custom taught by Moses, you cannot be saved"** (Acts 15:1). Paul and Barnabas challenged this teaching. **Sharp dispute and debate** entered the church (15:2). The Jewish teaching had disturbed the new believers, troubling their minds (see 15:24). To establish an atmosphere of unity in the church that would enable continued individual and corporate growth, a resolution to the debate was essential.

This matter was of overwhelming importance to the future of the church. On a practical note, would Christianity remain a sect under the umbrella of Judaism[2]? If so, its growth potential would be restricted. Or would the church move forward as a new community with appeal to people from all backgrounds? More importantly, on what theological base would the church build? What would be the basis of the salvation it proclaimed? Grace through faith alone, or grace, faith, *and* works?

To help better understand this, a brief summary of "salvation history" is appropriate.

Even under the old covenant, God's people were saved not through keeping the Law,[3] but through grace. They received God's grace through faith, in a manner foundationally similar to salvation under the new covenant.[4] Genesis 12:1-3 describes how God chose Abraham and his descendants. Centuries later, Paul pointed out how Abraham was saved by grace, through faith (see Galatians 3:6-8, 18; also Romans 4). It is significant that Paul most likely wrote his letter to the Galatians at the very time of the controversy Luke describes in Acts 15.[5]

To Abraham and his descendants, God graciously offered the covenant of salvation. As Paul writes in Romans 4:9-11, Abraham's submission to circumcision (see Genesis 17:1-14, 23-27) came *after* God's unconditional promise to bless Abraham and his descendants. The full Law came much later, not as a condition for God's redemption of Israel from slavery, but after God had rescued His people from Egypt. God gave the Law not as the means of salvation, but as an expression of His will for His people. God said to them, "Because you *are* my people, here is how you should live. Here is how you can show your acceptance of My covenant. Following My directions will give you the best relationship with Me and with others around you."

God promised to bless or to punish His people as they obeyed or disobeyed His Law. But that promise of blessing or punishment would not come from God arbitrarily. That blessing or curse would be the natural outcome of principles God had placed within the very constitution of the world He made. God graciously gave the Law to His people as a guidebook to life in His world.

In the centuries following God's gift of the Law at Mount Sinai, how did the nation of Israel treat God and His Law? In very general terms, we see two extremes in two broad time periods.

The first period came between the two exiles, during the time in Canaan between the "first exile" in Egypt and before the "second exile" in Assyria and Babylonia. During this period, there were many exceptions, but overall, Israel associated too closely with neighboring countries. This led the people to idolatry—the neglect of God and His will. In time, God punished His people with exile, of the Northern Kingdom to Assyria first, and of the Southern Kingdom to Babylon later.

After this "second exile," there were again many exceptions, but as a whole, God's people gave greater attention to the Law. In doing so, however, they often separated themselves too rigidly from everyone else. The nation's loyalty to the Law was manifested particularly in the period known as "the Maccabean revolt." Led by an old priest and his sons,

God's people said that they would remain loyal to God and His will, even to the point of death. But, across the years, the dynasty that arose from that movement gave more concern to maintaining the Law for its own sake and the privilege it gave to the those who kept it, than to maintaining a good relationship with God.

By the time God's people entered the New Testament time period, the tradition of loyalty to the Law had broadened even further. For many leaders, faith had largely degenerated into legalism. Law had taken the place of God (see Matthew 23:2-25). For many in leadership, the Law became a weapon with which to beat people, to keep them in subjection, rather than a means by which they all served God together.

Then Jesus came on the scene. In His preaching, He supported the Law (see Matthew 5:17-20). He also corrected the current interpretation of the Law. For example, He showed people how to internalize principles behind the Law (see 5:21-48). He pointed out that some aspects of the Law were more critical than others (see 23:23-24). But overall, He remained a loyal Jew. His followers also remained loyal Jews.

The Jewish authorities in Jerusalem did not recognize the Son of God because He did not fit their picture of the Messiah. Jesus threatened their authority and did not keep their Law. (Many of the common people more quickly responded to Jesus. They had less to lose. In general, they had remained more open to God.)

In the early years of the Christian church, the apostles did not immediately change their attitude toward their Jewish heritage. Peter and John continued to worship in the Temple (see Acts 3:1). Peter continued to keep the Jewish dietary laws (see 10:14). The church, at first, preached the faith almost exclusively to Jews.

Stephen, a Hellenistic Jew, seemingly was one of the first to grasp that Christianity was much bigger than its Judaistic base. He strongly attacked overstrong Jewish loyalty to the Law and the Temple (see Acts 7). The Jerusalem Jews recognized this as something new and quickly killed him. A greater persecution arose which sent many Christians away from Jerusalem.

Some of these scattered Christians preached to Gentiles in Antioch of Syria, where a Gentile church formed (see 11:19-21). It was this Antioch church which sent Paul and Barnabas on their first missionary journey. These men preached to Jews first (13:15; 14:1), but also to Gentiles (13:46; 14:1, 11). In time, the Christian church found itself divided into two segments: a Jerusalem-based church that worshiped Jesus, but also remained loyal to the Law and Judaism; and an Antioch church (and its daughters) that worshiped Jesus, but had a much looser relationship with Judaism.

This summary brings us to the period of time that Paul and Barnabas spent in Antioch after their second trip (see 14:28). During this time, Peter showed up to consult the missionaries and check out the scene in Antioch. During Peter's visit, he and Paul experienced a significant encounter, described in Galatians 2:11-14. Peter had been willing to interact with Gentile Christians until members of a Jewish "circumcision group" came from Jerusalem. After their arrival, Peter shied away from contact with any but Jewish Christians. Also during this time, Judaizers (a term scholars have given to Jewish Christians who tried to push Jewish legalism on *all* believers) had been active in the new churches in Galatia (see Galatians 1:6; 5:12).

Thus, we see the problem in place. What was the disagreement? The strongly Jewish Christians ministering within the Jewish context wished to maintain the old covenant *in addition* to the new covenant of grace. It's as if they were saying, "We have the main book, and God has now offered an authoritative supplement." Luke summarizes their viewpoint in 15:1, 5: **Unless you are circumcised, according to the custom taught by Moses, you cannot be saved. . . . The Gentiles must be circumcised and required to obey the law of Moses.**

On the other side, Hellenistic Jewish Christians were ministering within a Gentile context. These people thought that the new covenant largely replaced the old (at least the old covenant as the Jews had come to interpret it). Paul summarized this perspective in his letter to the Galatians: ". . . A man is not judged by observing the law, but by faith in Jesus Christ. . . . If righteousness could be gained through the law, Christ died for nothing" (Gal. 2:16, 21b).

What motivated the holders of these two opinions? If we give the Jewish Christians the benefit of the doubt, they were concerned that if they became outnumbered, the church might lose its moral standard in a largely pagan context. But Paul saw that if people had to become Jews to become Christians, then Christianity would remain a Jewish sect. He saw Christianity as much more than that. Judaism was tied to a race, a national tradition; but Christianity transcended its Jewish origin. It was a universal faith. And, even more critically, if Christianity remained Jewish, then Christians would be tempted to depend on Lawkeeping rather than on grace (certainly a primary message in Paul's letter to the Galatians). Paul emphatically stated that those who depend on the Law do not experience God's justifying grace (see Galatians 3:10-11).

How did this disagreement lead to a church council? It appears that the Antioch church took the initiative, sending Paul, Barnabas, and others to Jerusalem, **to see the apostles and elders about this question** (Acts 15:2). They wished a decision from "headquarters," to know how to instruct new Christians and handle any visiting legalists.

Paul could have merely asserted his apostolic authority over churches where he had been active. But he either suggested a council or humbly submitted to the Antioch church's decision to appeal to the Jerusalem church. There was risk involved for Paul. It was possible that the Jerusalem church could have supported the position of the legalists. (What would Paul have done if it had?)

Paul, Barnabas, and the others left for Jerusalem. As they traveled, they visited several local congregations in **Phoenicia and Samaria,** reporting on their missionary journey to Cyprus and Galatia. The news of their success **made all the brothers very glad** (15:3). The missionaries gave a similar report to the church in Jerusalem. (Luke gives no mention of the response there. Were some less than pleased?)

The Jerusalem Council itself evidently began with much debate (see 15:7). Many people spoke. Opportunity was given for all opinions, including the position of the Judaizers, to be aired. Luke spotlights three speakers.

Peter reviewed the lesson God had taught him in his significant rooftop vision: "God showed me that he makes **no distinction between us and them** [Gentile believers]. . . . **It is through the grace of our Lord Jesus that [each of us is] saved. . . . Why do you . . . test God by putting on the necks of the [Gentile] disciples a yoke that neither we nor our fathers have been able to bear?** (15:9-11). There can be no doubt which side of the debate Peter, the original leader of the church, supported. (On a side note, this is Peter's last appearance in Acts.)

Paul and Barnabas apparently spoke only briefly. They reflected on their experience of God's working among Gentiles, mentioning His **miraculous signs and wonders** (15:12). They did not specifically take sides in the debate, perhaps feeling that their position was obvious to all. Wisdom may have suggested that they allow Peter's strong words to speak for them, too.

James, who evidently had by this time become the leader of the Jerusalem church, spoke last. Reflecting on Peter's experiences (see 15:14) and offering Old Testament support for a mission among the Gentiles, he stated his opinion: "We should not ask them to do what Peter has called impossible and unnecessary" (see 15:19). To maintain peace among all parties, James suggested a compromise. Gentiles would not have to become Jews to join the church, but should avoid four actions particularly vulgar to Jews: eating **food polluted by idols, . . . sexual immorality, . . . the meat of strangled animals, and . . . blood** (15:20).[6] Even there, James was not suggesting that submitting to these four restrictions would be necessary for salvation, but that it would prevent offense to Jewish Christians. The two groups would thus be able to remain one body.

Did James decree this for the entire church? The church eventually adopted his suggestions, but the Christians made the decision they did because **it seemed good to the Holy Spirit and to [them]** (15:28). No single person decided, not even a single person who felt led by the Spirit. God participated, but He was gracious enough to give a sense of unity to the body. God can do the same for His church today.

What was the significance of the four specific restrictions?

The first one mentioned was **food polluted by idols.** When pagan worshipers offered animal sacrifices to their gods, their priests kept only a portion of the meat. The worshipers were free to eat or sell the rest. How should the Christians respond when offered this meat? By not buying or eating it, they could avoid any taint of idol worship.

The Gentile Christians were also to abstain from **blood.** Leviticus 17:10-11 shows the importance of blood within the Jewish culture. The only appropriate use of blood was for sacrifices to God. It was not to be eaten. This concern also explains the prohibition against **meat of strangled animals.** The carcass of an animal killed by strangling would retain its blood. Eating the meat from such a carcass would involve eating blood.

Finally, there was a restriction in regard to **sexual immorality.** In one sense, this regulation does not fit with the other three. The other three fit neatly into the category of what we would call "ritual law," specifically related to Jews under the old covenant. Christians of all times and places have seen the need for sexual purity. So why was it necessary to list this concern here? Possibly the Council saw the need to emphasize an appropriate sex life in the face of Gentile immorality, often a common part of pagan life, not to mention a frequent component of pagan worship. It is also possible that Jewish Christians hoped that Gentile Christians would heed all the Levitical laws prohibiting marriage with one's relatives (see Leviticus 18:1-18). If the latter was a primary concern, then all four issues (participating only in *proper* animal sacrifices, eating blood, eating meat from which the blood has not been drained, and entering only appropriate marriages) would relate to material covered in two sequential chapters in Leviticus (see 17:8, 10, 15; 18:1-18).[7]

The Council then chose clearly to communicate its decision to those who had most been affected by the controversy. In case some Jewish believers would not listen to Paul and Barnabas, the Council also sent **two [other] men who were leaders among the [Jerusalem] brothers** (Acts 15:22). It would be hard for anyone to dispute a decision unanimously proclaimed by a quartet of Council participants. Despite the Judaizers' previous statements to the contrary, no one could authoritatively proclaim that Gentiles who believed were not saved. The church had spoken. God welcomed all who believed. Grace, God's gift of salvation, precedes personal transformation.[8]

Note not only the authority, but the warmth of the communication. First, **the apostles and elders** described themselves as **brothers** of the Gentile believers (15:23). The Jerusalem leaders left no doubt as to their affection for Paul and Barnabas. The latter were **dear friends, . . . who have risked their lives for . . . Jesus** (15:25-26). Notice also that the headquarters group evidently chose its added representatives well. The extra two men, **Judas and Silas, . . . were prophets,** able to **encourage and strengthen the brothers** (15:32).

What had been the foundational problem? Once again, some within the early church had taken God-given "means" and made them "ends." The early church continually struggled with this problem. Today's church does, too. We all need to keep on asking ourselves what means we have made into ends. What unnecessary (and harmful) walls do we build that separate us from other believers or potential believers?

ENDNOTES

[1]In chapter 15, Luke does not specifically mention Galatia, the mainland area where Paul and Barnabas had just established new churches in Iconium, Lystra, and Derbe. But it appears that Paul wrote his letter to the Galatians in the time between the establishment of those churches and the Jerusalem Council. (The letter mentions no dates, but we can with reasonable certainty establish a window of time in which it was written. It obviously was written after the first missionary trip, during which the Galatian churches were established. Paul wrote it to counter a movement of Jews to subvert the free gospel of Jesus. If the Jerusalem Council of Acts 15 had already taken place, then Paul would have used its conclusions as supporting argument in the letter. Thus, the letter to the Galatians must have been written during the "long time" Paul and Barnabas spent in Syrian Antioch between the first trip and the Council, a time mentioned

in Acts 14:28.) Luke does tell us that Paul delivered the decisions reached by the apostles and elders to the people of Lystra and Iconium.

[2]Judaism is the life and belief system of the Jewish people and involves a covenant relationship with God. Though there are various branches of Judaism, the underlying theme among them has been monotheism and a recognition of the Law, or the Torah. The Hebrew word from which *Torah* comes is translated *law* and refers to divine instruction and guidance. The Torah is comprised of the instructions and directions given to Israel by God. Torah is another name for the Pentateuch (the first five books of the Old Testament: Genesis, Exodus, Leviticus, Numbers, and Deuteronomy), also known as the Law of Moses. It is considered the most important division in the Jewish Scriptures, with highest authority, since it was traditionally thought to have been written by Moses, the only biblical hero to have spoken with God face-to-face.

[3]Law refers to either the Levitical Code (all God's rules and regulations), the Ten Commandments, or the Pentateuch (the first five books of the Old Testament: Genesis, Exodus, Leviticus, Numbers, and Deuteronomy); it is often capitalized when it means the Pentateuch or the Ten Commandments.

[4]A covenant is a solemn promise made binding by a pledge or vow, which may be either a verbal formula or a symbolic action. Covenant often referred to a legal obligation in ancient times. In Old Testament terms, the word was often used in describing the relationship between God and His chosen people, in which their sacrifices of blood afforded them His atonement for sin, and in which their fulfillment of a promise to live in obedience to God was rewarded by His blessings. In New Testament terms, this relationship (the new covenant) was now made possible on a personal basis through Jesus Christ and His sacrifice of His own blood.

[5]See evidence described above in footnote 1.

[6]M. Robert Mulholland suggests that James was recommending that Gentile believers keep the standards set for God-fearers. See "Acts" in *Asbury Bible Commentary,* Eugene Carpenter and Wayne McCown, eds. (Grand Rapids, Michigan: Zondervan Publishing House, 1992), p. 955.

[7]Warren Woolsey, of Houghton, New York, pointed out this connection with Leviticus 17 and 18.

[8]You might be interested in what finally became of this decision. Unfortunately, the Council did not finally settle the controversy. On the one hand, the issue of food polluted by idols remained a live one. Paul needed to deal with it again several years later, when he wrote his first letter to the church at Corinth. (Ironically, Paul there permitted the consumption of such meat under special conditions [see 1 Corinthians 8]). On the other hand, Luke himself mentions a group of Jewish Christians who remained "zealous for the law," circumcision in particular (Acts 21:20-21). Despite its tragic results for the Jews, the destruction of Jerusalem significantly decreased the Jewish/Gentile Christian debate. The church went on as a group quite distinct from Judaism.

14

THE SECOND MISSIONARY TRIP

Acts 15:36–18:18a

On their first missionary trip, Paul and Barnabas succeeded in planting several new churches. At the Jerusalem Council, they succeeded in seeing a "Charter of Freedom" ratified for those new churches. After the conference, Paul and Barnabas were ready to set out on yet another missionary adventure.

1. PAUL SETS OUT AGAIN 15:36–16:10

A headline description of Paul's second missionary journey would read "Paul planted five churches in Europe!" Luke affirms that summary. In the three paragraphs Luke uses to introduce the second trip, he passes quickly over some crucial events. He must have been thinking, "Let's get Paul to Europe as quickly as we can." He could not, however, merely start this story with Paul in Philippi. Luke recognized the necessity of answering three key questions. Who went with Paul? By what route did Paul and company go to Europe? How did they sense God's plan for their travel? Let's see how Luke answers these questions.

Question 1: Who went with Paul? The quick answer is not Barnabas or John Mark, but instead, Silas and Timothy. Why so much change in personnel from the first trip?

To this point, Paul had worked well with the man who had been first his mentor and then his colleague—Barnabas (see chapter 10 of the commentary). Quite naturally, Paul asked Barnabas to accompany him as he revisited the towns where they both had **preached the word of the Lord** (15:36). Barnabas thought Paul's idea a good one and agreed to go. Barnabas then had a great idea of his own: "This next trip will give us another chance to mentor my young cousin, John Mark." Paul was not so sure. They had given John Mark one opportunity to work with them. He had failed. Early on the first trip, he had **deserted them** (15:38).

What had happened? Luke does not give the details (see 13:13). But Paul evidently felt that the factors causing Mark to desert them the first time might cause problems again. (Colossians 4:10 tells us that Barnabas and Mark were relatives. Mark may have felt that Paul, taking leadership of the team, had slighted his cousin. Or perhaps Mark, whose home was in Jerusalem [see Acts 12:12], had thought that Paul should not be sharing the gospel so freely with Gentiles. Mark even may have been simply homesick for Jerusalem.)

Like Barnabas, Paul saw the value in mentoring younger traveling companions. For this reason, Paul rarely traveled alone. But Barnabas, the "son of encouragement" (see 4:36), may have had a higher patience level than Paul. In contemporary terms, Barnabas may have been a "people person," while Paul was more task oriented. In any case, Paul and Barnabas **had such a sharp disagreement that they parted company** (15:39).

So, who traveled with Paul? Neither Barnabas nor Mark.[1] Instead, Paul **chose Silas** as his companion. Silas entered Luke's account earlier in Acts 15. The Jerusalem Council chose Silas as one of its representatives to communicate its decision to the Christians of Syria and Galatia (see 15:22). In that context, Luke describes Silas as one of the **leaders among the brothers** (15:22).

Then, early in the trip, Paul recruited Timothy to join them. It appears that Paul wanted Timothy to play the assistant role from which John Mark had deserted. Who was Timothy? A young man. (Years later, Paul still called him a young man; see 1 Timothy 4:12.) Perhaps a young man whom Paul had led to the Lord on the first missionary trip. (Paul calls Timothy his "true son in the faith" [1 Tim. 1:2].) A young man who grew up learning from a godly mother and grandmother (see 2 Timothy 1:5). We know nothing about Timothy's father except that he was not a Jew (see below). It was clear that Timothy was a highly recommended young man whose potential had become obvious during the interim since Paul's last visit to Lystra (see Acts 16:2).

When you are involved in ministry, do you follow Paul's example and get double effectiveness from ministry time? Paul sought to minister to a target group—a church or potential church. But he also gathered around him one or two associates (for example, John Mark, Silas, Timothy) who ministered with him. Paul could then accomplish two goals: minister to the target group *and* train his associates as ministers. Paul had learned this strategy from Barnabas, his mentor.

The only other Timothy-related detail that Luke gives at this point is the fact that Paul thought it best to circumcise Timothy (see 16:3). What was Paul's reason? Had not the Jerusalem Council, with God's help, just decided that circumcision was not necessary for salvation (see 15:1, 28)? Yes. Paul circumcised Timothy not so Timothy could become a Christian, but **because of the Jews who lived in that area.** In this way Timothy would avoid causing needless offense to area Jews. (Jews saw children born of marriages between Jews and Gentiles as Jews. Therefore, Timothy should have been circumcised as a Jewish infant.[2] The Jews, among whom Paul was ministering, knew that Timothy's father was a Gentile, and thus might have suspected that Timothy had not been circumcised. Paul wanted to remove any possibility that Timothy's noncompliance with Jewish custom would hinder anyone's movement toward faith in Jesus.) In 1 Corinthians 9:19-23, Paul laid out the principle behind this thinking. He sought to become "all things to all men"—that is, conforming where he could, when among Jews *or* Gentiles, so that he "might save some."

Question 2: What route did Paul and his companions take? His original idea had been to **go back and visit the brothers in all the towns where we preached the word [on the first missionary journey] and see how they are doing** (Acts 15:36). That likely would have included the island of Cyprus. But when Paul and Barnabas **parted company** (15:39), they divided the task. Barnabas took John Mark and revisited the new believers in Barnabas's home territory (see 15:39). Paul and Silas, later joined by Timothy, **went through Syria** [the province around Antioch] **and Cilicia** [the area around Tarsus, Paul's home town, where he likely had planted churches long before the first missionary journey; see 9:30; 11:25]. Paul then returned to Derbe and Lystra (16:1), and then through other towns where churches had been planted (16:4). (Not only did they practice evangelism—the planting of new churches—but they also discipled the new believers. Strengthening the already existing churches was a central part of Paul's ministry.)

Had Paul and Barnabas's original strategy of concentrating on population centers worked well (see commentary on 13:1-3)? It had been a year or more since their first visit, more than enough time to give a test to their strategy. Their plan had worked well! It appears likely that churches in the other unnamed towns (see 16:4) had been planted not by the apostles, but by the new believers of Galatia!

This tour of churches, allowing Paul and Silas to deliver the decisions reached by the Jerusalem Council, resulted in the strengthening and growth of the new churches (see 16:5). Paul saw the Jerusalem Council as providing crucial assistance to his mission. Some of us today look rather skeptically at the value of church business meetings. I doubt that Paul would share this opinion. Perhaps we should pray that our church business sessions could have as positive an effect as the Jerusalem Council.

As Paul, Silas, and Timothy continued west, they considered turning to the southwest and north. God had other ideas and prevented them from moving in those directions (see below). The travelers must have been a bit puzzled, but evidently assumed that God wanted them to move straight ahead. This they did, finally arriving at **Troas,** on the Aegean Sea (16:8). There, God responded to their puzzlement by giving them instructions to cross that sea and move toward **Macedonia** (16:9). (Hopefully, as you've read these paragraphs, you have been consulting maps. If you have, you see that Macedonia is an area now part of modern Greece.) Paul and friends thereby found themselves on the continent of Europe.

Question 3: How did Paul and his companions sense God's plan for their travel? Paul sensed God's plan via several different means. If God gave any special directions at the beginning of the trip while Paul was still in Antioch, Luke does not record this fact. It appears that two factors originally motivated the trip. First, the Jerusalem Council had instructed Paul and the others to travel a wide area in order to communicate its decision (see 16:4; God can communicate His will through the church body as a whole). Second, Paul used his own God-given reasoning abilities. He and Barnabas had planted churches in new areas. Paul wanted to do what he could to ensure that these churches were not only planted, but continuing to grow. A personal visit appeared the best means of accomplishing that goal. Likewise, common sense dictated that if Paul and Barnabas were going to separate, they should not duplicate their ministries. Paul headed northwest via a land route. Barnabas boarded a ship for Cyprus.

After Paul visited the Galatian churches, founded on the first journey, he moved toward what he thought was the next logical step. It seemed best to him to sweep systematically across the peninsula, hitting key population centers, as he had on the first trip. This, as indicated above, led Paul's thinking to the southwest, the area around Ephesus. While common sense had led Paul appropriately to this point in the journey, God here saw fit to overrule Paul's well-intentioned plans. **Paul and his**

companions [were] kept by the Holy Spirit from preaching the word in the province of Asia (where Ephesus was located; 16:6). Likewise, **when they . . . tried to enter Bithynia . . . the Spirit of Jesus would not allow them to** (16:7).

Why was Paul prevented from entering these fields of ministry? We don't know. It may have been that God had other people in mind for planting churches in these locations. It may be that the timing for Paul's ministry was not right. Near the end of this second trip, Paul briefly visited Ephesus (see 18:19), the capital of its province, Asia. At that time, he left Aquila and Priscilla, who were instrumental in founding the church there. A few years later, Paul himself ministered effectively in Ephesus in Asia, the province to the southwest. It appears that Paul never reached Bithynia, but that Peter may have later preached the gospel in that area (see 1 Peter 1:1).

It may have been that God needed to urge Paul and friends to move on to new territory they might not have otherwise tackled. A brief review of previous occasions when God intervened with such specific directions proves insightful.

God told Philip to go to the Gaza road, so that Philip might interact with the Ethiopian (see Acts 8:26); told Ananias to go to blind Saul (9:11); told Cornelius to send for Peter (10:5); told Peter to go to Joppa, to meet with Cornelius (10:20); and told the Antioch church to send Barnabas and Paul (Saul) for purposeful missionary travel (13:1-4).

On what occasions did God jump in with special instructions? It seems that He did so each time the church was breaking new ground. In each case, the Spirit was directing the church to new places or new people: a God-fearer (proselyte; 8:26); a persecutor (9:11); Gentiles (God-fearers; 10:20); the west (13:1-3; see Acts 13–14); farther to the west, across the Aegean into Macedonia (16:6-7, 9).

In any case, while Paul was in Troas, awaiting further instructions, God gave him a vision. In this vision, Paul saw **a man of Macedonia standing and begging him, "Come over to Macedonia and help us"** (16:9). Paul heeded the vision, **concluding that God had called [them] to preach the gospel to** the people there (16:10).

To direct Paul and his friends, God used a church decision, common sense, and direct communication through the Spirit. Today, God is still free to use each of these methods to instruct us.

Why does Luke include a detailed description of this second missionary journey? In many ways, the second trip is merely a rerun of the first trip (at least its second half, more devoted to evangelism and church planting). Thus, a summary of this second trip greatly mirrors the summary of the first.

- The Antioch church sent Barnabas and Paul out on purposeful evangelistic travel.
- Paul and his companions entered population centers.
- They preached the good news first to the Jews and then to the Gentiles.
- Some people responded positively and became the core of new Christian churches.
- Others responded negatively. Those who rejected the message usually rejected the messengers.
- Persecution arose.
- Paul and Barnabas moved on to another site.
- Paul and Barnabas returned to their base in Syrian Antioch, rejoicing over their success.

Several factors do make the second trip distinctive, however.

As mentioned above, Paul devoted the first half of the second trip to *strengthening* churches which he and Barnabas had planted earlier. And, of course, the specific events of the entire second trip were different. But, perhaps more crucial for Luke, this trip took Paul farther west, nearer the geographical, commercial, and political hub of the Roman Empire. In this section of Acts, Luke records events occurring in cities his readers were sure to recognize.

Another key contrast relates to the persecution that Paul and his companions received. On the first trip, certain Jews always instigated the persecution, focusing on matters concerning their religion. But events at Philippi, the first new stop on the second journey, set a new pattern. There, the persecution of Paul and Silas came from Gentiles and arose over an economic issue (see 16:19). In subsequent locations, Jews also actively participated in the resistance, but in most cases, rather than resorting merely to mob action, the offended parties took the matter to Roman authorities (16:20; 17:6; 18:12), accusing the missionaries of breaking Roman law (17:7; 18:13). The fact that Paul was able to leave each city with no charges against his name gave him credibility and lends support to the theory that Luke was writing a defense document.

Notice also the prominence of the new believers mentioned on the second trip. On the first trip, Sergius Paulus, the proconsul on Cyprus, is the only prominent believer Luke describes.

Philippi:	Lydia, a relatively wealthy local merchant (16:14)
	The Roman jailer (16:30, 33)
Thessalonica:	**Prominent women** (17:4)
Berea:	**Prominent Greek women and many Greek men** (17:12)
Athens:	**Dionysius, a member of the Areopagus** (17:34)
Corinth:	**Crispus, the synagogue ruler** (18:8)
	Aquila and Priscilla, a relatively wealthy couple (18:2)
	(Possibly Sosthenes, a replacement synagogue ruler [18:17; see 1 Corinthians 1:1])

Another new factor involves Paul's use of "reasoning," rather than proclamation, as his form of presenting the gospel. Luke notes Paul's reasoning in Thessalonica (17:2), Athens (17:17), Corinth (18:4), and Ephesus (18:19). Why might Paul have moved to this dialogical form? It is likely that in these larger urban centers, Paul dealt with better educated hearers. Perhaps he felt that reasoning might better enable them to receive the gospel which was so new to them.

Before moving on, we should note one other difference. By the time Paul reached Macedonia, Luke himself had joined the missionary team. Note the initial appearance of the first person plural pronoun **us** in 16:10. Luke also says, **From Troas *we* put out to sea . . .** (16:11, my emphasis). Luke's vivid memory of his own involvement in at least a portion of this journey may have contributed to his decision to include accounts of this second trip in his book.[3]

This overview better prepares us for a look at the six primary new locations Paul visited on this trip.

2. PHILIPPI 16:11-40

Paul's first destination was Philippi, **a Roman colony and the leading city of that district of Macedonia** (Acts 16:12). Cities which had been declared Roman colonies could relate more directly to Rome as they were not governed by the local provincial officials. (Pisidian Antioch, Lystra, Troas, and Corinth, among others, were all Roman colonies.) Philippi was a major trading center on the Ignatian Way, the main land route across Macedonia, between the Aegean and Adriatic Seas.

Luke summarizes the missionaries' time in Philippi by reviewing, in sequence, their interaction with three key individuals.

The first was **Lydia, a dealer in purple cloth from the city of Thyatira, who was a worshiper of God** (16:14). She and other women gathered each week by the river for a time of prayer. Paul had already established his pattern of beginning, in each new center, at the Jewish site of worship. Usually this was the synagogue, but evidently Philippi did not have the ten Jewish males required to establish a synagogue. Inquiries in the city likely gave the missionaries the information they needed to find the local group of Jews and God-fearers.

What does Luke tell us about Lydia? She was originally from Thyatira, a city across the Aegean Sea, north of Ephesus. (A church there was one of the seven the Spirit addressed through John the apostle; see Revelation 2:18-29.) The area around Thyatira was known for its purple dye. Lydia was likely the local "agent" for the home company. She owned a house large enough to host a team of at least four, which means she must have been reasonably wealthy. No husband is mentioned, so it is possible she inherited her business from a husband who had died.

Lydia was a God-fearer (those attracted to Judaism's God and moral principles, but not all its laws and sacrifices[4]). Such people were often prime candidates for belief in Christ. Lydia allowed God to open **her heart to respond to Paul's message** (Acts 16:14). She quickly manifested her new faith by receiving baptism and offering hospitality to the missionaries.

Luke describes the baptism of the **members of her household** (16:15). Proponents of infant baptism often use these "household" passages (see also 11:14; 16:31; 18:8) to support their practice. It is possible that young children or even infants were involved, but the evidence is not conclusive.

Lydia's warm hospitality may have set the precedent for the strong relationship Paul subsequently enjoyed with the Philippian church. Years later, he wrote a most affirming letter to this group: "I thank my God every time I remember you . . . because of your partnership in the gospel from the first day until now" (Phil. 1:3, 5). The church had expressed its "partnership" concretely, attempting to support Paul financially over the years (see 4:10, 14-18).

The second key individual Luke includes in his Philippian account was not a wealthy businesswoman, but **a slave girl** (Acts 16:16). Nor was she a God-fearer, but one possessed by a spirit. Her life likely had not been pleasant. As a slave, she could have been taken from her parents at an early age, to be raised by schemers planning to use her for their own personal profit. As the story unfolds, we see that her owners were more concerned with **making money** than with her well-being (16:19).

Paul and his partners first encountered this girl one day while **going to the place of prayer** (16:16). She immediately recognized them and announced that they were **servants of the Most High God** (16:17).[5]

Paul put up with her distracting shouting for several days, but then he became **troubled** enough to intervene. Not in his own power, but through Jesus Christ—One stronger than the forces of evil—Paul commanded the spirit to **come out of her** (16:18). It had no choice but to obey.[6]

The owners of the slave girl were not impressed. She had been earning **a great deal of money** for them; they had just lost a key source of income (16:19). But when they brought Paul before the authorities, they knew they needed a more substantial, less self-centered accusation. They quickly concocted one: **These men are . . . advocating customs unlawful for us Romans to accept or practice** (16:20-21).[7]

The crowd joined in the attack against Paul and Silas (16:22). Why? The others had suffered no economic loss. A general anti-Jewish feeling may have swayed the crowd. Citizens of a city which had been declared a Roman colony often felt quite patriotic and sought to maintain their pure Roman-ness. Charges of perverting Roman society were sure to attract attention.

The magistrates certainly took the charges seriously. We see this both in the immediate punishment and the subsequent high-security imprisonment they ordered. Assuming that the crowd of Roman citizens could not be wrong, the authorities ordered the prisoners **to be stripped and beaten** (16:22). Paul later picked up on the illegality of the treatment he and Silas received (see 16:37). At least for Roman citizens, the "innocent until proven guilty" principle should have held sway. Paul may have protested the injustice before the flogging, but in the midst of the mob's shouting, his words were ignored. Or his words might have been heard, but not believed.

The jailer was commanded to guard the prisoners carefully. From one perspective, this was hardly necessary. A Roman flogging, in itself, was enough to kill a man. The prisoners would have been weakened by a loss of blood and in severe pain. Their local friends were few and not strong enough to attempt a jailbreak.

At the time of their arrest and punishment, where were Timothy, Luke, Lydia, and others? Evidently, their role in the Philippian ministry had been more low-key. When they were not arrested, they may have thought their best move was to return to Lydia's house and pray.

Paul and Silas definitely were praying (see 16:25). God heard their songs of praise and engineered a miraculous release. An earthquake strong enough to open doors and free chains from walls so impressed all the prisoners that they sat there in awe of Paul, Silas, and their God. The **jailer** did not know if the prisoners had escaped and did know the punishment he faced if they had (16:27). Suicide looked to be a better option than facing Roman execution.

Fortunately for this third key figure in the Philippi story, Paul's shouts prevented any hasty harmful action. The jailer, too, joined the others there in amazement. The miracle of the earthquake and the prisoners' all staying in their places shocked him to the core: **"What must I do to know your God, to experience His salvation?"** (16:30). Paul bore no grudge and was quite willing to offer salvation to the man who had held him prisoner[8]: **Believe in the Lord Jesus Christ, and you will be saved** (16:31). Those words, read ever since as a wonderful summary of salvation, required further explanation, of course. Paul and Silas, despite their exhaustion and pain, which perhaps had been inflicted by the jailer himself, were willing to offer further explanation. As he heard, the jailer believed and was saved. He immediately offered washing to his new friends, before they offered him the washing of baptism. A joyful meal together finished an eventful night.

The magistrates also were impressed by what they must have seen as a divine sign of the prisoners' innocence. They ordered that Paul and Silas be released. But Paul refused to leave quietly (see 16:37). Why? What was to be gained by winning this legal technicality? No decision at that point would remove the previous day's scars from Paul's back. Paul was once again thinking of others. If the authorities publicly apologized for their illegitimate actions, then everyone in Philippi would understand that Christian faith did not violate Roman law. The infant Philippian church would be able to move forward unhindered.

The three Philippian individuals Luke features offer an amazing vignette of the breadth and power of the gospel. One can hardly picture three more different people. Consider their differences: perceived needs, age, gender, family status, wealth, position in society, and religious background. God employed human, spiritual, and natural resources to bring unique healing to each life.

Notice also the variety of forces that God overcame in Philippi. As so many people are today, most Philippians Luke describes were concerned with hanging on to their livelihood, money, and power. When Paul arrived, he may have wondered where he would find people interested in his message, those symbolized by the Macedonian man who had beckoned him to Europe. When Paul and company left the area, a church had been formed that would be a model for us two thousand years later. We, too, can believe for unbelievable manifestations of God's power today. No situation is too dismal for Him to redeem.

3. THESSALONICA AND BEREA 17:1-15

What do we know about the next places Paul and his companions visited? **Thessalonica** (Acts 17:1) was the capital city of the province of Macedonia. A key center of travel and trade, the city was located about one hundred miles west of Philippi on the main highway across the peninsula. **Berea** (17:10) was a smaller town, approximately fifty miles further to the southwest.

Compared to his account of events at Philippi, Luke provides less detail about the next two ministry locations. At both locations, Paul and Silas began at the synagogue (see 17:2, 10). Jews in both cities gave them opportunity to proclaim the life and message of Jesus who was the Messiah (see 17:3, 11). As Jesus himself had said, **the Christ had to suffer and rise from the dead** (17:3; see also Luke 9:22; 24:26). The Old Testament, sacred to the Jews of course, supported these claims (see Acts 17:2, 11). In both cases, there was a positive response from both Jews and Gentiles (see 17:4, 12).

The similarities end there. In Thessalonica, the Jews who did not freely accept the gospel rejected it strongly. Perhaps they sensed a theological threat to their belief system. They were certainly jealous of the positive response some local Jews and **a large number of** Gentiles gave to the new teaching (17:4). In any case, the skeptical Jews **formed a mob and started a riot** (17:5). In Berea, however, the Jews who did not readily believe were at least more open. Rather than flatly rejecting the message, the synagogue group encouraged the missionaries to continue preaching. The Jews wanted more time to examine their Scriptures, in order to evaluate the new message Paul proclaimed.

What was the result of the persecution in Thessalonica? When the mob sought Paul and Silas at the home of Jason, one of the new believers, the Jews **did not find them** there (17:6). Either the missionaries were out somewhere, or the new believers, more likely, were protecting Paul and Silas from the mob attack, even at risk to themselves. The angry Jews did not give up easily. Not finding Paul and Silas, they grabbed **Jason and some other brothers,** dragging them **before the city officials** (17:6). The Jews accused the new Christians of harboring Paul and Silas. They saw the latter as well-known criminals,[9] guilty of disloyalty to

Caesar. Certainly anyone proclaiming a rival king (perhaps the second coming of Jesus[10]) was potential trouble. The Romans in Philippi had flogged Paul and Silas for upsetting the economic and religious order; treason was an even more serious charge. But the officials may have felt that the charges were not a matter of major concern to them. (Thessalonica was a "free city" and not a Roman colony; thus, the city leaders were not so tightly tied to Rome and Caesar.) Or perhaps they postponed any major decision until they had a chance to consider the case. In any case, the lack of definitive action gave opportunity for the brothers to sneak Paul and Silas out of the city, protecting them from any further unruly crowd action.[11]

When Paul arrived in Berea, he continued his evangelistic ministry. The Berean Jews were more open. They wished to hear the message daily, rather than merely on the Sabbath. Paul and Silas could have carried on a long, fruitful ministry there. However, the Jews of Thessalonica heard that Paul, the criminal, had not left the area. Still upset at the new church in their home city, they traveled to Berea, **agitating the crowds** there (17:13). Yet, another group of new Christian brothers felt the missionaries were in danger. They sent Paul, the leader, away to the coast and then on to Athens (see 17:15).[12] It appears that Timothy, after a stay of unknown length at Berea and Athens, returned to Thessalonica for a period of ministry, before rejoining Paul at Athens (see 1 Thessalonians 3:2). Might Silas have returned to Philippi to help strengthen the church there?[13] In any case, Paul and company were not merely concerned with birthing new Christians; they wanted to help establish strong, self-propagating churches.

Note the persistence of Paul and his team. Despite being pushed out of Philippi and Thessalonica, the group went right on to the next town, preaching again the gospel which had had them railroaded out of the last two cities. The variety of charges against them (upsetting the economic, religious, and political systems) shows both the universal prejudice against their message and the resulting risk they took in proclaiming it. Despite this, the missionaries saw a positive response. They had planted new churches in key cities. But they and the new Christians paid the price of being ostracized from society.

Note also the great contrast between the response of the Jews in the two cities. One group rejected the new teaching because it was new and popular. The second group wanted time to evaluate the new teaching by means of the Scriptures' standard. When today's church encounters new ideas or practices, we should all be "Bereans." Consulting the Scriptures (as both our "textbook" and our "court of appeal"[14]) enables us to overcome the opposite dangers of gullibility *and* unnecessary resistance. Through His book, God can help His people to discover and follow the truth.

4. ATHENS[15] 17:16-34

Luke records accounts of Paul's preaching in many cities. Quite often, a violent negative reaction pushed Paul out of those towns. But, in almost every situation, Paul appears to have left behind a strong group of Christians. Athens came closest to being the exception. The response there seemed largely to have been one big yawn. But even there, Paul was not a failure. **A few men** and **a number** of women believed (Acts 17:34).

Should we place all the blame on Paul for the limited response at Athens? No. Athens was a unique city; it was the Roman "mall" of philosophy shops. Luke himself notes this: **All the Athenians . . . spent their time doing nothing but talking about and listening to the latest ideas** (17:21). The people of Philippi persecuted Paul for proclaiming new ideas. Would the people of Athens have done that? No. They more likely would have offered him another shop in their "mall." Would they have gotten excited about the truth he proclaimed as lifechanging? "No," they might have responded. "All we have heard is another **babbler** [17:18] offering his set of wild ideas."

Athens offers a picture of contemporary Western society. Thirty years ago, young people were much more likely to flatly reject Christianity. Today's generation would more likely see the Christian gospel as one option among many. In their minds, Christianity, like many other philosophies, might be right for a few, but is by no means the *only* truth for all people. Much of North America is, as Athens was, **full of idols** (17:16). Yesterday's idols no longer top the charts. Westerners continually look for a fresh idol, enjoy him or her a few weeks, and then become bored, ready to move on to something new. It's almost as if contemporary people have built their own altars **to an unknown god** (17:23)—that is, the next idol to be discovered. Life for Athenians or modern Western society appears to have no enduring meaning.

How did Paul respond to such a setting? You'd think he would have marveled at the astounding learning and architecture of this famous city. Instead, he was **greatly distressed** at what he saw (17:16). Luke records no other occasion when Paul first responded to a city in such a manner. Paul sensed the difficulty of preaching to people not committed to anything. How would he lead them to commit themselves to Christ?

Paul began as he usually did, **in the synagogue** (17:17). There the Jews might at least take him seriously. Then Paul went on to **the marketplace,** reasoning with those **who happened to be there** (17:17). He apparently attracted no continuous group of listeners. A few became interested enough **to dispute with him** (17:18). Even these did not truly take him seriously. They called him a **babbler,** literally a "seed-picker," a country bumpkin. These philosophers[16] took Paul to **the Areopagus,** a group which acted somewhat as the local "thought police." Those who proposed a new way of thinking ("a new shop in the philosophy mall"), helped their cause by gaining approval from the Areopagus.

The group there appeared mildly curious: **May we know what this new teaching is that you are presenting? You are bringing some strange ideas to our ears, and we want to know what they mean** (17:20). Here was Paul's best opportunity. He was given the podium, not merely at the local Rotary Club, but before the intellectual elite in the intellectual capital of the Empire.

Luke records Paul's address to the Areopagus at some length. We may assume that he was summarizing Paul's approach to an educated Gentile group. (Contrast this presentation with what Paul spoke to Jews in a synagogue [Pisidian Antioch—13:13, 16-47] or to an uneducated group of Gentiles [Lystra—14:15-17].)

In good preaching style, Paul began where his hearers were. He even complimented them: **You are very religious** (17:22). He noted their interest even in **an unknown god** and offered to enlighten them at this point. Who was the unknown god?

The god they did not yet know, Paul explained, was the One God **who made the world and everything in it** (17:24). Perhaps sweeping his hand around in the direction of the Parthenon or other such Athenian temples, Paul pointed out that God could not be contained in any single building. (Was Paul remembering words from Stephen's last "sermon" [see 7:48]?) Paul went on to describe in several other ways God's supremacy and self-sufficiency, and also His approachability. God had arranged life in the world He made **so that men would seek him and perhaps . . . find him** (17:27).[17] On this last point, Paul reached as far as he could to the Athenians, quoting great thoughts, not from the Old Testament, but from their very own libraries: **In him we live and move and have our being** (17:28). These words came from an earlier writer named Epimenides.[18] Likewise, **We are his** [God's] **offspring** (17:28), is a quotation from another ancient poet named Aratus.

How high a grade would you give Paul so far? To this point, Paul had done well. He had accomplished the two primary goals of any sermon introduction: he had attracted his hearers' attention and appropriately set groundwork for laying out his message. He also had attracted their attention by showing that this "seed-picker" knew a thing or two, even of Greek literature. Paul demonstrated that he was an educated thinker whose ideas were worth considering. The foundation for his message? He placed his God in the context of their own gods, showing that the God he proclaimed was not merely another god to add to their collection, but the *unique* One. Paul was then ready to move toward proclaiming Jesus, as he had in his sermon to the Jews at Pisidian Antioch.

Did he do so? We can give Paul the benefit of the doubt, for Luke likely does not record *everything* Paul said there.[19] In the summary Luke gives, we see Paul moving next to the foolishness of worshiping man-made objects, and then quickly through the need for repentance to a word about Jesus' resurrection (see 17:30-31). Note that Paul did not give a *detailed* description of salvation in the life and crucifixion of Jesus. (Paul himself may have reflected back on his Athenian sermon. Note his later description of his preaching to the Corinthians during the next stop on this tour: "When I came to you, brothers, I did not come with eloquence or superior wisdom. . . . For I resolved to know *nothing* while I was with you *except Jesus Christ and him crucified*" [1 Cor. 2:1-2, my emphasis]).

If, in Athens, Paul omitted mention of "Jesus Christ crucified," he did so not because he feared persecution or ridicule. His mention of Jesus' bodily resurrection certainly laid him open to mockery. Many ancient Greeks believed in the eternal existence of the human soul, but they thought resurrection of the body a fairy tale.

The response to Paul's preaching? **Some . . . sneered** (17:32). Others offered to listen to Paul's new ideas again. Did Paul go back to the Areopagus? Luke doesn't tell us. Luke finishes his account describing those who *did* believe. Among them were **Dionysius** (a member of the Areopagus) and **a woman named Damaris** (a woman of some repute, perhaps; 17:34).[20]

How do we evaluate Paul's ministry in Athens? He certainly did well at building bridges to the Athenian minds. "It has always been good missionary policy to express the gospel in terms that would be intelligible to the hearer without . . . altering the essence of the message."[21] After hearing Paul, a number of people, local leaders among them, did believe. Would Paul have received a stronger response (positive or negative) if he had more boldly proclaimed Jesus? Athens might have been a pretty tough audience, no matter how Paul had preached. Many of the people there were more interested in novelty than in truth. Even the best seed produces various types of growth (see Luke 8:4-15).

If we judge Paul's preaching in each city merely by the number of visible salvations, we come close to the Athenian sin of idolatry. Looking for big, instant results is a modern Western phenomenon, not God's standard for evaluating His servants.

Remember that what *impressed* Paul's world (and ours today) did not draw his *approval*. He may have flattered his hearers by praising their religious appearance. But his true evaluation of that city's apparent glory was deep distress (see Acts 17:16). He saw that its residents worshiped gods other than Jesus. Paul offered the true God to them. We, too, must look beyond superficial spirituality and bring people into deep relationship with Jesus Christ the Lord.

5. CORINTH 18:1-18a

Paul wrote two of his longest letters to the church at Corinth. His relationship with this group was not always smooth. In Acts, Luke offers information that gives helpful background. What do we know about this city and the establishment of this Christian church?

Politically, Corinth was a Roman colony. It was the capital of its province. Commercially, Corinth was a key center. It was located on a narrow strip of land connecting the mainland of Greece with a smaller area of land known as the Peloponnesian Peninsula. All land travel between mainland and peninsula moved through Corinth. The city was also a crucial seaport. Sailing around the peninsula was treacherous. Traders often preferred to unload their cargo on one side of the isthmus, carry it across the strip of land, and then reload it on the other side. Even small ships were often moved manually over the land and then set into the water again.

Corinth was also a key center for pagan worship. As in other locations, local worship here involved temple prostitutes who offered themselves as part of the pagan rituals. The city became known for its sexual immorality. The city's reputation even offered a new word to the Greek vocabulary. One could describe orgy activity as "corinthianizing."[22] (A review of Paul's letters to the Corinthians shows that, unfortunately, some of the believers, even after coming to salvation, still had a hard time maintaining sexual purity.[23])

Paul spent at least eighteen months in Corinth (see Acts 18:11). Luke's overview of that time includes several vignettes. Together they highlight the usual combination of positive and negative responses to Paul's presence and preaching. The Lord's assuring words to Paul seem to summarize the contrast: **Do not be afraid; keep on speaking, do not be silent. For I am with you, and no one is going to attack and harm you, because I have many people in this city** (18:9-10). Some Corinthians rejected Paul. He was at least tempted to fear them. He felt the possibility of harm. Yet, God was with him and would enable a fruitful ministry in this important pagan center.

Let's focus first on those with whom Paul interacted positively.

Luke opens and closes his description of the Corinthian visit with mention of Aquila and Priscilla (see 18:2-3, 18). Paul first met this couple soon after his arrival in Corinth. The three of them developed a strong relationship. A few years later, he told the Roman Christians that "all the churches of the Gentiles are grateful to them" (Rom. 16:4). Who were they, and what did they do to receive such praise?

Aquila was a Jew from the area of Pontus, in the northern part of what is now Turkey. For reasons unknown to us, he moved to Rome. It was probably in Rome that he met his bride, Priscilla. She was likely a Gentile. Together they were tentmakers.[24]

In the year A.D. 49 or 50, the Roman emperor Claudius ordered all Jews out of Rome (see Acts 18:2). Suetonius, an ancient Roman historian, wrote that Claudius took this step because of disturbances among the Jews on account of one called "Chrestus." It is likely that this Chrestus was none other than Jesus Christ. (Claudius evidently misinterpreted the Jewish-Christian disagreement as a threat to himself.) But what is significant for church history is the knowledge this gives us that the gospel had apparently reached Rome. A church had been established. Some Jews in Rome had evidently responded violently to the arrival of Christianity, just as many Jews rejected Paul and his message when he took the gospel into new territory. The emperor did not distinguish Jews from Christians and evicted all who were potentially involved. Aquila and Priscilla were in this group (see 18:2). Had they come to Christ and joined the new Christian church in Rome? We can't be sure. At minimum, they were open to the Christian message when they heard it from Paul in Corinth.

Aquila and Priscilla were relative newcomers to Corinth when Paul arrived. Either because of their common interest in tentmaking[25] or possibly a common faith in Christ, Paul was attracted to them. They opened their home and a partnership in their business to him.

Paul and this couple became close friends. When Paul left Corinth, he asked them to accompany him to Ephesus (see 18:18-19). (At least Aquila had made several moves by now; the couple felt free to move once again.) It appears that during their hours of working together, Paul taught them much and helped them to become strong leaders. "They were already expert tentmakers. They now became expert evangelists."[26] They later helped to plant the church in Ephesus. Luke specifically describes how they taught Apollos, one who already knew the Scriptures well (see 18:24-26).

Paul later greeted Aquila and Priscilla in several of his epistles,[27] and called them both his coworkers (see Romans 16:3).[28] They appear to have ministered in several more locations. (When Aquila and Priscilla were thrown out of Rome, they must have questioned what God was doing. Years later, they must have been grateful for this apparent tragedy, which God used for their good and the benefit of many churches.) Aquila and Priscilla may offer the New Testament's best model of a Christian couple who worked well as a team.[29]

With whom else did Paul interact positively? Team members Silas and Timothy rejoined Paul after having spent time in Macedonia (the area including Philippi, Thessalonica, and Berea). Their arrival brought encouragement and financial support (see 1 Thessalonians 3:6-8; 2 Corinthians 11:9). Before they arrived, Paul had evidently been giving more time to tentmaking, either as a short break from more public ministry or for the income it produced (see Acts 18:5).

Paul proclaimed Jesus in the synagogue at Corinth. That provoked a negative response (see below) but also belief from some Jews and God-fearing Gentiles. **Titius Justus,** one of the latter, responded positively and offered his house as a preaching point for Paul (18:7). **Crispus, the synagogue ruler, and his entire household believed** (18:8). Many other Corinthians also **believed and were baptized** (18:8; see 1 Corinthians 1:14-16 for another account of the church's first days, which lists the names of several other new believers). It is possible that Sosthenes, the man who replaced Crispus as synagogue ruler, also later became a believer (see Acts 18:17; also 1 Corinthians 1:1). Yes, God did have **many people in this city** (Acts 18:10).

Paul stayed on for at least eighteen months, much longer than he had stayed in any of the stops on his first two missionary journeys which originated from Antioch. Did he stay because of the fruitful ministry or because no persecution pushed him out of town? Perhaps both.

Paul did face some negative response early in his time in Corinth. While some Jews in the synagogue accepted his message, others **opposed Paul and became abusive** (18:6). Paul's reaction shows the strength of their opposition. He shook out his clothes (an action similar to shaking the dust off one's feet; see 13:51; Matthew 10:14). He laid all responsibility for the Jews' rejection of the gospel on them: **Your blood be on your own heads!** (Acts 18:6; see Matthew 27:25 for similar wording).

The Jews could not have been pleased with Paul's determination. (Notice his courageous action, setting up his next teaching location in the house next door to the synagogue.) The Jews, like their brothers in Thessalonica, may have attempted to expel Paul from the city. (The fear Paul felt in Acts 18:9 may indicate that the Jews attempted to harass him, but without success.)

After a year and a half of relative quiet, the Jews' patience ran out. It appears that a new Roman governor had arrived. Perhaps he would hear them and take the anti-Paul action they desired. They **made a united attack on Paul and brought him into court** (18:12). (Had their attacks to this point been less than "united"?) In order to gain a hearing with the governor, they accused Paul of breaking Roman law: **This man is persuading the people to worship God in ways contrary to the law** (18:13; see commentary on 16:11-40).

Gallio,[30] the new governor, refused to hear the Jews. He saw their argument with Paul as purely a matter of Jewish religion, one which did not relate to Roman law or his own duties. Evidently, feeling that he had more important things to do, Gallio sent away both the accusers and the accused (see 18:14-16). His decision took the previously set pattern even further. To this point, no government official had interfered with Paul's mission. But here, an important Roman leader had, at least indirectly, given his approval to Christianity and its proclamation.

The beating of **Sosthenes** is a bit of a puzzle (18:17). Who beat him and why? Perhaps Gentiles were so upset with the Jews that they went after the Jewish leader. Within the Empire, there was a common dislike of the Jews. Or it may be that the Jews were the instigators of the beating, going after one who had been their synagogue ruler, but who had recently converted to Christianity. Luke, however, makes it appear that when Sosthenes was attacked, he was still the synagogue ruler. This would argue for the theory that Gentiles attacked the Jewish leader.

Paul, acquitted by the Roman governor, likely stayed on in Corinth for a further period of ministry. Luke gives no details of this time. His account of Paul's stay finishes with another minor puzzle, relating to a haircut at Cenchrea (a suburb of Corinth down near the water) and **a vow [Paul] had taken** (18:18). Perhaps Paul had made a vow to God that if God gave him a fruitful, safe ministry at Corinth, Paul would not cut his hair as long as he stayed. As he left the area, Paul gratefully fulfilled his promise. Such vows were not uncommon among first-century Jews; it was likely a temporary Nazarite vow (see Numbers 6:1-5).[31]

God had reassured Paul of protection and fruitfulness in Corinth (see Acts 18:9-10). God kept those promises. To this point in Paul's missionary journeys, fruitfulness in evangelism and church planting had been the major themes, with protection being the enablement for future fruitfulness. In Luke's record, Corinth was the last new church that Paul himself planted. Was his work finished? No. God continued to protect Paul to enable him to participate in the strengthening of individual Christians and the churches that Paul and others had planted. Both ministries were and are essential.

ENDNOTES

[1] Who was right? Barnabas or Paul? Maybe Paul correctly sensed that Mark was not cut out for the rigors of life as a traveling missionary. Mark did later find his most enduring work in writing the gospel that bears his name. But Barnabas continued to invest himself in this young man. Years later, Paul commented on the result. In 2 Timothy 4:11, Paul describes John Mark as "being helpful to [him] in his ministry." Barnabas's people skills paid off again.

[2] I. Howard Marshall, *Acts* (Grand Rapids, Michigan: Wm. B. Eerdmans Publishing Co., 1980), p. 259.

[3] Other "we" passages in Acts are 20:5–21:28; 27:1–28:16.

[4] Judaism is the life and belief system of the Jewish people and involves a covenant relationship with God. Though there are various branches of Judaism, the underlying theme among them has been monotheism and a recognition of the Law, or the Torah. The Hebrew word from which *Torah* comes is translated *law* and refers to divine instruction and guidance. The Torah is comprised of the instructions and directions given to Israel by God. Torah is another name for the Pentateuch (the first five books of the Old Testament: Genesis, Exodus, Leviticus, Numbers, and Deuteronomy), also known as the Law of Moses. It is considered the most important division in the Jewish Scriptures, with highest authority, since it was traditionally thought to have been written by Moses, the only biblical hero to have spoken with God face-to-face.

[5] It is often noted in the Gospels (see, for example, Luke 4:34; the Gospels include the New Testament books of Matthew, Mark, Luke, and John), that persons possessed by spirits recognized and proclaimed the presence of God's ambassadors.

[6] The slave girl disappeared from the story at this point. What became of her? One would hope that she believed and joined the church, but Luke does not say.

[7] In actual fact, there might have been some truth to their charges. Rome required that all religions be "licensed." Judaism, within the Roman system, was a legal religion. As long as the Romans saw Christianity as a subdivision of Judaism, then it, too, was legal. As Christianity spread, and the Romans saw that it was a strong new force to deal with, then the Romans could use this "religious license law" against the believers. In this case, however, no one in Philippi noticed or cared that Christianity was new and different until the owners of the slave girl needed a charge to bring against Paul.

[8]William Barclay, *The Acts of the Apostles* (Philadelphia: The Westminster Press, 1976), p. 126.

[9]See F. F. Bruce, *The Book of the Acts* (Grand Rapids, Michigan: Wm. B. Eerdmans Publishing Co., 1988), p. 324. Perhaps Paul himself had become renowned. Or possibly the Thessalonian Jews were referring to Christians more broadly. The Roman emperor had recently expelled all Jews from Rome (see Acts 18:2). A Roman historian told how Claudius had done this because of problems among the Jews raised because of one "Chrestus." More than likely, this would refer to a Jewish-Christian controversy relating to Christ.

[10]Ibid., p. 325. See 1 Thessalonians 4:16; 2 Thessalonians 2:5.

[11]How long did Paul stay in Thessalonica? Likely, more than the three weeks implied by the three Sabbath days (see Acts 17:2). Paul stayed long enough to receive at least one gift from the church in Philippi and probably to work at tentmaking (see Philippians 4:16; 1 Thessalonians 2:9).

What happened to the Thessalonian church? Within months, maybe from Corinth, Paul wrote at least two letters back to the Thessalonian Christians. Because he had to leave them after such a short time, and at such short notice, he felt the need to supplement teaching he had given them during his short stay. The Thessalonians were especially confused about the Lord's second coming. They felt special concern for "those who fall asleep"—that is, some who had died—since Paul's visit (1 Thess. 4:13). It is possible that some of the Thessalonian Christians had been martyred for their faith (1 Thess. 2:14). But, despite their "severe suffering," the Thessalonian Christians had endured and thrived in their faith (1 Thess. 1:3-8).

[12]The church at Berea drops from the biblical picture at this point. Luke did mention Sopater, a member of the Berean church, accompanying Paul on his last trip to Jerusalem (see Acts 20:4).

[13]This possibility is raised by Marshall, p. 281.

[14]John R. W. Stott, *The Spirit, the Church and the World* (Downers Grove, Illinois: InterVarsity Press, 1990, p. 274.

[15]Of all the cities Paul visited, with the exception of Rome, you are most likely familiar with Athens. It still appears occasionally in our news. You certainly have seen pictures of the Parthenon and other ancient ruins of the city. Paul would have walked among these buildings while they were still in use.

[16]Verse 18 mentions two specific philosophical groups. The Stoics saw "reason" as the principle underlying the world. They did their best to live in accordance with reason. The Epicureans gave more emphasis to living the life of pleasure, but that did not necessarily mean wine and women. Some among them saw that the life of greatest pleasure was the life governed by good sense. Members of both groups would likely have been good people, would likely have worshiped their chosen god(s), but saw little need to live lives of submission to any one god.

[17]Johannes Munck, *The Acts of the Apostles* (New York: Doubleday, 1967), p. 172. Munck points out the similarity between Paul's thinking here and what he wrote in Romans 1:19-20.

[18]Interestingly enough, Paul quotes from the same writer, the same poem in fact, in Titus 1:12, when he writes, "Cretans are always liars."

[19]See Marshall, p. 291. Marshall raises the possibility that Luke, in his record of the sermon, purposely omitted teaching on Jesus that his readers would have

found repetitive. But elsewhere in Acts, Luke saw no problem in being repetitive (see the double account of Peter's vision in chapters 10 and 11, also the triple account of Paul's in chapters 9, 22, and 26).

[20]We unfortunately know little more of Christianity in Athens during the first century. One ancient tradition says that Dionysius became bishop of the church there.

[21]Marshall, p. 282.

[22]In 1 Corinthians 6:9-11, Paul points out the many sins from which God had saved the Corinthian believers.

[23]See 1 Corinthians 5:1, 9-11; 6:13-20; 2 Corinthians 12:21.

[24]This word can describe either the activity of weaving the goat's hair cloth from which tents were made, or the sewing together of large pieces of such cloth into actual tents.

[25]Bruce, p. 346. It appears that Paul practiced tentmaking as a means of supporting himself throughout his ministry (see Acts 20:34; 1 Corinthians 9:6-12, 15, 18; 1 Thessalonians 2:9; 2 Thessalonians 3:8).

[26]A. T. Robertson, *Types of Preachers in the New Testament* (Grand Rapids, Michigan: Baker Book House, 1972) , p. 61.

[27]Paul's epistles are comprised of the New Testament books of Romans, 1 and 2 Corinthians, Galatians, Ephesians, Philippians, Colossians, 1 and 2 Thessalonians, 1 and 2 Timothy, Titus, and Philemon (some consider Paul to be the unknown author of Hebrews as well). Paul's epistles include two categories: the Pastoral Epistles—1 and 2 Timothy, Titus; and the Prison Epistles—Ephesians, Philippians, Colossians, and Philemon (these letters were most likely written during the Roman imprisonment Luke describes in Acts 28:30).

[28]See 1 Corinthians 16:19; Romans 16:3-5; 2 Timothy 4:19.

[29]There is much debate in some churches today over the role of women in ministry. Luke offers no hint that women should play any subordinate role. He shows Priscilla as playing a role of equal if not greater importance than her husband. Of the six times they are mentioned in the New Testament, her name is mentioned first on four of those occasions. For first-century writing, this is quite unusual. "There is no hint here or elsewhere in Acts that a woman should be subordinate, be silent, and not teach a man." Evelyn and Frank Stagg, quoted in Janice Nunnally-Cox, *Foremothers: Women of the Bible* (New York: Seabury Press, 1981), p. 131.

[30]This Gallio is known from the secular history records of the day. His appointment to the post in Corinth can be dated to the year A.D. 51. This helps us date Paul's time in this city and other locations on his missionary journeys. For more information, see Bruce, pp. 352–53.

[31]Barclay, p. 138. Temporary Nazarite vows had apparently become common. Such vows involved fasting from meat and wine and allowing one's hair to grow uncut. At the end of the vow, the hair was offered to God as a burnt offering.

15

SUMMARY OF TRAVEL AND MINISTRY

Acts 18:18b-28

This section of Acts serves as a transition between Paul's second and third missionary journeys. Luke devotes all 41 verses of chapter 19 to Paul's extended period of ministry in Ephesus. In contrast to that detail, Luke gives only five verses to Paul's thousands of miles of travel and ministry between the time he left the Corinth area and his long stay in Ephesus. Luke may have seen this time as less eventful, or he may have known less information about this period in Paul's life.

Paul, Priscilla, and Aquila **arrived at Ephesus** (Acts 18:19). Ephesus was another of the great metropolitan centers of the Eastern empire. Like Corinth, it played a major role in the political, economic, and religious activities of its region.

Upon arriving in Ephesus, Paul, as was his custom, entered **the synagogue and reasoned with the Jews** (18:19). They were intrigued by Paul's message, and they asked to hear more. Despite the fact that the Ephesians were as needy as those in other places where Paul had ministered, he didn't feel Ephesus was God's call for him. Perhaps he still felt forbidden under the directive he had received earlier in this trip (see 16:6). Ephesus was the greatest city in Asia, and yet was an area he previously had been told to bypass. His promise to return, *if* that was **God's will** (18:21), may indicate that he felt that an immediate long-term stay was not God's plan.[1] Paul certainly felt concern for the people of Ephesus. He must have felt relieved that he could trust this key city to teachers whom he had trained: Priscilla and Aquila.

Paul stayed in Ephesus only a short time. Priscilla and Aquila stayed in Ephesus indefinitely. Paul probably asked his friends to come to Ephesus to help plant and establish the church there, sensing that he himself could not have that privilege. He left, hoping he could soon return.

Perhaps Luke felt he could not leave his readers hanging in suspense. Perhaps that motivated him to pass quickly over Paul's travels to Caesarea, Jerusalem, Antioch—the Galatian/Phrygian churches—in order to get Paul back to Ephesus as quickly as he could.

What can we say about those intermediate stops?

Caesarea was the Roman capital of the province of Palestine (18:22; see 10:1). It was also the major port. (Palestine had few natural harbors of any quality. Caesarea, with its man-made breakwaters, offered the best Mediterranean entry point into Palestine.) **When he landed at Caesarea, he went up and greeted the church and then went down to Antioch** (18:22). The church where? This wording could refer to greeting the believers in Caesarea, but more likely indicates a visit to the church in Jerusalem. (Ancients always spoke of going **up** to Jerusalem. If Luke had intended his readers to picture any other place, he would have used language more specific than **the church.** Likewise, the words **went down to Antioch** would more likely describe a trip from Jerusalem [in hill country] rather than from Caesarea [on the seacoast]).[2] Why did Paul wish to visit Jerusalem? Perhaps he wished to report on how the Gentile churches had received the decision of the Jerusalem Council (see Acts 15).

Paul **then went down to Antioch.** As at the end of the first trip, Paul would have "gathered the church together and reported all that God had done through them" (14:27).[3]

After some time of "home ministries," Paul headed back out on the road. At the beginning of his third trip, Paul traveled some of the same territory (Derbe, Lystra, Iconium, and Pisidian Antioch) he had covered on the first two (see 13:13–14-26; 16:6). He wished to continue his work of **strengthening all the disciples** there (18:23).

Paul was not the only minister active during this time.[4] While Paul was traveling, Priscilla and Aquila were busy ministering in Ephesus. They were likely quite pleased for their church to receive a "transfer member" named Apollos. Who wouldn't rejoice to welcome one who **had been instructed in the way of the Lord,** who **spoke with great fervor and taught about Jesus accurately** (18:25)? But then Priscilla and Aquila discovered that his teaching, although accurate, was incomplete. Apollos **knew only the baptism of John** (18:25).

How could this be? Perhaps Apollos had never had any firsthand contact with John the Baptist or Jesus. (He was from Alexandria, then the largest city in Egypt.) Perhaps his knowledge of these two men and their teaching came secondhand, fourthhand, or sixthhand. If so, his mentors had accurately grasped John's ministry and perhaps even the early teaching of Jesus. But maybe they had not heard about or fully comprehended Jesus' later ministry, death, and resurrection, and the outpouring of the Spirit. Apollos did not yet see Jesus as Savior and Lord.

Perhaps Apollos believed all he had heard.[5] He then did his best to proclaim Jesus as the one who had brought God's kingdom. Unfortunately, however, Apollos could proclaim the gospel only to the limited degree of his knowledge.

When Priscilla and Aquila sensed the inadequacy of Apollos's gospel, they wisely did not push him away or even rebuke him publicly. **They invited him to their home and explained to him the way of God more adequately** (18:26). "The cure for error is [not rejection, but] more truth."[6]

As Paul's teaching of Aquila and Priscilla had been effective, so was their teaching of others. Luke mentions **the brothers** in Ephesus, evidently referring to an active church there (18:27). And then, of course, there was Apollos. The church in Ephesus sent him as an ambassador to Achaia (more specifically, Corinth; see 19:1; 1 Corinthians 1:12). When he arrived there, he was a great help to the church, both in discipling believers and in refuting nonbelievers. His previous knowledge of the Old Testament, which was the only written Scripture the churches had at that time, combined with his newly enriched understanding of Jesus, equipped him well for effective ministry. Paul later described Apollos as watering seed that Paul himself had planted (see 1 Corinthians 3:6). (Martin Luther and many others have thought that Apollos wrote Hebrews.[7])

These incidents give an example of a principle Paul later wrote to Timothy: "The things you heard me say . . . entrust to reliable [people] who will also be qualified to teach others (2 Tim. 2:2). Paul taught Aquila and Priscilla. They taught Apollos. Apollos taught others in Corinth. The ideal place for each of us is in the middle of the chain of discipleship. We all need to continually receive teaching from mentors who have walked farther than we have. At the same time, we need to pass along to others what we have received. Continually be discipled; continually disciple.

ENDNOTES

[1]William Ramsay, *St. Paul the Traveler and the Roman Citizen* (London: Hodder and Stoughton, 1907), p. 263. There is some ancient evidence that Paul wanted to reach Jerusalem in time for one of the annual Jewish festivals, perhaps the Passover.

[2]I. Howard Marshall, *Acts* (Grand Rapids, Michigan: Wm. B. Eerdmans Publishing Co., 1980), pp. 301–302, and F. F. Bruce, *The Book of the Acts* (Grand Rapids, Michigan: Wm. B. Eerdmans Publishing Co., 1988), pp. 356–57.

[3]Paul appears to have traveled alone for a time. The last time Silas and Timothy were mentioned was back in Corinth (see Acts 18:5). Perhaps Paul left them there to continue discipling the believers.

[4]You might be excused if you thought that Paul was the only one. In the last sixteen chapters of Acts, these next five verses (18:24-28) are the longest description of events in which Paul does not appear.

[5]See Marshall, pp. 303–4, and Bruce, pp. 359–60. Some scholars even argue that Apollos had received the Holy Spirit. The phrase which the New International Version translates, **He spoke with great fervor,** could be translated "He spoke in the Spirit."

[6]A. T. Robertson, *Types of Preachers in the New Testament* (Grand Rapids, Michigan: Baker Book House, 1972), p. 65.

[7]Bruce, p. 361.

16

THE THIRD MISSIONARY TRIP

Acts 19:1–21:16

L uke hardly took time to set down his pen as he finished recording
his account of the second missionary journey and started his record
of the third. Seeking to maintain his readers' interest, he kept the
action going. Did Paul take a vacation on the Mediterranean between
periods of ministry? Let's hope he took some breaks, but Luke keeps our
attention on the continued outward movement of the gospel.

1. EPHESUS 19:1–20:1

Paul spent three years ministering in Ephesus (see Acts 20:31). A
year and a half (possibly two years) in one location (Corinth) had been
Paul's previous record (see 18:11, 18). Why did Paul spend so much
time in Ephesus?

Luke follows Paul by writing a longer account of Paul's time in Ephesus.
Including Paul's farewell to the Ephesian elders (see 20:17-38), Luke
devotes 63 verses to Paul's ministry to the church at Ephesus. All the rest
of Paul's third journey receives only thirty-six verses. Why was Ephesus so
important? Like Corinth, Ephesus was a city of worldwide renown. It was
the Roman provincial capital. It was a center of trade for the entire region.
Periodic games were held in this city; people from all over the region came
to participate and watch. It was also the site of the temple of Artemis (also
known as Diana; see 19:27-28, 34-35), a pagan goddess of fertility. This
temple was revered as one of the seven wonders of the ancient world.[1] Her
devotees believed that her image had fallen from heaven (see 19:35). Likely
a meteorite had at some time fallen into the area. Locals marveled and
mistook this natural event for a divine visitation.

The first incident during Paul's Ephesian visit raises as many questions as it answers. Paul encountered a number of **disciples** in the same situation Apollos had faced: **Did you receive the Holy Spirit when you believed?** (19:2a). These believers followed God as best they could. But their knowledge and experience went no further than **John's baptism** (19:3).

Why hadn't Aquila and Priscilla enlightened this group, as they had Apollos? Ephesus was a large city; perhaps their paths had never crossed. This group of believers evidently stayed off to themselves.[2] But God discerned their sincerity and sent Paul to them in Ephesus. Paul gave them the essential sequel to John the Baptist's teaching (the full ministry of Jesus, His death and resurrection, and the outpouring of the Holy Spirit), and they gladly received it. They must have been glad to hear that God offered not only a call to repentance, but offered salvation through grace. **Paul baptized them into the name of the Lord Jesus** (19:5). God baptized them with **the Holy Spirit** (19:6). As the first Samaritan believers and the first Gentile believers had received the Holy Spirit at their moment of faith (see 8:16-17; 10:44), so did these dozen Ephesians.

The only problem with this interpretation of the text is that Luke calls these men **disciples** even before they received a fuller understanding of Jesus and the Holy Spirit (19:1). It appears that they, like Apollos, knew of Jesus, but no more than John the Baptist had known. These Ephesians did not worship John. They realized that John had come to prepare the way for One who would be far greater. To this extent, these Ephesian men did believe in Jesus. In that sense, they were disciples. Paul accepted them where they were. He did not criticize them, but rather enabled them to become disciples of Jesus in a much deeper sense.

Jesus cared for Apollos, and He cared for these men who knew of Him, though they did not know Him fully. This serves as a wonderful reminder to us that God cares for all people, no matter what their present level of knowledge and commitment. At the same time, these stories remind us of our responsibility. God calls us, like Aquila, Priscilla, and Paul, to help others gently to a stronger relationship with the God who loves them.

After his encounter with the dozen "incomplete" Christians, **Paul entered the synagogue and spoke boldly there for three months** (19:8). There was nothing unusual about Paul's starting in the synagogue. He did so in nearly every place he visited. Acts 19:8 does, however, raise a couple of questions.

First, why didn't Paul go to the already existing Christian church? Aquila and Priscilla had ministered effectively in Ephesus. They led a church large enough to include at least a group of "brothers" (18:27).

Why did Paul, then, go to the synagogue? Quite simply, Paul had promised the inquiring Jews of Ephesus that he would return to them (see 18:20-21). Also, perhaps the size of Ephesus and the competence of Aquila and Priscilla contributed to Paul's decisions. Rather than build on the foundation Aquila and Priscilla had already established (see Romans 15:20), Paul felt he could start a second local church body. This second group would not compete with, but would complement the already functioning church.

Second, what enabled Paul to spend **three months** in the synagogue (19:8)? The Ephesian Jews must have given Paul a warmer welcome than other synagogues he visited. Perhaps many Jews in Ephesus, like those of Berea, "were of more noble character," recognizing that Paul's preaching correlated well with their Scriptures, the Old Testament (17:11).

But, after some time, the seemingly inevitable happened once again. Some Jews rejected Paul; they **publicly maligned the Way** (19:9).[3] From this signal, Paul sensed that he had given the Jews their chance. Taking the Jewish believers with him, he would turn his ministry to the local Gentiles.

During his three months in the synagogue, God had evidently brought a large number of Jews to salvation in Jesus. For, when Paul left the synagogue, he established local Christian headquarters not in a house, as had been his custom (see, for example, 16:40; 17:5; 18:7), but in a public lecture hall. (An ancient tradition describes how Paul had access to this hall in the middle of the day. During each day's hottest hours, the hall otherwise might have been empty. The rent might have been quite cheap.) As in Corinth, God protected Paul in Ephesus over a long period.[4] Again, God had **many people in this city** (18:10).

But Paul's vision was bigger than even the large city of Ephesus. During Paul's two years in Tyrannus's lecture hall, **all the Jews and Greeks who lived in the province of Asia heard the word of the Lord** (19:10). Paul's strategy of planting churches in large centers so that the gospel could radiate out from the cities worked well here. It was likely during this time that one of Paul's disciples, Epaphras, took the gospel to the people of the nearby city of Colossae (see Colossians 1:7). Other neighboring churches that Paul mentions (Laodicea and Hierapolis in Colossians 4:13, as well as the other area churches Jesus addresses in Revelation 2–3) may have been established during this time.

God's extraordinary miracles through Paul would have confirmed the power of Paul's message (Acts 19:11-12). (Note that even Luke calls these miracles, associated with Paul's handkerchiefs and aprons, extraordinary.) As God had used a vision to encourage Paul in Corinth,

God by these miracles confirmed, both for Paul and others around him, God's participation in Paul's Ephesian ministry.[5] (Compare this to God's display of power through Peter, which attracted the notice of surrounding areas; see 5:15-16].)

In Ephesus, the miracles attracted the attention of at least two broad groups. One group jealously tried to imitate Paul's power ministries. Other Ephesians wished to receive the benefits of the real thing.

The jealous imitators? Some Jews, sons of a (false?) high priest named Sceva, observed Paul driving out evil spirits. They decided that Paul's words must have magical power, so they tried them, too: **In the name of Jesus, whom Paul preaches, I command you to come out** (19:13). Their use of Paul's words backfired on them. Even the evil spirit to whom they spoke recognized that they only had what Paul calls in 2 Timothy 3:5 a "form of godliness," but not true "power." With words that sound quite humorous, the spirit replied, **Jesus I know, and I know about Paul, but who are you?** (Acts 19:15). The evil spirit was not laughing, however. He then attacked the impostors, giving **them such a beating that they ran out of the house naked and bleeding** (19:16).

God gives His power to those whom He can trust. Others can superficially imitate the words and actions of godly people. But, true godliness results not from mere mimicry, but from a deepening relationship with God himself.

Another group responded to God's display of power through Paul with true submission. Among these were people who had previously employed magic to control their world. At this point, they wished to repudiate the evil powers they had used. They turned to the God who manifested His power not for people's harm, but for their good (see 19:11-12). In contrast to the sons of Sceva who wished to gain easy power at no cost to themselves, these people saw God's desire for true inner change. Their external actions demonstrated their inner desires. They burned their entire libraries of magic formulas (see 19:19). Perhaps they could have sold their books for tens of thousands of dollars. They rejected that possibility, seeking to join their new God in His efforts to destroy evil.

In this way [true submission—likely followed up by teaching from Priscilla, Paul, or other mature Christians—not superficial formulas or quick fixes], **the word of the Lord spread widely and grew in power** (19:20). A local pagan tradesman, **Demetrius,** later noted that Paul had **led astray large numbers of people here in Ephesus and in practically the whole province of Asia** (19:26). Even allowing for some exaggeration in that propaganda statement, the gospel had produced a significant impact on the region.

As Paul observed the ashes of the bonfire, his memory of the new Christians' commitment to Jesus must have moved him. He surely felt some sense of completion. God had enabled him to plant churches across Asia Minor (Turkey) and Greece. Having introduced the gospel in major centers there, the new Christians would complete the task of evangelizing other cities and rural areas around them. Paul now cast his eyes farther west. "Rome! The very center of the Empire! But first I must revisit some of the last churches I have planted: Philippi, Thessalonica, Berea, Athens, Corinth.[6] By **Timothy and Erastus,** I will send word that I am coming" (19:21-22).[7]

Circumstances confirmed that it was time for Paul to move on. Apparent disaster struck. A riot threw the city into confusion and led to Paul's withdrawal from the area. The cause of the **great disturbance** (19:23)? The number of people turning from pagan idols to Jesus threatened the profits of local businessmen. As these people learned **that man-made gods are no gods at all** (19:26), the makers of the man-made gods feared their business would decline. As if that weren't enough, the local chamber of commerce saw that current Christian trends might discredit their "patron saint," **the great goddess Artemis** (19:27). That could damage their city's worldwide reputation.

Demetrius, a maker of expensive local "souvenirs," grasped all these dangers and spoke with great power to his colleagues. They responded with fury and **uproar** (19:28-29). The crowd swept up two of Paul's companions and would have taken Paul, too, if his friends (even some among the local officials) had not restrained him (see 19:29-31).

Confusion reigned. **Most of the people did not even know why they were there** (19:32). Some Jews pushed forward one Alexander who hoped to **make a defense before the people** (19:33). These Jews were not believers. They were hoping to disassociate the local Jewish community from the Christians allegedly causing the current furor. The crowd had no interest in such distinctions; the confusion excited them. For **two hours,** the people shouted the praise of their goddess (19:34).

Then, like the Roman governor in Corinth, the city clerk (who would have been a key local leader), Gallio, gained the mob's attention and began reasoning with the people. In effect, he said that the Christians could in no way damage the glory of their goddess. He carefully pointed out that Roman law offered established procedures for dealing with lawbreakers. If the crowd continued to act irrationally, it would be in danger of breaking the law (see 19:40). He by no means declared Paul innocent, but he certainly called for a cautious response to the perceived threat. The crowd dispersed. Paul and the Christians were free, at least for the short term, to continue their ministry. Paul, however, soon chose to move on. After encouraging the disciples, he **said good-by and set out for Macedonia** (20:1).

Luke includes this story as evidence of several facts. First, Christianity was (and is now) to be distinguished from magical attempts to control God. There are no easy formulas which produce instant spiritual power. Second, decision moments can radically change the direction of a person's life. As it was essential for the pagans to burn their past (see 19:19), it is necessary for people today to turn their focus from the ways of this world toward true relationship with God. Third, while true Christianity may oppose ingrained human ways (Demetrius's greed and our own), it does not contradict the best principles of human government.

2. FROM EPHESUS TO "EPHESUS" 20:2-15

The first sixteen verses of Acts 20 offer only one incident in any detail. With that exception, they offer a mere diary of travel between a number of relatively quick stops. The following table shows how many places Luke fit into this short record:

LOCATIONS ON THE GREEK PENINSULA	
Macedonia 20:1 (Philippi, Thessalonica, Berea) Greece 20:2 (Corinth) Macedonia 20:3 Philippi 20:6	
LOCATIONS ON THE WEST COAST OF ASIA MINOR/TURKEY	
Troas 20:6	Kios 20:15
Assos 20:14	Samos 20:15
Mitylene 20:14	Miletus 20:15

A quick look at a map shows that during this time, Paul and company traveled twice in an upside-down U shape. They started on the right side, went up, over, and down, and then reversed that route in nearly identical form on the way back.

These verses raise several questions. Why does Luke give such detail, naming even the places Paul visited for one night? On the other hand, why does Luke not give any more detail on what happened in any of these locations?

The first question offers a fairly simple answer. Luke offers more detail of travel, particularly on the second half of this upside-down U, because he once again accompanied Paul. (Notice the use of **we,** starting in 20:6.)

The second question? Luke already has set the pattern of highlighting story details only in places where Paul visited for the first time. Return visits rarely merited more than brief mention (for example, 14:21b-24; 16:6). The one exception was Ephesus, where Paul's first short visit received only three verses (see 18:19-21), while his return visit (of three years' duration) merited a full chapter (Acts 19).

What was Paul accomplishing on these quick stops?[8] He was **speaking many words of encouragement,** obviously seeking to strengthen the churches in Macedonia and Achaia (20:2-5).

Luke, in giving more detailed coverage to Paul's first visits to various places, may have fallen into the trap of glorifying the spectacular work of preaching for conversions and planting new churches. Paul (and hopefully Luke, too) would want to say that the less visible work of discipling individuals and churches is just as necessary. Would Paul's churches have lasted as they did, had it not been for his ongoing encouragement?

During this time, Paul was also collecting an offering for the church in Jerusalem. Apparently because it does not fit his purposes for writing, Luke all but ignores this collection of money. Luke's only hint at the offering is in 24:17. In contrast, Paul mentions this "service to the [Jerusalem] saints" in all three of the letters from this period (see 1 Corinthians 16:1-4; 2 Corinthians 8–9; Romans 15:25-28).

There was a longer-than-usual list of men (see Acts 20:4) accompanying Paul who apparently were carrying their churches' portions of this offering. (Paul offered the Corinthian Christians the option of sending some of their members as part of the offering process; see 1 Corinthians 16:3). Notice that Paul was accompanied by members of at least five churches (20:4): **Sopater** (Berea), **Aristarchus and Secundus** (Thessalonica), **Gaius** (Derbe), **Timothy** (although not mentioned explicitly, Timothy was from Derbe), and **Tychicus and Trophimus** (from Ephesus in Asia). In addition to these, Luke may have been the representative from Philippi, a place where he had apparently spent several years (see 16:6, 40; 20:6). These offering-bearers were there not only to insure that the money arrived at its intended destination; they may have been necessary because of the *weight* of the coins.

The purpose of the offering? The Jerusalem church, for some unknown reason, was facing economic stress. Perhaps its members faced discrimination in the local (Jewish-dominated) job market. In any case, Paul applauded the generosity of those churches that contributed to the offering, and strongly encouraged the others to join in (see 2 Corinthians 8:1-15). Despite the miles and ethnic differences separating the Asian believers from those in Jerusalem, all believers bore responsibility for one another. (Today, many North Americans are following the model of the one who, "though he was rich, became poor for our sakes" [2 Cor. 8:9], a familiar verse from Paul's appeal for the offering.)

Luke also hints at some stories of interest, but gives no details. The Jews of Corinth somehow plotted to capture Paul, but he eluded them (see Acts 20:3).[9] As a result, Paul took the longer route back up, across, and down, while others (who perhaps did not want to carry the weight of the coins any farther than they had to) took the more direct route across the Aegean Sea (see 20:3, 5-6). Later in the journey, Paul again chose, for an unknown reason, to walk rather than sail (see 20:13), despite the fact that he was **in a hurry** (20:16). Perhaps he wanted time alone to think and pray through his uncertain future (see 20:22).

Luke interrupts his speedy account of this journey to describe one incident in some detail (see 20:7-12). When we read it, we don't know whether to laugh or cry. At Troas (where Paul had had opportunity to preach, on the outward portion of the journey; see 2 Corinthians 2:12), Paul stopped to visit the church. That church gathered **on the first day of the week . . . to break bread** (20:7). Both of these phrases are likely significant. Were churches then meeting regularly on "the Lord's Day"? It appears that way. When the church gathered, its members celebrated the Lord's Supper. Despite the significance of Paul on this particular day, Jesus the Lord was still central.

Paul and the group there may have sensed they would not see each other again (as Paul and the Ephesians did a few days later; see 20:25, 38). In any case, Paul decided to take advantage of this time to say many things. It was long after dark, and smoky torches lit the room. (The group may have met at night so that more people, undistracted by their employment, could attend.[10]) People would have packed in to hear Paul. The room would have become stuffy. **A young man** [a Greek word used here indicates that he was likely between the ages of eight and fourteen[11]] **named Eutychus** moved to an open window (20:9). Unfortunately, this window, at which he sought some fresh air, was on the third floor. He was attempting to stay awake. His strategy failed.

The next thing Eutychus knew, he was no longer listening to Paul preach, but to the angels singing. Paul came down from the third floor to bring Eutychus back from the dead. (There's a question I have always wanted to ask: Did Eutychus go back upstairs and listen to the rest of the sermon, or did he decide he'd had enough for one night? Notice that Paul **went upstairs again and broke bread and ate** [20:11]. Maybe you are wondering if they closed the window to prevent any further incidents.) No one there ever forgot that evening. But did anyone remember what Paul *said?*

From this story, what's the lesson for today's preachers? I will let you decide.

3. A REVIEW OF PAUL'S MINISTRY 20:16-38

In contrast to Luke's hurried account of Paul's travels away from and back to Ephesus, up around the horn and back down again, Luke again slows down to detail Paul's interaction with the church at Ephesus. Words usually described as "Paul's farewell to the Ephesian elders" are actually an excellent summary of Paul's past ministry and future possibilities. These words may have been Paul's farewell to the Ephesians; they could also have served as a final statement to all the churches.[12] Within Luke's account, this talk helps move Luke's readers from the period of Paul's active evangelistic ministry to the time of his arrest and imprisonment.

In his travels, Paul chose to **sail past Ephesus** (20:16). Luke states that Paul wanted to get to Jerusalem for **Pentecost** (fifty days after the Passover mentioned in 20:6).[13] Paul may also have taken a step of caution to avoid Ephesus since it had been less than a year since the riot there.

The elders of the [Ephesian] church came to the seaside city of Miletus to meet Paul (20:17). There he spent some last moments with them. He portrayed his ministry as a model for theirs. Paul looked back without shame. His first and last words reflect this sentiment: **"You know how I lived the *whole time* I was with you, *from the first day . . ."* (his first words; 20:18, my emphasis); *In everything I did* [while I was with you], I showed you that by this kind of hard work we must help the weak** (his last words; 20:35, my emphasis).[14]

"Hard work that helps others"—this phrase could summarize the ministry that Paul gave to the Ephesians and that he hoped the church leaders would then give to others:

> **WORK**
> For God—Serving the Lord (20:19)
> Not serving self—Paying his own way by tentmaking (20:34)
> Offering the Truth—You **must turn to God in repentance and have faith in our Lord Jesus** (20:21) . . . **the gospel of God's grace** (20:24) . . . **[God's] kingdom** (20:25) . . . **the whole will of God** (20:27)

> **HARD WORK**
> **Tears** (20:19, 31)
> Risking physical harm—(**severely tested;** 20:19)
> **From house to house** (20:20)
> **Night and day** (20:31)
> Images Paul used: a **race** to be finished, a **task** to be completed (20:24)

> **HELPING OTHERS**
> **Humility**—not serving self (20:19, 33)
> Paul felt he had done all he could for them; he bore no more responsibility (20:26)

Paul knew, both through his own ministry and through hearing from Jesus, that **it is more blessed to give than to receive** (20:35).[15] Paul knew this from past experience, but he was not done giving to others. He planned to continue the hard work of serving. He would willingly face **hardships,** considering his **life worth nothing.** He wanted to **complete the task the Lord Jesus [had] given [him]—the task of testifying to the gospel of God's grace** (20:23-24).

Paul asked the same commitment from those who stood before him:

> **WORK**
> **Keep watch. . . . Be shepherds** . . . (20:28).

> **HARD WORK**
> **Savage wolves** would attack and **distort the truth** (20:29-30).[16]
> The elders would need **to be on [their] guard** (20:31).

> **HELPING OTHERS**[17]
> **All the flock** (20:28; see 20:29). **. . . the church of God** (20:28)

Paul, the elder statesman, was not retiring. He was not asking for a gold watch. He was asking for others to take his place, to continue building on his foundations, so that he could go and begin again somewhere else.

As he left, he felt deep concern. You can hear it in his tone of voice. Yet, he trusted God to carry on His work through them (see 20:32, 36). Paul also must have felt deep satisfaction. He would face more trying days ahead (see 20:22-23), but he had finished this portion of his race. He had been faithful (see 20:18, 35).

As I come to each milestone in my life, I want to feel that same satisfaction. In areas such as diligence in service, content of teaching, and even handling of money, I hope (with God's help) to come to the end being able to say to younger leaders around me, "Follow my example."

Paul's departure at the beach that day was "such sweet sorrow." The elders **grieved . . . that they would never see [Paul's] face again** (20:38).[18] Yet they had had the privilege of knowing one of God's saints. He left a model for them and us to follow.

4. THE FINAL JOURNEY TO JERUSALEM 21:1-16

After a break for the farewell to the Ephesian leaders, Luke's account follows Paul's hurried pace to Jerusalem. Nothing would stop Paul from reaching his goal (see Acts 21:4, 11-13). He was heading there, **compelled by the Spirit** (20:22). Luke and Paul both were following a model set in Luke's gospel. Luke describes the heroes of his gospel and Acts as they made their final trips to Jerusalem (see Luke 9:51–19:44): Jesus and Paul both "resolutely set out for that city" (Luke 9:51).

Why must Luke's heroes so determinedly head toward the "home" that would not welcome them? Jesus realized that "no prophet can die outside Jerusalem" (Luke 13:33). Jesus knew He was heading toward His death. Paul was not so sure. But he did not shy away from the harsh welcome he expected from the city that had killed his Master (see Acts 20:23-24; 21:13). Why was Paul hurrying toward Jerusalem? He and his friends carried an offering to deliver to Jerusalem, but that alone cannot explain his urgency. Paul may have wished to describe to the Jerusalem leaders his recent missionary efforts, but that doesn't seem urgent either. Paul wished to reach Jerusalem by the time of Pentecost (see 20:16), but why? It seems Paul somehow sensed that Jerusalem, though hundreds of miles out of his way, was on his route to Rome (see 19:21). Rome, he hoped, was the gateway to the unevangelized field of Spain (see Romans 15:23-25).

Whatever unknowns lay in his future, Paul now recognized that *a change was coming*. Earlier in his ministry, he took persecution as the signal to move on to a new site of church work. Now he chose to follow Jesus right into the face of suffering.

Perhaps Paul felt directed toward Jerusalem because arrest there was part of God's mysterious plan for Paul. God had told Ananias, at the time of Paul's conversion, that Paul would speak before **kings** (Acts 9:15). Paul wouldn't have dreamed that he might speak to Caesar himself! For Paul (and sometimes for us today), apparent disaster was the route to significant witness.

Luke details their travels through this chapter. (Luke accompanied Paul here; note his use of the pronoun **we** [21:1-3, for example]). They first stopped at **Cos, Rhodes,** and **Patara** (21:1). The first two were islands in the Aegean Sea; the third was a port on the southeastern coast of Asia Minor. All evidently were overnight stops for the ship's crew and passengers.

For his sea travel, Paul and his companions booked berths on cargo vessels. The captains of such vessels carried passengers for extra profit. Note that, in the travel described in Acts 21:1-8, Paul may have sailed on as many as three ships: one from Miletus to Patara, another from Patara to Tyre, and another from Tyre to Ptolemais and on to Caesarea. God helped His team to travel safely and efficiently.

Paul had a layover of seven days in **Tyre,** a Phoenician seaport north of Palestine. A church had been planted there at some time; Luke does not tell us when or by whom. Paul likely had visited the church there previously. When traveling from Antioch to Jerusalem for the church conference, Paul and Barnabas had "traveled through Phoenicia," bringing joy to that area's believers as Paul described their first missionary journey (15:3). On that visit, joy would have been mixed with sorrow. Paul would have told many more stories of new churches established. But tears would have far outnumbered smiles in the scene which Luke (obviously an eyewitness) poignantly portrays at the beach. Men, their wives, and even their children walked with Paul as far as they could, to the water's edge. There they must have sung the first-century equivalent of the hymn, "Blessed Be the Tie That Binds." Everyone **knelt to pray** together (21:5). The locals would have prayed for Paul, and he for them. Then they said **good-by** and parted (21:6).

Note the involvement of children on Paul's farewell tour. As we have seen, at least one young lad participated in Paul's last service in Troas (see 20:9-12). The parents in Tyre made sure their children interacted with and said good-by to Paul. Today's church practice of separating children for their own teaching and worship times certainly has its value. Children may feel that adult meetings go on forever, and there is some danger in boring them (see 20:9). But there is also great value in allowing our children to become acquainted with great men and women of God. Sometimes we try too hard to "protect" our children from anything they might not find scintillating. We also isolate respected church leaders from children, feeling the children might distract them from their tasks. This segregation harms both children and leaders. Remember that the greatest leader, the One who bore the responsibility of saving the world, wanted time with children (see Luke 18:15-16).

Before Paul left their area, **through the Spirit they** [the believers in Tyre] **urged Paul not to go on to Jerusalem** (Acts 21:4). A couple of stops later, the prophet Agabus,[19] also speaking under the influence of the **Holy Spirit,** predicted Paul's upcoming arrest in Jerusalem (21:10-11). As a result of this, all those gathered around Paul urged him to go anywhere but Jerusalem (see 21:12). But the same Spirit who warned of the dangers Paul faced in Jerusalem was compelling Paul to move that way (see 20:22). Was the Spirit contradicting himself? No. The Spirit was giving the same information to all His people.

Paul would face a hard time in Jerusalem. But God's people, on the basis of identical accurate information, reached quite different conclusions. Those with deep concern for Paul's safety and ongoing ministry wished to save him from pain and imprisonment. Paul, however, trusted God to work out His plan even in the midst of danger. Paul was **ready,** if this was God's will, **not only to be bound, but also to die in Jerusalem for the name of the Lord Jesus** (21:13).

Paul had previously raised dead Eutychus. His handkerchiefs were the means to miracles (see 20:9-12; 19:12). In a manner similar to Jesus' experience, Paul could "save" others, but could not protect himself (see Luke 23:35, 39). From Corinth, only a few months before this last trip to Jerusalem, Paul had written the strong words of Romans 8. At that point of the trip, as Paul traveled toward pain, he had opportunity to prove that those words were more than rhetoric: "Who shall separate us from the love of Christ? Shall trouble or hardship or persecution or famine or nakedness or danger or sword? . . . No, in all these things, we are more than conquerors through him who loved us" (Rom. 8:35, 37).

Others around Paul, catching his peace, despite the risk he faced, gave in (Acts 21:14). Paul himself would not have relished the thought of potential pain, but everyone in the company echoed words Jesus had spoken in Jerusalem a few years before: "Not my will, but yours be done" (Luke 22:42).

Are we willing today to follow the models of Paul and Jesus, or are we too addicted to the comfortable "Christian" life? Those who truly engage in the battle against evil will not escape battle wounds.

Looking back over the time of Paul's three missionary journeys, we notice a variety of patterns for resolving church conflict. The believers of that time experienced disagreement just as contemporary churches do. What methods did they use to maintain unity despite conflict?

Acts 15 depicts two major disagreements. The majority of the chapter deals with the issue of Gentiles becoming Christians: Must Gentiles become Jews before they could join the Christian community? In this situation, the leaders felt they had to reach an agreement. We don't know how easily the conference reached a consensus. Did it take half an hour, a week, or more? We don't know. But, in time, the believers made a compromise that pleased them and God. The work of the church went forward.

The end of Acts 15 (verses 36-41) describes a more personal, yet significant, conflict. Paul and Barnabas, two great missionary pioneers of the church, both wanted to continue in the work God had given them, fulfilling the Great Commission. Their disagreement focused on John Mark. Paul felt that Mark would be a burden, hindering their ministry among the churches. Barnabas felt that investing in Mark's personal development was a key part of their ministry. In this case, the two leaders could reach no consensus. Yet, they did agree that their disagreement must not stand in the way of continued ministry. They divided the work and went in separate directions.

As seen above, Acts 21 offers a third major disagreement. Paul was determined to go to Jerusalem (see 20:22; 21:13). Luke and others around Paul were equally convinced that he should not. Luke writes, **When he would not be dissuaded, we gave up and said, "The Lord's will be done"** (21:14). In this case, there was no compromise, but neither was there separation. Luke and the others accompanied Paul to the place they thought he should not go (see 21:15). In this disagreement, one side chose to yield.

Paul and friends used three quite different methods to resolve disagreements. All three apparently resulted in the accomplishment of God's will. Disagreement was resolved by (1) the parties' reaching a compromise agreement; (2) separation of the disagreeing parties; or (3) one party's submitting to the will of the other.

In any given church disagreement today, how do we decide which method of conflict resolution is best? Is one method always best? It would be ideal, but too simplistic, to say that agreement is always the best way. Agreement is not always possible. Because of our humanness, our inability to hear God perfectly (which is quite different from God's ability to communicate perfectly), situations arise where we may have to separate or give in.[20]

Nevertheless, in all three situations, all parties upheld central Christian principles: open communication, mutual respect, and a joint desire for God's will and glory.

Another factor of note in this last leg of Paul's journey to Jerusalem was the hospitality believers offered Paul (and, possibly, the large company of associates traveling with him; see 20:4). The group **stayed with** the disciples in Tyre and Ptolemais (21:4, 7). They **stayed at the house of Philip** in Caesarea (21:8).[21] In Jerusalem (or possibly on the final leg of their journey to that city), at least some from the group stayed in **the home of Mnason** (21:16).

What do we see in these verses? First, the faith had spread to a network of towns, all across the area. Second, the Christians in these locations were a hospitable bunch. With today's levels of stress in ministry (although Paul, even in the "good old days," experienced a fair bit of stress), our church leaders may prefer hotels (and potential hosts may not want the bother of welcoming others into their homes), but we all may lose opportunity to give and receive ministry.

Paul knew that he would face hard times ahead. The hospitality and prayer support offered by Christians all through this journey no doubt greatly encouraged him. His upcoming suffering could not separate him from the love of God or from the love of his friends in the many places he had ministered.

ENDNOTES

[1]William Barclay describes why in *The Acts of the Apostles* (Philadelphia: The Westminster Press, 1976), pp. 140–41. The Temple "was 425 feet long by 220 feet wide by 60 feet high. There were 127 pillars, each the gift of a king. They were all of glittering . . . marble and 36 were marvelously gilt and inlaid."

[2]It's possible that these twelve Ephesians had been taught their incomplete information by Apollos himself. But, if that were the case, it would be hard to understand why Apollos did not return to them and pass on the fuller picture that Aquila and Priscilla had given him.

³Luke refers to Christianity as **the Way** here and several other places in Acts. It was one of the early names given to this new walk with God (see 9:2; 19:23; 22:4; 24:14, 22).

⁴Luke selected those incidents during Paul's Ephesian ministry that best fit his purposes. Paul, in his epistles (consisting of the New Testament books of Romans, 1 and 2 Corinthians, Galatians, Ephesians, Philippians, Colossians, 1 and 2 Thessalonians, 1 and 2 Timothy, Titus, and Philemon [some consider Paul to be the unknown author of Hebrews as well]), alluded to other stressful events during this time. These likely preceded the riot and its aftermath, described in verses 23-41. In 1 Corinthians 15:32, Paul mentions fighting with beasts in Ephesus. This may be a symbolic expression, and not a description of actual persecution. Note the **savage wolves** against whom Paul subsequently warned the Ephesian elders. On a later occasion, Paul alluded to a time in Asia (likely Ephesus) when he even despaired of life (see 2 Corinthians 1:8-11). His language here is vague. It could refer to persecution, physical illness, or possibly discouragement caused by his broken relationship with the Christians in Corinth. It also may have been at Ephesus that Aquila and Priscilla risked their necks for Paul (see Romans 16:3-4).

See also 1 Corinthians 16:8-9, written during this time period: "I will stay on at Ephesus until Pentecost, because a great door for effective work has opened to me, and there are many who oppose me."

⁵John R. W. Stott, *The Spirit, the Church and the World* (Downers Grove, Illinois: InterVarsity Press, 1990), p. 306.

⁶Paul likely wrote his letters to the Corinthians during and just after his time of ministry in Ephesus. The relationship between Paul and that church was quite strained during this time. He likely interrupted his Ephesian ministry to visit Corinth. In 2 Corinthians 2:1, he spoke of his painful visit to this church. He would not have used those words to describe his first visit to Corinth; he must have returned at least once (see also 2 Corinthians 13:1-2). The time in Ephesus appears to have been the best opportunity for such a visit.

⁷Another purpose for this return visit to already established churches was the collection of an offering for the Christians in Jerusalem (see endnotes in chapter 17 of the commentary).

⁸The longest stop was three months in Greece, likely Corinth, where the relationship between Paul and the church there needed some healing (see, for examples of the strained friendship, 1 Corinthians 1:10-13; 4:8-21; 2 Corinthians 2:1-14; 7:5-13). Paul wrote the first of these letters while he was in Ephesus (see Acts 19) and the second while on his way from Ephesus to Corinth on the journey described in Acts 20:1-2.

⁹Barclay, p. 148. Jews could easily have plotted to capture and kill Paul, while they were together with him on the ship. It would have been difficult for Paul to escape their grasp.

¹⁰Ibid., p. 149.

¹¹I. Howard Marshall, *Acts* (Grand Rapids, Michigan: Wm. B. Eerdmans Publishing Co., 1980), p. 326.

¹²Stott, p. 323. Stott makes the point that this is the only address recorded in Acts that was originally intended for Christians. It may be the one most appropriate for most of us.

[13]In the New Testament, Pentecost primarily refers to the event when the Holy Spirit was given to the church; this occurred on the day of Pentecost. It is also known as the Jewish Feast of Weeks. This day is part of the Jewish observances, and was the beginning of the offering of first fruits.

[14]Marshall, p. 330. Marshall notes the similarities between the themes of this address and what Paul wrote in 1 Thessalonians 2.

[15]This is the one of the few times in Acts that anyone directly quoted a line from Jesus' earthly teaching. The others are 1:4-8 (an account of Jesus' interaction with His disciples before His ascension) and 11:16 (where Peter quoted 1:5). Acts 20:35 is the only New Testament quotation of a statement from Jesus' earthly ministry that does not appear in the Gospels. (It is not likely that any of the Gospels had yet been written. [The Gospels include the New Testament books of Matthew, Mark, Luke, and John.] Jesus' teaching would have been passed from Christian to Christian via word of mouth.) Other nonbiblical ancient documents, such as one called "the Gospel of Thomas," potentially offer other statements from Jesus, but no one can document their authenticity.

[16]As they had in Galatia (see Galatians 1:7-9) and Corinth (2 Corinthians 10:10-12; 11:4-6, 13-15).

[17]Paul would not have denied his need, at appropriate times, to take care of himself. For example, he had not sought an early martyrdom. He also, in this very address, told the leaders that they needed to **keep watch over** *themselves,* in order to be in a condition where they could take care of others (21:28).

[18]Paul was not certain what faced him in Jerusalem, but he did feel that his work in this area was done. God was leading him onto new territory (see Romans 15:23).

[19] Agabus makes his second appearance in Acts (see 11:28). On this occasion, he not only spoke his message. Like Old Testament prophets often did, he acted out his message (see similar actions in 1 Kings 11:29-32 and Isaiah 20:2-6). Stott, p. 331.

[20]There may be other options, including a phrase my father, an experienced church administrator, likes: "agreeing to disagree agreeably." But usually, that option includes some form of compromise, or one side giving in.

[21]Luke's allusion to Philip's four prophetess daughters documents the church's openness to ministry from people of both genders.

Part Four

GOD ENABLES PAUL SAFELY TO REACH ROME

Acts 21:17–28:31

In the first three parts of Acts, the church's progress is obvious. The first quarter of the book describes the establishment of the church in Jerusalem. The second quarter sees it moving out into **Judea and Samaria,** and beginning to reach toward **the ends of the earth** (1:8). The third part documents the growth of the church in Asia, Macedonia, and Achaia. In the last quarter of the book, Luke's account seems to show the church (at least Luke's hero, Paul) stuck in jail cells in Jerusalem and Caesarea. Only the last two chapters of Acts show Paul moving toward Rome, though even in those chapters he remains a captive. What was God doing? Why does Luke give so much attention to Paul the prisoner?

For his contemporary readers, Luke gives evidence to show that Paul the prisoner was innocent of crimes against the Jews and the Romans. For us today, other key points stand out.

- The fact that Paul was facing very hard times does not refute the fact that he was doing God's will.
- The fact that Paul was facing very hard times does not refute the fact that God was working out His plan.
- The fact that God appeared to be absent does not refute the fact that God was quite active.

All through these trials, God was preparing the way for Paul to proclaim the gospel in Rome, the capital city of the Roman Empire. God's plan, God's power, could not be defeated.

PAUL
IN JERUSALEM

Acts 21:17–23:11

P aul's trip to Rome began with his last recorded visit to Jerusalem. Paul had received his education in Jerusalem. The city had for centuries been the worship center for Paul's people. Likely Paul prayed for at least one more chance to preach the good news of Jesus to his home city. He received that opportunity, but, unfortunately, Paul's ministry there did not produce new converts or establish a new church. Instead, God allowed His servant, for all practical purposes, to be laid aside for several years. Even so, God still fulfilled His plan.

1. PAUL'S ARREST 21:17-36

Paul's first day or two in Jerusalem flowed smoothly. Mnason, an otherwise unknown local believer, opened his house to Paul (see Acts 21:16). A group of unnamed brothers **received** Paul, Luke, and the others **warmly** (21:17). Paul reported, to **James and all the elders,** the details of his last missionary journey (21:19).[1] (Paul had visited Jerusalem, apparently giving such a report at the end of the previous two trips [see 15:4; 18:22]). Paul's report resulted in a praise meeting. So far, so good.

Then James turned up the tension level at least one notch. Paul had reported on his work **among the Gentiles** (21:19). James took his turn and reported on the work among the Jews: **Thousands of Jews** had become Christians (21:20). This was great news that would have caused Paul to rejoice. But, according to James, **all** these Jewish Christians were **zealous for the law**[2] (21:20). Despite the broad-minded decisions of the Jerusalem Council (see commentary on Acts 15), these Jewish Christians evidently saw Gentile Christians, who did not keep the full requirements of the Jewish Law, as second-class believers. Certainly some of the Jewish converts could have viewed the Law in a more flexible manner, as Stephen, Paul, and others had; James may have exaggerated with the word **all.** But it might not be surprising if a majority of the Jewish Christians maintained strong loyalty to the Law.

Remember these facts. First, many Jews in Galatia and Greece (an area where the Jews tended to be more flexible than the Jews in Jerusalem) had violently rejected Paul's message, fiercely hanging onto their distinctively Jewish ways. Second, other more conservative Jews had become Christians, but had tried to impose the full Jewish tradition on Gentile believers (see, for example, 15:1). Third, the Jerusalem Council (see Acts 15) gave indirect approval to Jewish Christians who wished to continue living within the Law; it merely forbade them from forcing the complete Law on Gentiles. Thus, it is possible that there were a large number of Jews in the Jerusalem area who believed in Jesus *and* still maintained their ancient traditions. (If these Jewish Christians lived in accordance with the Jerusalem Council decision, they did not require Gentile Christians to conform to all the requirements of the Law, such as circumcision, dietary laws, and Sabbath restrictions. In fact, if the Jewish believers had kept the Law rigidly, they may have conveniently stayed away from most Gentiles, whether Christian or pagans.)

But then Paul, a Jew (more than that, a Pharisee) came to town. Rumors started circulating that he not only had violated the Law, but had told other Jews that they could do the same (see 21:21). When they heard this news, Jewish Christians undoubtedly asked questions. It is possible that James himself was one of these Jewish Christians who felt uncertainty about Paul's teaching.

In any case, James devised a plan. He sought to prove to everyone that Paul was a Christian *and* a loyal Jew. James suggested that Paul visibly participate, along with four Christian Jews, in **Jewish purification rites** (21:24). A generous contribution to the Temple treasury (**pay[ing] their expenses** [21:24]), perhaps another ritual haircut (another temporary Nazarite vow? [see 18:18]), and hopefully everything would be okay. James continued, **"As for the Gentile believers,** we here in Jerusalem are complying with the mandate of the Jerusalem Council. We are not forcing the full Law upon them" (21:25; see Acts 15).

How did Paul respond? He may have considered James's test of loyalty unnecessary, but appears to have conceded graciously to the request (see 21:26; also 1 Corinthians 9:19-22—This may be an occasion when Paul chose to "agree to disagree agreeably" [see commentary on 21:1-16].)[3]

Paul, in his missionary teaching and strategy, had undoubtedly moved away from much current Jewish teaching and practice. In doing so, he was following the steps of his Master who had also challenged contemporary Jewish thinking and actions. But both Jesus and Paul would have claimed that they, and not their contemporary critics, were more loyal to the ancient God-given traditions.

In any case, Paul's last encounter with the Jerusalem apostles was a positive one. The Jerusalem leadership joined the host of previous witnesses (Gentile officials, as well as Jewish and Gentile believers) who had affirmed (or, at minimum, had not hindered) the ministry of Paul.

Paul, in accordance with James's plan, visited the Temple with the four Jewish Christians. But, around the city, he still conversed with his Gentile Christian friends. Jews who were not Christians misinterpreted (innocently or purposely?) Paul's friendship with Gentiles. These Jews' reaction brought trouble to Paul.

Jews from the province of Asia (an area in what is now southeastern Turkey; Ephesus had been Paul's primary target for ministry in that region) took matters into their own hands. (If Paul accomplished his goal of reaching Jerusalem by Pentecost [see 20:16], then Jews from all over would have been gathered in the city, as they were for a previous Pentecost[4] [2:9-11].) Jews from this region had no love for Paul. They had fought him during his time in Ephesus (see 20:19). These Asian Jews, now in Jerusalem (for Pentecost? [see 20:16]) **seized** Paul, accusing him of speaking against the Jewish people, Law, and Temple (21:27-28; compare this with the accusation against Stephen in 6:13-14).

What truth did their accusations contain? Very little. There is no evidence that Paul had, in Jerusalem, spoken directly against Jewish customs. Yet, these Jews may have known that Paul had previously taught Gentiles that circumcision was no longer necessary as a means to God (see Galatians 5:6; Romans 2:25-29).[5] In any case, the Jews in Jerusalem followed the pattern their brothers elsewhere had followed. They became jealous of Paul and afraid of his message. They feared that Judaism[6] would lose influence as numbers of Jews and Gentiles moved toward Christian faith.

These Jews in Jerusalem grasped at any charge they thought plausible. They accused Paul of taking Gentiles into the Temple. If this charge were true, then he had violated a major taboo. Gentiles were allowed only in the outer court of the Temple area. A large sign, written in both Greek and Latin, warned Gentiles that they risked their lives if they went into the inner courts. These courts were reserved for Jews alone.[7]

The Asian Jews recognized Trophimus, a man from their own area, as one of Paul's traveling companions. They put two and two together and got five. Paul had visited the Temple. Trophimus had accompanied Paul in the city. Therefore, Trophimus had visited the Temple. Their skill in logic did not match their zeal for Judaism.

Once again, a riot developed. Paul could have compiled a scrapbook of the riots he "caused": Lystra (14:19), Philippi (16:22), Thessalonica (17:5), Ephesus (19:29), and, at this point, Jerusalem. If guilt came by association, Paul deserved judgment. Paul had broken no law, Jewish or Roman, but the Jesus he proclaimed did bring radical change to both individual lives and to society. And this change, as always, produced stress.

Throughout Paul's ministry, many Jews and Gentiles had struggled to respond to that stress. In some cases, leaders lost control of themselves and the people around them. Riots broke out. In other cases, angry leaders purposely incited crowds of bystanders into a frenzy. The Asian Jews in Jerusalem appear to have known exactly what they were doing. They may not have been able to destroy Paul when he was in Ephesus, but they would finish the job in Jerusalem.

The local Roman headquarters sat adjacent to the Temple grounds. Stairs connected the two[8] (see 21:40). A riot near the Temple certainly would have brought out the Roman legions. If everyone were pointing fingers at Paul, his guilt would be obvious, the Jews hoped. If the mob had not yet lynched him, the Romans would be obligated to rid Jerusalem of this threat to peace. (Jerusalem was always a troublesome hotbed for the Romans. Any Roman governor's primary task was to keep things under control. His commission? Try not to upset the Jews, and keep those taxes coming. Potential disturbances? Do everything to nip them in the bud.)

When the soldiers arrived, **the whole city of Jerusalem was in an uproar** (21:31). The riot instigators smiled smugly. They had accomplished their task. Paul was **arrested** and **bound with two chains** (21:33).[9] But, the mob continued to attack. The soldiers attempted to protect the prisoner from his enemies. Even when their sticks and stones could not harm him, the crowd carried on with its words: **Away with him!** (21:36; this happened near the location where Jesus had heard a similar cry from an angry mob [see Luke 23:18]).

Paul's faith angered the Jerusalem crowd. An angry response might not be the goal we seek. But, with God's help, it is our goal to live for Him in a way distinct enough to draw some response. If we disappear into the crowd, we betray our calling to be light and salt (see Matthew 5:13-16).

2. PAUL SPEAKS TO JERUSALEM 21:37–22:22

Paul knew what the next step would be. The Roman commander would interrogate him, seeking to uncover the reason for the riot. Perhaps Paul concluded that he could get double duty from his statements in self-defense. Before the commander could ask, Paul could answer the questions he knew were coming.[10] At the same time, Paul's words could be his witness for Christ to the entire city. More likely, however, Paul sensed that this might be his last chance to speak to the Jews of the city he called home. He wanted to seize this final opportunity.

When Paul asked permission to speak, the commander responded with a question of his own. He, too, had been thinking, "Who could this prisoner be?" The commander guessed: **Aren't you the Egyptian who started a revolt and led four thousand terrorists out into the desert some time ago?** (Acts 21:38).

Josephus (pronounced Jo-see´-fus), a Jewish historian writing about the end of the first century, gives us more information about **the Egyptian.** This individual had claimed to be a messiah. He led thousands of Jews to the Mount of Olives, adjacent to Jerusalem. He promised that his followers would see the city walls fall. Roman power over Jerusalem would also fall. However, the Roman army, directed by Felix (who remained the Roman governor at the time of Paul's arrest [see 23:24]) squashed this revolt. In the process, many innocent citizens were massacred. The Egyptian leader, however, escaped. Those Jews who survived this event remained angry at this "false prophet" who had led many astray. As the Roman commander observed the crowd's vicious behavior toward Paul, he assumed that only this Egyptian could provoke such brutality. Jerusalem was seeking revenge against an enemy. Yes, Jerusalem was seeking revenge on an enemy, but not an Egyptian. The enemy was an educated citizen of Tarsus (note that Paul spoke Greek in 21:37).

The commander might have thought Paul foolish to desire any further contact with a murderous crowd, but permitted him to speak. Paul showed his versatility by changing his language to **Aramaic** (21:40), the common tongue of the people of Palestine. (Paul's strength, after he had nearly been beaten to death [see 21:31], must have been divinely supplemented.)

The crowd could not attack Paul; undoubtedly he was still heavily guarded by the Romans. Being unable to get at him, they decided to listen to him, perhaps hoping that he would incriminate himself (see 22:2).

Luke's record of Paul's **defense** (22:1) offers little information not already included earlier in the book. Luke has already given his own account of Paul's conversion (see 9:1-19). In Acts 22, Luke allows Paul to tell the story in his own words. Paul did so in words quite similar to the earlier record. In this retelling, Paul "compressed or enlarged details [of his conversion story] according to the demands of his hearers"[11] (see yet another account of the same story in Acts 26:12-19).

What new information did Paul (Luke) include here? Largely, facts that emphasize the Jewish slant on Paul's biography, particularly his conversion.

Paul described three relevant facts relating to his early education. First, he received it in *Jerusalem,* not in Tarsus. Second, his teacher was the renowned **Gamaliel** (22:3). This same Gamaliel had remained active in the leadership of the Jewish community at least into the period of the early church. He had cautioned the Sanhedrin against overstrong persecution of the apostles (see 5:34-39). Third, Paul's curriculum was **the law of our fathers**[12] (22:3; see Galatians 1:14). Paul hoped that his strong Jewish background would sway the crowd at least slightly in his favor.

Paul described Ananias in such a way as to make him attractive to Jews: **He was a devout observer of the law and highly respected by all the Jews living there** (in Damascus; Acts 22:12). In Paul's retelling, Ananias emphasized that Paul had met **the God of our fathers** (22:14). Ananias referred to Jesus as **the Righteous One,** similar to Old Testament descriptions of the Messiah (22:14; see Zechariah 9:9; Isaiah 53:11). Both of these statements could have appealed to the Jewish mind.

The account of Paul's interaction with God in Jerusalem after Paul's conversion[13] offers further unique information (see 22:17-21). In this paragraph, Paul emphasized that he had been praying in the **temple** (22:17). For the second time, even in this brief account of Paul's defense, he described his active persecution of the church (see 22:19-20). Seemingly, Paul was emphasizing that nothing less than an encounter with God himself could have turned him around. (The current **high priest** and **council** [Sanhedrin] would have remembered Paul from the period when he persecuted, rather than spoke for, the Christians [Acts 22:5].) Such encounters had occurred both on the road to Damascus (22:7-10), through Ananias (22:14-15) and in the Temple itself (22:17-21). Meeting God had led Paul away from persecuting Christians. Divine direction had not only moved him to join **the Way** (22:4), but also to take the message of Jesus Christ **to the Gentiles** (22:21).

The crowd listened quietly until Paul mentioned his mission to the Gentiles (22:22). Mention of outsiders reminded Paul's hearers of why they were there. They remembered the rumor that Paul, among the Gentiles, had turned Jews **away from Moses** (21:21). They believed that he had taken one of his Gentile friends into the inner reaches of the Temple. No longer able to restrain their emotions, they returned to crying for his death.[14]

In his defense, Paul told the crowd who he had been—one of them. He went on to tell them who he had become—one quite different from the typical Jew. He also clearly announced that he had not engineered this revolutionary change in his character. He had merely obeyed God's commission.

Today, we, too, need to remember who we were, who we would be without Christ: "There but for the grace of God go I." Can we, like Paul, announce that we are *transformed* people? If so, do we follow Paul's example in giving appropriate credit to God and His grace? As Paul told the Corinthian believers, "By the grace of God I am what I am" (1 Cor. 15:10).

And, like Paul, if we are truly transformed, then we are obedient. If you have received God's calling to salvation, then you have also heard Him call you into service. God's offer of salvation brings happiness; service to and for Him also brings joy. But, as Paul so clearly portrays, true service of God can also bring pain. Others may misunderstand what we are doing. Our God-given ministries may upset their settled routines or their pictures of how life should flow.

Paul spoke plainly: "I have been changed. My direction for life has been changed. You may see God behind these changes or you can choose to reject that idea. But I have followed God and will continue to do so, no matter what you think." God calls us to follow Him with the same determination.[15]

3. THE TRIAL BEFORE THE SANHEDRIN 22:23–23:11

Once again, as the crowds called for Paul's death, Roman soldiers had to rescue Paul from the Jews' anger (see Acts 22:22-24; also 21:34, 36). It is hard for us to picture such violent rage directed at a man we admire. (But don't forget that twenty-five years before this, a similar crowd had struck out at One we admire even more.) Perhaps the mob was venting anger its members wished they could thrust directly at the Romans. An oppressed people can slowly build up "anger pressure" to the point of explosion. It was less than twenty years later that Jerusalem did revolt, only to see their city destroyed by the stronger Roman army. This psychological analysis does not, however, diminish the fact that Paul's message of grace was a threat to the Jewish religious system based on the Law. If large numbers of Jews continued to follow Jesus, who would be left to follow the high priest? If people could truly know God outside Judaism,[16] then Jerusalem would no longer be the center of the (religious) world!

Once Paul was taken to the safety of the barracks, the military commander **directed that he be flogged** (22:24). (On the seriousness of such floggings, see commentary on 16:11-40 and chapter 5 endnotes). This flogging likely was unnecessary. Paul had spoken freely to the crowd. He would have answered the commander's questions without the incentive of torture. (Evidently, other prisoners did not talk as freely. Flogging seems to have been a common practice [see John 19:1; Acts 5:40]).

Paul saw no value in added suffering. (Remember that Paul was still smarting from a beating received that very day; see 21:31-32.) In this situation, he claimed his rights as a Roman citizen: **Is it legal for you to flog a Roman citizen who hasn't even been found guilty?** (22:25). The answer was an obvious "no."

The thoughts Paul had recently written in Romans 13 would still be fresh in his mind: "Rulers hold no terror for those who do right, but for those who do wrong. Do you want to be free from fear of the one in authority? Then do what is right and he will commend you. For he is God's servant to do you good" (Rom. 13:3-4). At this point, God did use a Roman centurion to protect Paul from danger and to enable him further to proclaim his message.[17] Those words Paul wrote to the Romans are still true. If God could use the Roman government as His instrument, contemporary governments are not outside *His* power.

Luke gives several verses to the issue of Paul's citizenship (see Acts 22:25-29). If Acts was written as a defense document for Paul's Roman trial, then this discussion would have underlined that Paul was no ordinary criminal, but a man of some standing in Roman society. It appears that Luke is suggesting that ancient Christians could claim any governmental rights they possessed. If so, then by implication Christians today have the same privilege.

Paul gave the commander little choice. Paul's status as a Roman citizen mandated a fair trial for him. A fair trial necessitated a statement of the charges and evidence to support the accusations. The commander was not an expert in the fine points of Jewish religion. If the Jews wished to have Paul punished, then *they* needed to state a strong case: "The crowds of Jerusalem could not give a statement of the charges [see 21:34]. I will try **the Sanhedrin,"** the centurion thought. So, **the next day . . . he brought Paul and had him stand before them** (22:30).

Throughout this hearing before the Jewish authorities, Paul took the initiative. He did not wait for the Jews to accuse. He chose to speak first: **My brothers, I have fulfilled my duty to God in all good conscience to this day** (23:1; see also 24:16; 2 Timothy 1:3). In effect, he said, "Before I met Jesus, I persecuted the Christians as I thought I should. Since I met Jesus, I have changed my ways. All my service to him has been part of *God's* plan." With one sentence, Paul summarized his recent defense before the Jerusalem crowds (see Acts 22:1-21). Having taken this initiative, Paul awaited a response, perhaps hoping that it might be a reasonable one.

The high priest quickly dashed any such hopes. He ordered Paul to be struck **on the mouth** (23:2). To avoid flogging, Paul had recently claimed his rights as a Roman citizen (see 22:25). Here, to avoid a punch, Paul appeared to claim his rights as a citizen of the heavenly kingdom (see Philippians 3:20).

This reply and the exchange of words that follows do raise a number of questions. Why didn't Paul, as Jesus commanded, accept the blow and "turn the other cheek" (see Matthew 5:39; 1 Corinthians 4:12; also John 18:22-23)? How is it possible that Paul did not recognize the high priest (see Acts 23:5)? Was his "apology," the quotation of Exodus 22:28 in the second part of Acts 23:5, sarcastic or sincere?

Each of these questions has received a wide variety of answers.[18] Perhaps more important for us are the relevant contemporary questions. How do we relate to people who act unreasonably toward us? Do we move into passive mode and allow them to harm us? Or do we confront, and, if so, how? But, again, these questions are easier to ask than to answer.

How do we combine love and justice? Having a sincere desire to live out *both* those principles is the first step. There is danger on both extremes—always being hard or always being soft. What is the right path?

Perhaps it is safe to say that when others are being hurt by someone's actions, our thoughts and actions must lean more toward justice. We must attempt to control the offender. People need to be protected from abuse. Governmental police and court systems are set up with this goal in mind. Even so, mere revenge should never be the goal. Groups are called to act in love, even toward "enemies." On the other hand, when you as an individual are the target of abuse, you may have opportunity to manifest your faith by returning love for evil.

Why did Paul speak so harshly to the high priest? It is possible that, under the stress, Paul lost his temper. Our admiration for Paul need not require that he be sinless. Or, perhaps Paul's concern was not merely for himself, but for others. If the high priest, a person in legal authority, could mistreat Paul, then he would be setting a precedent for abusing all Christian believers.

In any case, Paul moved himself out of trouble by once again taking the initiative. He defused the attack against him by dividing the "enemy" force. Paul claimed that he stood **on trial because of [his] hope in the resurrection of the dead** (Acts 23:6). Paul was not lying. Jesus' resurrection from the dead was a key pillar of his preaching (see, for example, 13:30). But, at this point, the Jews were united in opposition to Paul's ministry *among Gentiles*. But with the question of the Resurrection, Paul cunningly moved attention away from his ministry to an issue that divided the Sanhedrin. The Pharisees among the Sanhedrin accepted the doctrine of eternal life. The Sadducees did not accept it (see 23:8; the Sadducees had played with this issue in a difficult question they asked Jesus in Matthew 22:23-28, near the end of His ministry).

A fierce theological argument arose. Paul might even have chuckled for a moment when he realized that this doctrinal division was also dividing the group over his guilt. Evidently some of the Pharisees somehow began thinking that if the Sadducees were foolish enough to reject the Resurrection, they might also have misjudged Paul. Some Pharisees actually began defending Paul (see Acts 23:9).

But Paul's trick nearly backfired on him. The Roman commander, observing the whole scene, realized that Paul faced great danger again. The commander feared that Paul might be **torn to pieces** by angry members of the Sanhedrin (23:10). So, for the third time (see 21:34; 22:24), the commander ordered Paul taken to the safety of the army barracks (23:10).

All the events of 21:27 through 23:10 had taken place on only two days. Paul had faced much stress in that short time. Prospects for future ministry may have looked bleak (see 20:22-24). God evidently sensed Paul's potential discouragement. God came to reassure Paul: **Take courage! As you have testified about me in Jerusalem, so you must also testify in Rome** (23:11). With these words, God both affirmed Paul for his recent actions ("Good job, Paul!"), but also assured him that he would not be killed as a result of the present situation ("Everything will be OK!"). Through the events of the next two years (see 24:27), those words must have strengthened Paul. At times during that long stretch, Paul may have felt deserted. But he could hang on to God's promise. God would bring him through.

Fortunately, God has given us many promises. In days that seem dark to us, we also can rest in Him.

ENDNOTES

[1]With verse 19, Luke drops into the background. Another "we" section has ended. Luke himself returns to the action in 27:1.

[2]Law refers to either the Levitical Code (all God's rules and regulations), the Ten Commandments, or the Pentateuch (the first five books of the Old Testament: Genesis, Exodus, Leviticus, Numbers, and Deuteronomy). Often capitalized when it means the Pentateuch or the Ten Commandments.

[3]See William Willimon, *Acts* (Atlanta: John Knox Press, 1988), p. 163. Willimon sees a pattern Luke includes in the midsection of his book dealing with outreach among Gentiles. His pattern looks like this: A Christian evangelist moved to offer, in a new way, the gospel to Gentiles. The Jerusalem leadership directly or indirectly challenged this advance. The witness(es) offered evidence that the new response from Gentiles was legitimate. The new Gentile converts (or their representative) responded with some "conciliatory gesture." The following chart displays evidence to support this pattern:

	Cornelius and Household	Gentiles in Antioch	Gentiles in Galatia	Gentiles in Asia, Macedonia, and Achaia
Evangelist(s) Acted Among a New Group	Peter (Acts 10:24-48)	Unnamed believers (Acts 11:20-21)	Paul and Barnabas (Acts 13:4–14:25)	Paul and others (Acts 16:11–21:16)
Jerusalem Church Challenged New Outreach	Direct challenge (Acts 11:1-3)	Barnabas sent to check things out (Acts 11:22)	Direct challenge (Acts 15:1, 5)	Some challenged Paul's ministry (Acts 21:21-22)
Jerusalem Church Accepted New Group	Leaders accepted Peter's explanation (Acts 11:4-18)		The Council came to a compromise (Acts 15:19-20)	
New Group Submitted Peace-making Gesture		Antioch sent an offering to offset a famine (Acts 11:29-30)	The Gentiles received the decision gladly (Acts 15:31)	Paul agreed to token ritual action (Acts 21:26)

The church moved cautiously, but it did move forward.

[4]"Pentecost" here refers to a celebration of the event when the Holy Spirit was given to the church: the day of Pentecost. The Greek term *Pentecost* comes from means "fiftieth" or "the fiftieth day" and is literally the fiftieth day after the end of the Passover. It is also known as the Jewish Feast of Weeks. This day is part of the Jewish observances, and was the beginning of the offering of first fruits.

[5]I. Howard Marshall, *Acts* (Grand Rapids, Michigan: Wm. B. Eerdmans Publishing Co., 1980), p. 344.

[6]Judaism is the life and belief system of the Jewish people and involves a covenant relationship with God. Though there are various branches of Judaism, the underlying theme among them has been monotheism and a recognition of the Law, or the Torah. The Hebrew word from which *Torah* comes is translated *law* and refers to divine instruction and guidance. The Torah is comprised of the instructions and directions given to Israel by God. Torah is another name for the Pentateuch (the first five books of the Old Testament: Genesis, Exodus, Leviticus, Numbers, and Deuteronomy), also known as the Law of Moses. It is considered the most important division in the Jewish Scriptures, with highest authority, since it was traditionally thought to have been written by Moses, the only biblical hero to have spoken with God face-to-face.

[7]F. F. Bruce, *The Book of the Acts* (Grand Rapids, Michigan: Wm. B. Eerdmans Publishing Co., 1988), p. 409. The Romans had given a blanket authorization for death sentences to Gentiles who violated this space sacred to the Jews.

[8]Ibid., p. 411.

[9]Ibid., p. 410. During the riot, Paul had been **dragged from the temple** and **the gates were shut** to keep Paul and the violent crowd out. This was Paul's last recorded visit to the Temple. It was also the last Temple incident that Luke describes. Perhaps Luke is saying that the Jews had shut Paul out of their system. Is Luke perhaps implying that the Jerusalem Jews had shut their doors to the Kingdom?

[10]This reconstruction of Paul's thinking requires that the commander either himself understand Aramaic or that someone could give him a summary of what Paul said.

[11]Frank Goodwin, *A Harmony of the Life of St. Paul* (New York: American Tract Society, 1895), p. 200. Goodwin helped me to see the Jewish flavor of this defense.

[12]See endnote 2.

[13]Bruce, p. 418. This experience in the Temple probably occurred during Paul's first post-conversion visit to Jerusalem, described in 9:26-30. During that first visit, Paul had attempted to offer the gospel to non-Christian Jews, but they had rejected his message and **tried to kill him** (9:29). This parallels Paul's story of receiving instructions from God to leave the city (22:18). Note also Romans 10:1. There, Paul described his great desire to see Jews come to the faith. He must have felt this concern for his own people from the beginning.

[14]John R. W. Stott, *The Spirit, the Church, and the World* (Downer's Grove, Illinois: InterVarsity Press, 1990), p. 348. Why? "In their eyes proselytism (making Gentiles into Jews) was fine, but evangelism (making Gentiles into Christians without first making them Jews) was an abomination. [This was like] saying that Jews and Gentiles were equal, for they both needed to come to God through Christ, and that on identical terms."

[15]Willimon, pp. 168–69.

[16]Johannes Munck, *The Acts of the Apostles* (New York: Doubleday, 1967), p. 219.

[17]Willimon, p. 168.

[17]Nearly all verse-by-verse commentaries detail the breadth of possible answers.

18

PAUL
IN CAESAREA

Acts 23:12–26:32

W hen newly elected President Abraham Lincoln approached
Washington, D.C., prior to his inauguration, assassins threatened
his life. He could not enter the capital with the honor he
deserved. Friends disguised Lincoln and smuggled him into Washington
under the cover of darkness. Even after safely arriving, his next few
years would be anything but glorious.

Paul, the great Christian statesman, deserved a hero's farewell as he
left Jerusalem the last time. But assassins' threats dashed any such
hopes. The Roman army packed Paul up and rushed him out of town
one night. Safe delivery to Caesarea did not move Paul into comfort,
however. He spent at least the next two years in prison there. Yet, God
remained in control.

1. PAUL IS MOVED TO CAESAREA 23:12-35

Looking back after this next story is finished, we see God's delight in
ironic twists. At nearly the same moment that God was promising to keep
Paul alive (see Acts 23:11), a group of forty or more Jews was
determining to kill Paul. The members of this group swore to each other
that they would not **eat or drink until they had killed Paul** (23:12). In
contests like this one between God and ordinary human beings, there can
be no doubt who wins. This reminds us of the contest between God and
the prophets of Baal in 1 Kings 18:16-40. If the forty Jews kept their
oath, they soon died of dehydration.

The plotters were not members of the Sanhedrin (see Acts 23:14), the
group who previously attempted to destroy Paul. Perhaps the plotters

were the Jews from Asia who had first stirred up the crowds in Jerusalem only two days before (see 21:27). In any case, they worked out their scheme in some detail. If the high priest could arrange for Paul to attend another hearing of the Sanhedrin, the murderers would ambush Paul between the army barracks and the Temple grounds (see 23:15).

Even if the Roman commander had agreed to such a request, would the plot have worked? The Romans had quite recently protected Paul from the murderous mob and the raging Sanhedrin (see 21:32-33; 23:10). If another attempt to kill Paul had arisen, the Romans would likely have protected Paul once again. But God intervened to avoid this next murderous confrontation.

To this point, God used many means to protect Paul, including earthquakes (see 16:26), decisions from Roman governors (18:14-15), and an unknown informant who told Paul of a plot to assassinate him (20:3). God had quite recently used the Jerusalem contingent of the Roman legion and its commander (23:10). At this point, a member of Paul's own family got in the act.

Somehow, Paul's nephew heard of the plan the forty Jews were putting together.[1] He told Paul,[2] who told a centurion, who took Paul's nephew **to the commander** (23:18). Luke describes this chain of interaction in some detail (see 23:17-23). Perhaps Luke thought it helpful to document the fact that the commander and those under his command showed great respect to Paul the prisoner. The centurion did exactly what Paul asked, taking Paul's nephew to the commander (see 23:17-18). The commander listened to Paul's messenger and later took the action necessary to protect Paul (see 19:22-24). At the same time, Luke records the unreasonable hatred the Jews felt toward Paul, twice describing the plot in almost identical words (see 23:14-15, 20-21).

Paul's calm courage (see 21:39) and his Roman citizenship (22:27) evidently had impressed the commander. Paul was evidently living by a principle Peter wrote in 1 Peter 2:12: "Live such good lives among the pagans that, though they accuse you of doing wrong, they may see your good deeds and glorify God on the day he visits us." We, too, need to live our lives before nonbelievers in a way that helps them see Christ in us. Such behavior may work for others' benefit, not to mention our own.

Luke's description of the commander's respect for Paul (and the Jews' fanatical anger at Paul) continues. How large a military escort was needed to deliver Paul **safely to Governor Felix** in the Roman capital of Caesarea? Four hundred seventy men (Acts 23:23-24)! The commander took no chances; he ordered maximum security. There were at least forty wild Jews out for Paul. Just in case, the commander made sure that even four hundred attackers would have little chance against the might of the Roman guard.

Luke's quotation of the commander's letter adds little new information.[3] Luke includes the letter's text merely to summarize, for further emphasis, information he has already given.

REFERENCE IN ACTS	INFORMATION GIVEN	PREVIOUSLY STATED
23:27	The Jews' seizing of Paul in Jerusalem	21:30
23:27	The first attempt to kill Paul	21:31
23:27	The commander's rescue	21:32
23:27	Awareness of Paul's Roman citizenship	22:27
23:28	Desire for knowledge of accusation	22:30
23:28	The "trial" before the Sanhedrin	22:30–23:10
23:29	Paul's innocence of any charge	*new*
23:30	The plot to kill Paul	23:12-22
23:30	The sending of Paul to Felix	23:23-24
23:30	Jewish accusers' presentation of charges	*new*

Note the new information Luke does include via this letter.[4] For the first time, Luke gives the information telling us that the commander saw Paul as innocent, at least by the standards of Roman law (see 23:29). Since the commander could find no fault in Paul, nor charges to press against him, he required the Jews also to travel to Caesarea. There, they could state their accusations against Paul. Had it not been for their accusations (dealing with **questions about their law**[5] [23:29]), and their intense desire to kill one the commander saw as innocent, Paul could have been set free. But, Paul remained a prisoner and was about to leave Jerusalem (as far as we know) for the last time.

Luke describes, again in detail, Paul's journey to Caesarea (a destination from which Paul, Luke and others had come just a few days before; see 21:15). The first day's journey took the military escort and Paul to **Antipatris,** a distance of roughly thirty-five miles (23:31). At that point, more than halfway from Jerusalem to Caesarea, and safely out of the reach of the angry Jews, part of the troop **returned to the barracks** in Jerusalem (23:32). The next day, **When the cavalry arrived in Caesarea, they** (the other half of the **cavalry**) **. . . handed Paul over to [the governor]** (23:33). He took no immediate action, but chose to wait for the Jews to arrive with their complaints against the prisoner (see 23:35). If they refused to come (perhaps the governor's secret hope), then he could free Paul and avoid a confrontation with the troublesome Jews.

What is the significance of this lengthy portion of Acts? Through the actions of the Roman commander, God won a major contest. Jews in Jerusalem had determined to kill Paul, but God had determined that Paul would safely reach Rome (see 23:11). Despite the fact that Paul, God's servant, faced difficult days, God himself would not be defeated! Today, even when our circumstances look daunting, God remains in control.

2. THE TRIAL BEFORE FELIX[6] 24:1-27

Luke has finished Acts 23 by describing how Felix postponed Paul's trial until his Jewish accusers arrived. Paul did not have to wait long. Within five days, the accusers appeared before Felix in Caesarea. Who came? Among others, the high priest himself (see 24:1)! The fanatical forty (see 23:12-13) were not the only ones who wanted to see Paul dead. This desire went to the top of the Jewish hierarchy. Other **elders and a lawyer named Tertullus** accompanied the high priest (24:1; the practice of bringing in expert attorneys to plead important cases began before the twentieth century).

Tertullus evidently possessed both knowledge of the law (both Jewish Law and Roman law) and skills in speaking. In Luke's account, Tertullus's speaking ability appears first. Notice the smooth manner in which he approached the governor (see 24:2-4): **Everywhere and in every way, most excellent Felix, we acknowledge [your virtues] with profound gratitude** (24:3).[7] Would you buy a used car from Tertullus? Felix had to know Tertullus was lying. (To soften our criticism of Tertullus, Paul also "buttered up" the governor before he spoke, although to a much smaller degree [see 24:10].) Tertullus was also aware of the political tightrope the Roman governor had to walk, trying not to upset either the Romans or the leading Jews. In demonstration of his knowledge of the law, Tertullus raised the charges against Paul in 24:5-6: (1) Paul was a **troublemaker;** (2) Paul had stirred up **riots among the Jews all over the world;** (3) Paul was **a ringleader of the Nazarene sect;** and (4) Paul **even tried to desecrate the temple.**

After stating the accusations, Tertullus tried to make Paul's guilt obvious.[8] It's almost as if he said, "Speak to the prisoner, even briefly, and you will see what a dangerous figure he is" (see 24:8). If that weren't enough, the other members of the Jerusalem delegation all **joined in the accusation asserting that these things were true** (24:9).

What was the truth of the charges against Paul? Luke intended to show his own contemporaries (and us today) that Paul had broken no Roman law. Luke prepares his readers for this trial scene with a previous description of recent events. This, combined with Paul's self-defense here before Felix, shows Paul's innocence. The lack of evidence supporting each charge leads directly to this conclusion.

First, they said Paul was a **troublemaker** (24:5). Paul pled "not guilty" to this accusation: "No one found **me arguing with anyone at the temple, or stirring up a crowd in the synagogues or anywhere else in the city**" (24:12). (In 24:11, Paul mentioned that he had returned to Jerusalem **no more than twelve days ago.** The disturbance he had allegedly created was quite recent. If so, then the Jews should have brought witnesses to his "crime."[9]) If Paul's statement were not strong enough by itself, Paul repeated his plea of innocence to this charge a few seconds later (the second half of 24:18).

Second, Paul's accusers said Paul had stirred up **riots among the Jews all over the world** (24:5). All over the world? That's obviously an exaggeration. But Paul had been a factor in mob actions in a number of Roman cities (including Lystra [14:19]; Philippi [16:22]; Thessalonica [17:5]; Ephesus [19:23]; Jerusalem [21:30]). But in none of those cases had Paul himself caused the riot. He had peacefully been preaching fresh news from God when others around him worked the crowds out of control. Once again, not guilty.

Third, Paul was accused of being **a ringleader of the Nazarene sect** (24:5). No one could doubt that Paul acted as a Christian leader. (Note that the Jews avoided the title "Christian," a word that had arisen in the Gentile setting of Antioch. The Jews did not want to associate Paul with the Christ [Messiah]. While they did not want to give Jesus any theological importance, they had no problems in associating Him with His hometown, Nazareth. Thus, they found it more convenient to call Jesus **the Nazarene.**[10]) Paul, in effect, pled *guilty* to this charge. But the accusation was harmless. At this point, no Roman had stated it was illegal to be **a follower of the Way, which [the Jews called] a sect** (24:14). Paul no more broke the Law by leading the Christians than Ananias, the high priest, did by governing the Jews. Paul was a loyal Christian, but that did not prevent him from remaining a loyal Jew (see below). (Paul's Christian faith and action was obviously the primary fault the Jews found in him. Paul subsequently alluded to this fact when he mentioned **the crime** some had found in him—his proclamation of the Resurrection [24:21]. The Jews realized Felix would not condemn Paul for religious opinions, but perhaps they sought to discredit the entire Christian group by painting them all as "revolutionaries" like Paul.)

Fourth, Paul's accusers said that he **even tried to desecrate the temple** (24:6). This refers to the incident described in 21:28-29. Jews had seen Paul in the Temple and with Gentiles in the city. These Jews (from Asia; see Paul's challenge to them in 24:19) assumed that Paul had taken his Gentile associates into the Temple with him. Had he done so, at least the Gentiles entering the inner areas of the Temple would have committed an offense leading to their execution. Jews participating in such a desecration of the Temple also risked their lives. Luke has already carefully described Paul's innocence in relation to this charge (see 21:29).

Before Paul moved away from the charges, he countered Tertullus's summary statement with one of his own: **They cannot prove to you the charges they are now making against me** (24:13). Paul, however, moved beyond mere rhetoric to substantiate his claim.

A paraphrase of Paul's position in 24:17-21 would sound like this: "Why am I here? I have done nothing wrong. I came to the Temple, minding my own business. No, in fact, I came to Jerusalem, hoping to help the poor of the city.[11] I came to do nothing but good. If anyone has a problem with that, let him come and bring further charges. I am not guilty of any crime against Rome. If I'm guilty of a crime, then they are, too!"

Paul placed himself squarely among the Jews. He wanted Felix and everyone to know that "he worshiped the same God (**the God of our fathers** [24:14]), believed the same truths (**the Law** and **the Prophets**[12] [24:14]), shared the same hope (the **resurrection of both the righteous and the wicked** [24:15]), and cherished the same ambition (**to keep** his **conscience clear** [24:16])."[13]

Felix, by this time, had heard enough to know that Paul was not a political threat. But, Felix faced the same dilemma that his predecessor Pilate had faced twenty-five years before. Roman governors of Palestine needed to maintain good relationships with the Jewish leaders in order successfully to rule the area. (Tertullus, in his accusations, had played on this fact [see, particularly, charges one and two, listed above].) At the same time, the governor needed to rule Palestine in accordance with Roman law. What did the governor do when those two priorities conflicted with each other? Paul presented such a case.

The Jews desired the execution of a man whose presence was inconvenient to them. Yet, the one the Jews disliked had committed no true crime against Rome. Pilate had given in to the demands and ordered Jesus' execution. Felix evidently did not feel right about giving in to the

Jews, but neither did he want to antagonize those whose cooperation was quite important. So, he took the easy way out and postponed any decision: "Let's wait until **Lysias the commander comes. . . . [Then] I will decide your case**" (24:22). Could Lysias offer Felix information that would clarify the case? Perhaps Felix hoped so, but the commander likely had already written all the relevant information in his letter (see 23:25-30).

In the meantime, Felix gave Paul relative freedom. At minimum, Paul's friends had free access to him (see 24:23).[14]

Felix's wife, **Drusilla . . . a Jewess,**[15] evidently had some interest in the prisoner, for Paul was given an audience with the governor and his wife. Paul took this opportunity, outside the presence of his Jewish accusers, to preach the gospel with more directness. Paul proclaimed **faith in Christ Jesus, . . . righteousness, self-control and the judgment to come** (24:24-25). The wording in this text bears an interesting similarity to Jesus' prediction that the Holy Spirit would speak to the world about sin, righteousness, and judgment (see John 16:8). Felix, with a reputation for public cruelty and private immorality, needed to hear such preaching.

Felix responded with fear (see Acts 24:25). His fear may have arisen from interacting with a prisoner who felt *no* fear. Roman governors possessed power, but seemingly always faced the possibility of losing their position or even their lives if they were unable to walk the fine line—keeping both Rome and Jerusalem happy. A prisoner who felt no fear obviously had connections with One greater even than Caesar. Paul knew that even death could not separate him from his God (see Romans 8:38). Felix likely feared death and the judgment to follow.

What did Felix have? A position of human power he would hold for two more years. Beyond that, he did not know. What did Felix want? A bit more money (see Acts 24:26). In contrast, what did Paul possess? A relationship with the God of all power. A relationship that gave him more peace than the Roman governor probably ever knew. What did Paul want? To proclaim Christ (see 24:24) and to maintain a clear conscience **before God and man** (24:16). Felix clung to his life and ended up with nothing (see Matthew 16:25).[16] Paul had given up what he could not keep to gain what he could not lose.[17]

But, before we move Paul onto some superhuman level, notice that Paul, like Felix, found himself in a squeeze between Jerusalem and Rome. Although he had done nothing to harm those on either side, they both appeared out to get him. The Jews wanted him dead. The Roman governor largely ignored Paul during the time he held Paul prisoner.

During this standoff, Paul sat in a Roman prison for two years (see Acts 24:27). It takes us only a second or two to read those words. But try to feel what it would be like to spend two whole years confined to your house. Most twentieth-century North Americans go stir crazy after a day or two of being confined even to their entertainment-filled homes.

Paul, during this time, remained faithful to his God. When he was next given opportunity to speak, his message did not change. Did God let Paul down by leaving him to waste away in prison? If we were in Paul's position, we would likely come to that conclusion. But Paul stood firm, holding to the promise God had given him, that Paul would "testify in Rome" (23:11).

God has promised His faithfulness also to us. Can we hang on to God, even when our circumstances tempt us toward doubt? As Paul wrote in his letter to the Roman church, "Neither death nor life, . . . neither the present nor the future, . . . nor anything else in all creation will be able to separate us from the love of God that is in Christ Jesus our Lord (Rom. 8:38-39).

3. THE TRIAL BEFORE FESTUS 25:1-22

During his last two years in office, Governor Felix left Paul in prison. Felix may conveniently have forgotten Paul, but the Jews in Jerusalem did not. They kept him on their hit list. Soon after Festus,[18] the next governor, took office, he made a courtesy call on the Jewish leaders in Jerusalem (see Acts 25:1; it was in his best interests to meet quickly the leaders of the people he would rule). One item high on the Jews' agenda was prisoner Paul. Felix had not granted the Jews their desires for Paul's execution. They lost no time in stating their wishes to the new governor.

At minimum, the Jews wanted Festus to arrange a new trial for Paul. They also hoped the verdict would be a speedy "guilty." Then, by means of a legal execution, they could rid themselves of this national enemy. (This is not clearly stated in 25:2, but Festus later described the Jews' desire to King Agrippa in 25:15. See below for details of Agrippa's visit.) If Festus would not order Paul's death, the Jews then hoped to take matters into their own hands. Their plea went something like this: "Oh most excellent governor, we have one small favor to ask. This prisoner Paul—does he really need another formal trial? If so, wouldn't it be simpler for you both to come here to Jerusalem, than for us and all our witnesses to travel to Caesarea? That would make us so very happy."

Had the new governor granted that seemingly harmless wish, the Jews would have insured that Paul never saw Jerusalem. They planned to set up **an ambush to kill him** (25:3; we hear no repetition of vows that might cut off food and drink—perhaps they had learned a lesson [see 23:12]). Time had not diminished the Jews' hatred of Paul, their enemy.

Felix may have been new in the territory, but evidently someone in Rome had briefed him. He had heard of the Jews' skill at manipulating people and circumstances.[19] So, he quickly reminded them that he, not they, governed the area: **It is not the Roman custom to hand over any man before he has faced his accusers and has had an opportunity to defend himself against their charges** (25:16). (Did the Jews let Festus in on their plan to "take care" of Paul? Probably not. If they did, then at this point, very early in his term, Festus hung on to his idealism. He hoped he could handle the case in a way that would somehow please both Roman justice and Jewish desires.) His final response? "No. Paul's safe in Caesarea. I will return to my headquarters soon. If his case is so important to you, then you can make the trip" (see 25:4-5).

Eight to ten days later, the scene shifted to Caesarea (25:6). All the main characters were present. Festus called the court into session. Paul took his place in the courtroom. The Jews prepared to speak. Had they strengthened their case? No. They had either dropped some of the accusations relating to Roman law (Festus did not mention such charges when describing their case to Agrippa in 25:18-19) or else Festus, like Felix before him, quickly dismissed those charges as ones **they could not prove** (25:7). They did continue to accuse Paul of teaching false doctrine (see 25:19), perhaps of leading "the Nazarene sect" (24:5), but Festus felt he had no need or ability to rule on such matters (25:20).

With the Jews adding nothing new, Paul saw no need to change his strategy. He countered the charges with a strong "not guilty" plea: **I have done nothing wrong against the law of the Jews**[20] **or against the temple or against Caesar** (25:8).

Festus may quickly have realized that Felix had left him a no-win situation. It appeared he faced only two choices. He could deny Roman justice and order the execution of a prisoner who had broken no Roman law. Or, he could deny the Jews their wish to be rid of their pest. Neither option looked promising.

The Jews had, however, offered him another option that looked promising. They had offered to host Paul's trial, with Festus still acting as judge on their own home grounds. Perhaps their case would look stronger or it might fall apart completely, if the trial took place in Jerusalem, the scene of the "crimes." If the prisoner was so convinced that he had done nothing wrong, then perhaps he would consent to trial in Jerusalem. Festus saw nothing to lose in asking (see 25:9). If the prisoner permitted this plan, Festus could harmlessly win points with the Jews. Roman governors wisely seized such opportunities.

Paul, though, had everything to lose in being moved back to Jerusalem. Roman justice may have had its flaws since it left him, an *unconvicted* prisoner, sitting in prison. But he still preferred the objectivity of undergoing trial in a neutral city almost anywhere other than Jerusalem. In the Jewish capital, all the legal proceedings could be easily tainted by the Jews' scheming, especially since Festus was a newcomer to their strategies. In Jerusalem, Festus might even accept Jews as members of his legal council. Paul knew the strength of (and had felt on his body) the Jewish prejudice against him: **If the charges brought against me by these Jews are not true, no one has the right to hand me over to them** (25:11). Paul perceived that a move to Jerusalem would lead to his death. The Jews would pervert justice, as they had done in Jesus' trial a few decades before.

What choice did Paul have? Refusing trial in Jerusalem might have left Paul waiting another two years in jail in Caesarea, or, worse yet, he might have been offered as Festus's sacrifice to win the favor of the Jews. Neither prolonged imprisonment nor execution would further his ministry. He had earlier stated his desire to minister in Rome (see Romans 15:23-24). Paul could potentially escape his no-win situation by appealing to the highest court in the land.[21] That's just what he did: **I appeal to Caesar!** (Acts 25:11).

Luke tells us that Festus **conferred with his council** (25:12). How much thought would his response have required? Paul had just offered Festus a way out of *his* no-win situation. Festus could escape his dilemma without displeasing either Rome or Jerusalem: **You have appealed to Caesar. To Caesar you will go!** (25:12). Festus then dismissed the Jews and **ordered [Paul] held until [he] could send him to Caesar** (25:21).

Luke evidently saw this encounter with Festus as a crucial one. As you can see from this reconstruction of events, Luke tells the story twice: once as it occurred, and a second time as Festus recounted the incidents to King Agrippa and Bernice.[22] (Other such repetitions include Peter's vision and subsequent ministry to Cornelius [see 10:1-48; 11:1-17] and Paul's conversion [9:1-31; 22:4-16; 26:12-18].) The king and his wife had come **to pay their respects** to the new governor (25:13).

After Festus had told Paul's story to the king and his wife, Agrippa expressed his interest in meeting Paul, just as his great-uncle, Herod

Antipas, had been interested in meeting Jesus.[23] Festus saw no problem in such an encounter and promised that it would occur on the next day.[24]

4. THE TRIAL BEFORE AGRIPPA 25:23–26:32

In the chapters immediately preceding this encounter between Paul and King Agrippa, Luke has described several "trials" Paul faced.[25] In the first two, Paul took the initiative, seizing an opportunity to describe and defend his ministry. For example, Paul chose to speak with the Jerusalem Christian leaders (see Acts 21:17-19). Likewise, Paul asked for permission to address the angry crowd of Jews in the same city (see 21:40–22:21).

As the Roman military commander and governors became involved, two major changes occurred. First, people other than Paul set up the situations. Second, the encounters became legal trials, with Paul's future ministry, and even his life, at stake. Note the trials before the Sanhedrin (22:30–23:10), Felix (24:1-22), and Festus (25:6-12). At the end of the last of these trials, Paul grasped what power he retained, bypassed the local governors, and placed his future in the hands of Caesar himself (see 25:11).

But before Paul faced Caesar, he needed to take one more preliminary step. The plan required that Paul stand before King Agrippa. Whose plan? God's plan. God wanted to give this king a chance to hear the gospel. But it was also Governor Festus's plan. Why? Because Festus needed Agrippa's help. Festus realized that he no longer had power over Paul, the prisoner. But before he could send Paul to Rome, Festus needed to summarize the charges and the evidence supporting them. (Note 23:25-30 — as Claudius Lysias sent Paul to the governor, he wrote a similar legal brief.) Festus felt unsure what to write in his official letter to Caesar (see 25:20, 26-27). Festus had heard the charges, but lacked evidence to support them.[26] Perhaps Agrippa could help. After all, Agrippa had lived in the area longer than Festus. Agrippa was more familiar with Jewish affairs (see 26:3, 27). Agrippa was himself of Jewish blood.

Luke's account of this last "trial" includes features similar to those in previous trials, but the interaction with Agrippa also offers distinctive elements. Now we focus primarily on the uniquenesses of this event.

This occasion offered **great pomp,** perhaps the greatest Paul had ever witnessed (25:23). This hearing had become a great event on the Caesarean social calendar. Everyone but the prisoner came dressed in their best robes; he came in his chains. (Yet today, no one would remember any of the others were it not for the plainly dressed prisoner.)

Many **high ranking officers and the leading men of the city** flocked to the governor's chambers (25:23). They must have relished the chance to witness this "summit meeting" involving the governor, the king, and his wife. But this was also their last chance to see Paul, a prisoner whose local fame must have been growing. (Observe Festus's grand introduction of Paul in 25:24: **You see this man!**)

In his summary of Paul's case, Festus spoke more directly than in his previous public statements: **I found [Paul] had done nothing deserving of death** (25:25). Prior to Paul's appeal to Caesar, Paul's future weighed primarily on Festus. As described above (see commentary on 25:1-22), Festus had struggled between the demands of Roman justice (which called him to release an innocent prisoner) and the need to please the Jewish leaders (who wanted Paul executed; see 25:24). Those circumstances had prevented Festus from speaking freely. Now that his opinion no longer carried legal weight in the case, Festus could more freely announce his private thoughts—Paul was not guilty. In announcing this, even in these circumstances, he took the risk of telling everyone that he had considered an act of injustice (punishing or continuing to imprison an innocent man) to please the Jews.

But because of Paul's appeal, Festus now faced another dilemma, one "of his own making"[27]: "I think the prisoner is innocent. But he has appealed to Caesar. I must present a summary of the case that justifies Caesar's attention. **It is unreasonable to send on a prisoner without specifying the charges against him**" (25:27).

Note that Luke mentions no Jerusalem Jews in attendance at this hearing. Evidently Festus had not invited them. They had failed to prove their case against Paul. This hearing would not result in any official verdict; its only purpose was fact-finding. Festus saw Paul, the innocent prisoner who had appealed to Caesar, as the only necessary source of information. The presence of Jews might have prevented Festus and Paul from speaking freely.

Agrippa gave Paul **permission to speak** (26:1). Paul **motioned with his hand** (26:1). At the time, this was a common habit for formal speakers; Paul had begun his defense before the Jerusalem crowds with a similar motion (see 21:40). Paul opened his defense, following the appropriate protocol. He spoke words complimentary of King Agrippa (compare 23:26; 24:2-4, 10). Paul highlighted Agrippa's familiarity **with all the Jewish customs and controversies** (26:3).

What would have been Paul's goals for this hearing? Would he have been surprised to hear Festus's declaration of his innocence? With that information in hand, his strongest hope would have been to lead Agrippa to the same conclusion. If the two of them, high Roman officials familiar with the situation, agreed that he was innocent, then the brief they sent to Caesar would not accuse Paul, but exonerate him. Paul knew he had broken no laws (see 25:8). He had nothing to lose in straightforwardly proclaiming his biography and his Christian faith.

Paul started at the beginning: **Since I was a child** (26:4). In effect, he says, "No marks have appeared against me on anyone's record. I received A+'s on all my report cards. My performance even in **the strictest sect of our religion,** was outstanding. In accordance with my Jewish belief, I opposed **the name of Jesus of Nazareth"** (26:4-5, 9-10).

At this point, Paul gave a most graphic portrayal of his persecution of the Christians. Notice how hard he fought them. He alluded to the following: the quantity of believers he imprisoned—*many* **of the saints** (26:10); his determination to search out the Christians—even at **noon,** a time most ancient Middle Eastern travelers would have taken a break; riding on, eager to get on with his work (26:13)[28]; the severity of the sentence he sought—voting for their death (26:10); the pressure he applied—trying **to force them to blaspheme** (26:11), although apparently *without* success[29]); the strength of his **obsession against them**—going from synagogue to synagogue, even going **to foreign cities to persecute** the believers (26:11).

Luke, at this point in his account, includes yet another detailed description of Paul's encounter with Jesus on the way to Damascus. The details of this event are familiar to Luke's readers by now; he has already told the story twice (see 9:1-19; 22:5-16). The thrust of the story remains the same each time—Jesus intervened in Paul's life and dramatically reversed his direction. On this occasion before Agrippa, Paul needed to help the king and others present to understand how he changed his position so dramatically—from Jewish persecutor to recipient of Jewish persecution.

What factors are new in this retelling? First, a less Jewish slant. When speaking to the Jews of Jerusalem (see Acts 22), Paul identified himself with them (**I was just as zealous for God as any of you are** [22:3]). When Paul told the story to Festus and Agrippa, the Jewish accusers were absent. On this occasion, Paul saw benefit in identifying himself, even from the beginning, with the Christians. He referred to the people he persecuted as **the saints** (26:10).

What other differences appear in this narration of Paul's conversion? It is the shortest such account in Acts. It contains no reference to Ananias of Damascus. The story climaxes with Paul's question, **Who are you, Lord?**

The words that, in the other accounts, God gave to Ananias are here attributed directly to the second person of the trinity: **I am Jesus** (26:15).

That last statement illustrates the answers to two evangelical questions about Scripture. First, we believe that the words of Scripture are both human and divine. Who wrote Acts? Luke did. The Holy Spirit did. There is no contradiction between those two statements. In the case of the words that Ananias, under God's direction, spoke to Paul (see 9:15; 22:14-15), Paul and Luke felt free to attribute those words both to Ananias (22:14-15) and to God (26:16-18). Human words whose source is God are divine words. This illustrates the fact that words written by quite ordinary people like Luke can be and, in the case of Scripture, *are* the Word of God.

Note also the fact that these words, attributed either to God or to Ananias, do not appear in exactly the same form in the three accounts (see 9:15; 22:14-15; 26:16-18). Do the three accounts contradict each other because of their variation in detail? No. All three quotations center on similar thoughts relating to Paul's serving as a witness to Gentiles. More generally, must all Scripture descriptions of the same event (the resurrection of Jesus, for example) be correlated in every detail in order to present the event accurately? It appears that neither Luke nor Paul thought so. They felt free to paraphrase God's word through Ananias at least two of the times they quoted them.

In the Acts 26 account of Paul's conversion, God (through Luke) quite fully described Paul's mission.

What was God's role in Paul's ministry? God **appeared** to Paul in order to appoint him (26:16). This divine self-revelation gave Paul knowledge and authority. The appointment involved **sending** (26:17). Paul was under divine constraint to *go*. Paul, however, would not go alone. God would be there to **rescue** him (26:17).

What was Paul's role? He would be **a servant** and **a witness** (26:16). The first word describes his relationship with God and his hearers. The second unfolds the content of his message: to proclaim what Paul had seen (26:16).

Who were those who would hear Paul's message? His **own people** and **the Gentiles** (26:17).

The goal of Paul's mission? To bring enlightenment and true empowerment. To bring forgiveness for past sins and the potential for sanctification, true holiness, godlikeness.

By telling the story of how God appeared to him and gave him these specific instructions, Paul justified his Christian belief and activity. God had not only converted Paul, but commissioned him.[30] From this vantage point, Paul could look back and testify to his faithful submission to God's plan: **I was not disobedient to the vision from heaven** (26:19).

Our calls may bear similarity to Paul's commissioning. In various ways, God calls all His people to be servants and witnesses. At the end of our ministries, the question will not be the type or size of the call; it will be our obedience to God's instructions for us. Paul spoke firmly, declaring his faithfulness to his commission.

Just as Paul had traveled from city to city to persecute believers (see 26:11), he went after his conversion to those in Damascus, Jerusalem, and all Judea, and then to the Gentiles, proclaiming **that they should repent and turn to God** (26:20). As he told the rulers his story, what was Paul saying? "The Jews may not like me, because my teaching contradicts their system. I, too, remember fighting the Christians. But Jesus, the risen Lord, spoke to me. I cannot deny that fact. And I have since discovered that what we Christians teach accords precisely **with what God has promised our fathers . . . the promise our twelve tribes are hoping to see fulfilled . . .what the prophets and Moses said would happen"** (26:6-7, 22).

Paul, in his presentation before Festus, Agrippa, and Bernice, rightly saw the primary causes of the Jews' opposition to him. First was his proclamation of the Christian **hope,** the resurrection of the dead (26:6-8)[31]: **It is because of this hope that the Jews are accusing me** (26:7). If the Jews had accepted the doctrine Paul preached, the Sadducees would have been forced to reverse their theology of life after death, and all the Jewish leaders would have had to admit that they had made the overwhelmingly tragic mistake of murdering the Messiah God had sent them. Second was Paul's inclusion of the Gentiles in the inner circle of God's favor: **First to [the Jews] and to the Gentiles also, I preached that they should repent. . . . That is why the Jews seized me in the temple courts and tried to kill me** (26:20-21).

Peter and Paul may have varied the content of their preaching to make it relevant to their hearers, but no one can deny the overwhelming similarity of their messages. For both Peter and Paul, Jesus of Nazareth had come as the Messiah of God's people (see 26:9, 23; 2:22, 36). Both focused on the resurrection of Jesus Christ as the core of the good news (see 26:7-8, 23; 2:24, 32). Both saw Jesus' death and resurrection as the fulfillment of God's previous prophesy (see 26:6-7, 22; 2:25-31). Both preached that salvation was open to *all* people (see 26:23; 2:21, 39). Peter and Paul called people to repentance, a new beginning (see 26:20; 2:38). This message, preached by Luke's two heroes, is still our message today.

Paul felt quite certain about the validity of his message. Festus, however, was not so sure. He saw Paul as innocent of crime against Rome. In that sense, Paul was harmless. But Festus was a Roman aristocrat. If he was a typical Roman, he accepted only what he saw as reasonable. Thus, he must have struggled with the possibility of God's becoming flesh, of Jesus' physical rising from the dead, and of Paul's experience of truly seeing and hearing God. Paul may not have been a threat to Rome's peace (see 25:25; 26:31) but Festus concluded that Paul's beliefs did threaten sanity (26:24). Festus sounds quite like some people living around us today.

Festus had rejected Paul's message, but Paul still held out hope for Agrippa. Paul was even so bold as to reverse roles. He, the accused, became the questioner: **"King Agrippa, do you believe the prophets**, and thus, their support for what I say?" (26:27). He put the king on the spot, because (1) the king had lived for some time in the region (the events of Jesus' life did not occur **in a corner** [26:26]); (2) Agrippa was a Jew (**The king is familiar with these things** [26:26]); and (3) Agrippa would have known the Scriptures (**Do you believe the prophets?** [26:27]). A proconsul on Cyprus had believed Paul's message, even without all the background Agrippa had (see 13:12). If a Roman proconsul could believe, then Paul had faith for a king.

Paul had not mentioned to Festus or Agrippa that, back at the time of his conversion, God through Ananias had told Paul he would carry the name of Jesus even before kings (see 9:15; compare Luke 21:12). Paul, even as he spoke, believed that the salvation of this king was quite possible (see Acts 26:29). But, although Agrippa may have been more polite, he too refused the offer. He did so quite diplomatically. He could not refuse awareness of the prophet's message without denying his Jewish faith. He could not profess faith in their message without opening himself to the question Paul obviously would have asked, "Do you then believe in Jesus, the Christ?"[32] Agrippa politely asked for more time (see 26:28).

Paul, too, was polite. He did not condemn the rulers who had rejected Jesus. He continued to pray for all who heard him (see 26:29). If he were insane, he wished them all insane. Fortunately, he was not; he could pray that they, too, might enjoy all he had received from God, **except for these chains** (26:29).

How could anyone speak against Paul's wisdom and sincerity? The king and the crowd got up and **left the room** (26:31). As far as we know, Festus and Agrippa never did accept the gospel. Festus was dead within two years. Agrippa lived on, but not in the abundant life he could have known. The two rulers and the rest of the crowd did not accept Paul's faith, but they declared him innocent of crime against Rome. As Agrippa said it, **This man could have been set free, if he had not appealed to Caesar** (26:32).

So, Paul was on his way to Rome. Luke has nearly closed his recounting of legal evidence for Paul's Roman trial. By means of Paul's brief, the two highest Roman rulers in Palestine had testified on Paul's behalf. What basis would Caesar have for overturning their verdict?

ENDNOTES

[1]The nephew's presence and access to inside information raises several questions. Nowhere else in the New Testament do we see mention of any other member of Paul's family. The fact that Paul grew up in Tarsus suggests that his extended family lived in that same city. Did his nephew come to Jerusalem to receive the best education Judaism could offer (Judaism is the life and belief system of the Jewish people and involves a covenant relationship with God)? Was he perhaps in training to become a Pharisee, like his uncle? Those guesses might explain the young man's reason for being in Jerusalem and the opportunities he had to gain inside information. If this scenario describes what happened, the nephew may have betrayed his Jewish mentors in order to protect his uncle. Family ties won out over loyalty to Jerusalem's Jewish system.

[2]I. Howard Marshall, *Acts* (Grand Rapids, Michigan: Wm. B. Ecrdmans Publishing Co., 1980), p. 368. If this young man could have such easy access to Paul, then what prevented an assassin from reaching Paul? The Romans evidently had a system devised for checking out prison visitors.

[3]Although this letter is brief, it displays the same ancient format displayed in the New Testament Epistles (comprised of the New Testament books of Romans; 1 and 2 Corinthians; Galatians; Ephesians; Philippians; Colossians; 1 and 2 Thessalonians; 1 and 2 Timothy; Titus; Philemon; Hebrews; James; 1 and 2 Peter; 1, 2 and 3 John; and Jude). Note the sequence: (1) sender; (2) recipient; (3) greetings; (4) letter content.

[4]Luke here identifies the commander as **Claudius Lysias** (23:26). Perhaps, by clearly identifying this man, Luke intended to commend him for his kindness to Paul. Perhaps, but notice also that Luke describes how the commander shaded the truth to make himself look better. The commander stated how he rescued Paul from the Jerusalem mob because **I had learned that he is a Roman citizen** (23:27), while in actual fact it was later in that day that he learned of Paul's citizenship. (Earlier, Luke had described how the commander did not know Paul was a citizen until after Paul was in custody; see 21:33, 39.)

[5]Law refers to either the Levitical Code (all God's rules and regulations), the Ten Commandments, or the Pentateuch (the first five books of the Old Testament: Genesis, Exodus, Leviticus, Numbers, and Deuteronomy); it is often capitalized when it means the Pentateuch or the Ten Commandments.

[6]Felix, who had begun his working career as a slave, served as the Roman governor of Palestine for several years. His brother Pallas was friend to

Claudius and Nero, Roman emperors during this period. His brother's rank gave Felix an inside track to Roman position. A ruthless man, he was not known for his quality leadership. Tacitus, a Roman historian, described Felix as one who "exercised the power of a king with the mind of a slave." Neither was he known for his private morality; his present wife was his third.

[7]As you read these words, remember that Felix was a governor noted for his cruelty.

[8]Tertullus may also have stretched the truth to make the Jews look innocent. Notice the words the New International Version editors placed in the footnote (see 24:6b-8a): Some ancient manuscripts quote Tertullus as saying that Lysias, the Roman commander, used unnecessary force to disrupt the Jews, who were handling Paul justly. In actual fact, the commander rescued Paul from a Jewish mob about to lynch Paul (see 21:31-32).

[9]Marshall, p. 376.

[10]This, however, is the only place in the New Testament where the Christians are called "Nazarenes."

[11]As mentioned above, this is the only reference in Acts to the offering for the Jerusalem church, a task which was a major purpose for the third missionary journey.

[12]The Prophets here refer to the Old Testament classification of books comprised of Joshua, Judges, 1 and 2 Samuel, 1 and 2 Kings, Isaiah, Jeremiah, Ezekiel, Hosea, Joel Amos, Obadiah, Jonah, Micah, Nahum, Habbakuk, Zephaniah, Haggai, Zechariah, and Malachi. See endnote 5.

[13]John R. W. Stott, *The Spirit, the Church and the World* (Downers Grove, Illinois: InterVarsity Press, 1990), p. 361.

[14]These friends could have included Luke, who appears to have stayed in the area during the time of Paul's imprisonment in Caesarea (see 27:1); Philip and his prophetess daughters, who lived in Caesarea; as well as other local believers (21:8-9, 12).

[15]Drusilla was a daughter of Herod Agrippa I. He is the one who martyred James, imprisoned Peter, and subsequently suffered a rather stunning death himself (see Acts 12). Drusilla's marriage to Felix, when she was still less than twenty, was her second marriage.

[16]Felix remained governor of Palestine for two more years (see 24:27). He lost that position because of the way he had mishandled his position. Caesar recalled him to prevent him from further alienating the Jews.

[17]These words are quite similar to those written by Jim Elliot. His words are found in *Through Gates of Splendor,* by Elisabeth Elliot (New York: Harper and Brothers, 1957), p. 172.

[18]Marshall, p. 383. Festus served as governor of Palestine for two to three years. Historians view his leadership as adequate, but not spectacular. He died while in office. Had he lived longer, he might have left a more impressive legacy.

[19]It was in the transition between Festus's death and the arrival of the next procurator that the Jews did forcefully take matters into their own hands. While no Roman procurator was present to stop them, they stoned James, the brother of Jesus.

[20]See endnote 5.

[21]F. F. Bruce, *The Book of the Acts* (Grand Rapids, Michigan: Wm. B. Eerdmans Publishing Co., 1988), pp. 453–54. All Roman *citizens* had the legal

right to appeal their legal cases to Caesar at any point in the process of their trials. Perhaps during this two years' imprisonment, Paul had considered the possibility of appealing to the emperor for his own benefit, but also for the chance to proclaim the gospel to the most powerful person of his day. Also, if the emperor acquitted him, that would indirectly give legal authority to all groups of law-abiding Christians anywhere in the Empire. Interestingly, the Roman emperor at this time was Nero, the one who later executed Paul, Peter, and many other believers. During the first years of his reign, however, Nero ruled with much more wisdom and fairness than he did in his later years.

[22]Ibid., pp. 456–57. This Agrippa is known as Herod Agrippa II, the son of Herod Agrippa I. The latter is the Agrippa who executed James, the brother of John (see Acts 12:1). Herod Agrippa II did not immediately inherit his father's power, for he was only seventeen when his father died. When he was twenty-four, Caesar gave him his first kingdom. Agrippa II continued in Caesar's favor; the emperor several times enlarged the area he ruled. (Although Festus and not Agrippa ruled Judea, the Romans gave Agrippa power to select the Jewish high priests.) When the Jews revolted in A.D. 66, Agrippa sided with the Jews and was rewarded with more land and honor. He died around A.D. 100, having fathered no children, thus ending the line of the Herods.

Bernice was Agrippa's older sister and his mistress. She had first been married to her father's brother. When her uncle/husband died, she became her brother's partner. She interrupted that relationship for a marriage to the king of Cilicia, but soon returned to her brother.

[23]Stott, p. 368. Stott quotes R. B. Rackham who describes the sins of the Herod family. "Their founder, Herod the Great, had tried to destroy the infant Jesus. His son Antipas, the tetrarch of Galilee, beheaded John the Baptist. . . His grandson Agrippa I slew James the son of Zebedee with the sword. Now we see Paul brought before Agrippa's son" (from Rackham's *The Acts of the Apostles* (Methuen, 1909), p. 457).

[24]See Marshall, p. 386. Marshall asks how Luke could have gained authoritative information on this private discussion between Festus and Agrippa (see 25:14-22). The question is a good one. It is not likely that Luke was able to gain interviews with either Agrippa or Festus. Marshall guesses that Luke imagined the conversation that likely occurred. Many scholars debate how freely Luke used his imagination in reconstructing other narratives or speeches throughout the book. Evangelical scholars tend to believe that Luke, as far as possible, did consult witnesses to the events he described. In relation to many particular events, the scholars cannot state precisely what, if any sources Luke consulted. We prefer to take him at his word. At the beginning of his gospel, the first volume of his two-volume set, Luke states his procedure: "I have carefully investigated everything [so that I might write] an orderly account" (1:3).

[25]Not all the events described here were literal trials. But in each of these encounters, Paul was interacting with people who were checking out the validity of his Christian faith and ministry.

[26]Stott, p. 369.

[27]Marshall, p. 390.

[28]William Barclay, *The Acts of the Apostles* (Philadelphia: The Westminster Press, 1955), p. 195.

[29]Stott, p. 371.

[30]Ibid., p. 372.

[31]Marshall, p. 391. See 23:6, 24:15, and 28:20 for other Pauline references to the Christian hope as a theme in his trials.

[32]Ibid., p. 399.

19

PAUL REACHES ROME

Acts 27:1–28:31

n this final section of the book, Luke accomplishes at least one of his goals in writing: he shows how his hero Paul finally reaches and ministers in Rome. The last travel to that point was treacherous. Paul, upon arrival, remained a prisoner. Not only did Luke accomplish a goal at that point, but God did, too. In the further establishment of a church in the capital city, God was setting in motion yet another chain of events which has led to the conversion of "the ends of the earth" (Acts 1:8).

1. PAUL TRAVELS TO ROME 27:1–28:14a

In these final chapters of Acts, Luke shows his love for telling a good story. Paul's cruise to Rome reads with powerful suspense. (If you have any doubts, read these verses to an eight-year-old child.) Paul is finally traveling to Rome, the capital of the Roman Empire. You, the reader, know he is going to reach that goal; Luke has dropped enough hints to tell you that. Paul has safely come through several scrapes, but this one looks serious. You live the suspense; you experience the trauma with him. Then, you sigh with satisfaction when Paul marches into the great city.

While Luke was being discipled in his Christian faith, he must have heard the Old Testament sea epics of Noah and Jonah. Perhaps Peter had told him about the day Jesus walked on the sea and calmed the storm. Did Luke know that he was writing another sea adventure that would rank with the other biblical voyages? For Luke, however, this one was different. Luke did not need anyone to tell him the story of Paul's trip to Rome. Luke lived it! The detail in the account (the water **one hundred twenty feet deep** [27:28]; **the four anchors** [27:29][1]) and a return to the use of the pronoun **we** (for example, 27:1; 28:1[2]) convince us that we are reading an eyewitness account. Perhaps, even during this trip to Rome, Luke sensed that he himself was participating in no ordinary voyage, but in another *divinely guided*, history-making sea adventure in the tradition of Noah and Jonah.[3] God's continual intervention (rescuing Paul from the snake in 28:3-6 and, before that, rescuing the ship's entire company from the great storm in 27:44) assures us that this is *God's* story.

Luke's account of the journey breaks into three blocks:

- Forward travel in safety—27:1-6; followed by a transition (a time of slowed travel and the decision to go on)—27:7-13
- Being blown about in danger—27:14-32; followed by a transition (the survival of all on board and ministry on Malta)—27:33–28:10
- Forward travel in safety—28:11-14

Another list lays out the story's parallels more graphically.

- The voyage began in Caesarea (27:1)
  - Safe travel (27:2-6)
    - Meeting on dry land (27:8-12)
      - Disaster struck (27:14-15)
        - "We're all going to die!" (27:18-20)
      - The trauma eased (27:39-44)
    - Meeting on dry land (28:1-10)
  - Safe travel (28:11-13)
- The voyage ended in Rome (28:14)

Luke appears to have carefully laid out his exciting saga. What were his purposes in telling it? What features does he emphasize?

As Luke recounts the journey, he gives more detail when describing the disaster scenes. He passes quickly over the uneventful safe travel. Then, as now, readers had great interest in stories of people facing and overcoming disaster. (Each day in North America, thousands of airline flights reach their destinations without problem. That success never hits the news. But when a single crash occurs, the nation focuses on its victims.) Luke's own memory of the uneventful travel days may have faded. On the other hand, Luke could vividly remember each detail of the treacherous days.

Luke does summarize the course which the ship took before its engagement with the great storm.[4] (To make best sense of this paragraph, you should also be consulting a Bible map of Paul's journeys.) From

Caesarea, the ship hugged the Mediterranean shoreline as it traveled north and then east along the coast of what is now Turkey. As Luke puts it, **the ship set sail for ports along the coast of the province of Asia** (27:2). The land offered fixed points to help with navigation and shelter if a storm should arise. Luke specifically mentions a stop at **Sidon** (still on the eastern shore of the Mediterranean; 27:3). The ship then took a sweeping left turn and headed west between **Cyprus** and the mainland, on the northern side of the Sea (27:4). Luke mentions swapping ships at **Myra,** a spot on the coast about two-thirds of the way toward the southwesternmost point of Turkey (27:5). The settlement at **Cnidus** (27:7) marked the point on the southwest of the mainland. The captain of the ship may have hoped to stop at Cnidus and then travel on to reach Italy by winter. A strong northwest wind would not permit either of these goals (see 27:7).

Autumn, a period of increasing danger in sailing the open seas, was already upon them. Which direction should they head? West? No. The wind would not easily allow that. And also, traveling west would take them toward the area south of the Greek peninsula. Even in the best of times, the sea there was known for being treacherous. Rather than navigate that area, sailors often preferred to carry their cargo (and even small ships) over the narrow stretch of land near Corinth, rather than sail around the peninsula (see commentary on 18:1-18a). The risk of sailing near Greece and the strong northwest wind left the crew little choice. They took the safest route open to them—the long way around the east and south coast of **Crete,** a long, narrow island in the sea (27:7). The ship traversed that stretch of sea safely and was able to enter a harbor on **Crete** at **Fair Havens, near the town of Lasea** (27:8). **Lasea** was located about midway along the south coast of the island. That harbor was the best the ship had seen for some time, but not adequate for the winter.

Luke's attention throughout his record of this voyage is focused on his hero, Paul. Luke describes how Paul met with Christian **friends** (both at Sidon [27:3] and Puteoli [28:14]). (How and when were Christian communities established in these cities? We can only guess. Their existence, however, does remind us that the church was expanding far beyond what Luke could describe in a short book like Acts.) More significantly, Luke portrays Paul (a prisoner!) as a key member of this ship's crew. As the journey became more treacherous, Paul became the one that knew what lay before them. Three times, Paul accurately predicted major events.

While at **Fair Havens,** Paul warned the ship's company that they should go no further, even though the harbor in which they hoped to winter was only forty miles farther west. Paul sensed that sailing then would **be disastrous and bring great loss to ship and cargo, and to our own lives also** (27:10). The commander chose to ignore Paul's warning, and, from that point, the ship entered a stretch where nothing went right.

It's possible that Paul could have received this information directly from God. It's just as possible that Paul, an experienced sea traveler, sensed the danger without any divine help. He knew that it was autumn (**after the Fast** [27:9]—the Day of Atonement which occurred each year in September or October).[5] Paul had previously sailed through major Mediterranean storms (see 2 Corinthians 11:25). He did not relish the idea of another such experience.

But despite his warning of the likely danger, Paul and all on board ship soon faced nautical disaster!

Here Luke's memory served him well. With detail, he described **the gentle south wind** that convinced the captain he had made the right decision to sail on (Acts 27:13). The wind suddenly shifted into a storm so severe that no one doubted that it was the dreaded **northeaster** (27:14). Luke remembered the difficulty of hauling in **the lifeboat** (27:16; had Luke helped pull the ropes?). Next was the strain of **passing ropes under the ship to hold it together,** much as we might secure a package by tying string around it (27:17).

The dangers gradually increased. The captain took radical steps, hoping to save the lives of his passengers. He ordered the lowering of the anchor, hoping to slow the ship and avoid the dangerous sandbars of **Syrtis,** off the African coast (27:17). The crew discarded the ship's valued cargo of grain (see 27:18). They even went as far as throwing overboard the sailing gear not currently in use (see 27:19; perhaps the largest sails, as these would have dangerously weighed the ship down if they had become heavy with rain). For another ten hopeless days, the ship was carried wherever the nasty winds took it (see 27:19, 27).

The turning point in Luke's saga comes as Paul speaks words of assurance. God had promised Paul his own safe arrival before Caesar and also **the lives of all who sail with you** (27:24). Paul announced this good news to all his traveling companions. From that point on, momentum turned in favor of the company. The next detail in Luke's story is that **the sailors sensed they were approaching land** (27:27). How would they have come to this conclusion? Likely they could hear (or possibly see) waves breaking toward a shoreline.[6] Luke remembered even the decreasing depths of the water as the ship moved toward an area known to this day as St. Paul's Bay. The crew welcomed the thought of land, but not too quickly. Moving ashore at night would have involved the danger of hitting rocks while still at some distance from the safe coastline. The crew **dropped four anchors** to restrain the ship's landward movement until daybreak when the sailors hopefully could guide the ship through the rocks (27:29). The sailors, at that point, came close to forsaking all other passengers. If they could get down into the lifeboat, they could easily guide this smaller vessel to safety. Paul recognized this strategy and helped to forbid it (see 27:30-31).

Just before dawn, Paul once again spoke optimistically to the ship's company: **Take some food. . . . Not one of you will lose a single hair from his head** (27:33-34). By this time, everyone trusted Paul's wisdom and heeded his words. Everyone ate, and yes, all 276 on board did reach shore safely (see 27:44).

Details of the ship's last hours? Note the words Luke used to describe Paul's handling of the food. Paul **took some bread, . . . gave thanks, . . . broke it, and began to eat** (27:35). Note the familiarity of these words. They're associated then and now with the Lord's Supper. Did Luke intend this parallel? Did he, Paul, and Aristarchus (the only known Christians on board [see 27:1-2]) remember Jesus as they ate this meal? Undoubtedly, they knew that Jesus had protected His own. He was about to bring them safely to land.

The crew joined Paul in eating, although probably not in any understanding of the spiritual significance the Christians placed on the meal. The crew would not have had the opportunity to receive much teaching. But, as in Jonah's case, the pagan sailors must have seen that Paul worshiped a powerful God. The crew then tossed the remainder of the grain cargo overboard, to make the ship as light as possible for its landing on a beach (as opposed to a deeper harbor; see 27:38). The sailors guided the ship away from rocks, but could not see an underwater sandbar (see 27:41). The ship stuck there. The pounding waves began to break up the ship. After traveling all those miles, it could not make the last few hundred yards. As the ship broke up, it looked like it would be each man for himself. The soldiers feared that the prisoners might escape. The soldiers thought it best to kill Paul and the other prisoners. (By doing so, they were seeking to protect their own lives. Remember that soldiers who let a prisoner escape risked facing the punishment the prisoner would have faced [see commentary on 12:19].) The centurion, however, protected Paul (and the others) who by this time must have become something of a star (see 27:42-43).

By the time everyone reached safety on Malta, Paul was certainly treated as if he were a VIP. Despite the fact that Paul remained a prisoner potentially facing execution, his interaction with people (and wildlife!) on the island only verified his uniqueness. He was attacked by a deadly snake, but experienced no harm. The Maltese islanders decided that Paul **was a god** (28:6; compare 14:11). When Paul healed the chief official's father, as well as other needy people on the island, it appears the island declared a "Paul of Tarsus Day." Everyone **honored** Paul and his friends **in many ways,** and then offered supplies for the ongoing journey (28:10).

Paul completed the trip without incident. By late winter, it was safe to sail again. After several months to recover, the entire group was ready to board another ship and head for Rome. Luke remembered the highlights: three days in **Syracuse,** the capital city of Sicily, an island off the southwest coast of Italy (28:12); **Rhegium,** at the southern point of Italy was their next port of call (28:13); and the last two hundred miles to **Puteoli.** From there, Paul and his companions walked up the Appian Way, the most famous of ancient Roman roads, on toward the capital city.

Paul may have left Caesarea as merely another prisoner.[7] When the voyage was finished, Paul was a key member of the team.

Put yourself in Paul's place. How must he have felt throughout this trip? First, relief that finally *something* was happening—at least he was leaving Caesarea. Then, fear for himself and the safety of others on the ship, and calmness when God assured him that all would be fine, despite the fury of the storm. Finally, gratitude for all the miracles God performed around and through him.

If I had been Paul, I hope that I would not have complained, but I might have wondered why God had turned on the supply of miracles once again. For months and years, Paul had sat in prison in Caesarea. God had protected Paul from death, but there been no miraculous release. What made God modify His strategy? Had Paul changed? There's no evidence that his faith or his prayer life had improved. Had God himself changed? No. God had retained sovereign control throughout the entire period. During the time Paul spent in Caesarea, God chose to work through natural means. On the journey, it looked as if God jumped into the picture more often. What made the difference? We cannot know.

Today, we often wonder why God sometimes appears to step back, despite our pleas for His strong action. God loves us. As He did in Paul's case, God works out *His* plan, but He does not always explain His methods to us.

What do we learn from Paul's character and leadership in this situation of serious stress?[8]

- Faith—When God spoke, Paul believed. Paul risked looking the fool by announcing in advance what God had said would happen (see 27:24-26, 34).

- Concern for others—Paul was on his way to Rome with no way of knowing what his future held. We might excuse Paul if, under the circumstances, he had focused his attention on himself. Rather, he was continually seeking to encourage and minister to others (for example, 27:25; 28:8-9).

- Practicality—Paul was concerned not only about the spiritual welfare of others; he sensed the practical danger of sailing the sea in the fall (see 27:10). Nearing the end of the voyage, he encouraged the ship's crew and passengers to eat, so they might have physical strength for the test that was ahead (see 27:34). When the group needed a fire to keep warm and dry on a cool, rainy evening, Paul was out gathering sticks (see 28:3).

- Willingness to receive help—No pride kept Paul from depending on the help others offered. When his friends in Sidon wanted to **provide for his needs,** Paul allowed them to do so (27:3). Later in the trip, when the Maltese islanders wanted to do the same, Paul graciously received from their generosity (see 28:10).

- Authority—When the situation called for someone to take charge, Paul did not let his position as a prisoner stop him from acting. Paul risked taking the role of the captain, at least briefly. He spoke the strong truth people needed to hear (see 27:10, 21). Had it not been for Paul's insight, the ship's crew might have sneaked away in mutiny (see 27:31). (Don't be tempted to worship Paul. He remained a human being. Even he could not resist the opportunity to say, "I told you so—you should have listened to me in the first place" [see 27:21]).

- Desire to serve God—Was Paul ever afraid to proclaim his devotion to God? During this trip, Paul let everyone know that his inside information came from the God to whom he belonged and whom he served (see 27:23).

It appears that once again Luke has portrayed Paul in a way that he hoped would bring a verdict of "innocent" in Rome. In his account of the weeks preceding the voyage, Luke quotes Claudius Lysias, Festus, and Agrippa. These important men all vouched for Paul's innocence. The sea journey clinches the verdict, for it apparently shows *God himself* standing with Paul.

Was Paul the hero of this trip? Luke comes close to portraying him in this role. But Paul, even within this story, would have rejected such human hero worship (see 28:6). Furthermore, Luke wished to portray God as the hero. Look to what lengths God went to insure that his servant reached Rome, the destination. God arranged a free ticket, at Caesar's expense. God brought a whole ship's party through a fierce Mediterranean storm. God would not permit the soldiers to kill Paul. God protected Paul from a poisonous snake. Paul's way was not easy, but it was sure, for God was present and active. We, too, will face storms, but the ruler of the storms travels with us, as well.[9]

2. PAUL ARRIVES IN THE CAPITAL 28:14b-31

Luke finishes his two-volume work with Paul in Rome, **without hindrance** preaching **the kingdom of God** (Acts 28:31). Why does Luke not go on to tell the story of Paul's trial? There are several possibilities. One is that every story has to end somewhere. Or, more likely, Luke saw Paul's unrestricted preaching in Rome as the climax of his story. His hero had reached the biggest and best-known city in the world. There Paul had total freedom to preach Jesus.[10] And, of course, there is a chance that Luke ended his book with the latest available news. Paul had spent **two whole years boldly** (28:31) preaching **the kingdom of God** in Rome.[11] Perhaps as Luke laid down his quill, Paul was about to face Caesar.

Luke began Acts by portraying Jesus with His eleven disciples. Even the group of 120 in Acts 1 must have felt small, compared to the population of the Roman Empire. But Jesus had foreseen the day when His followers would preach the good news "to the ends of the earth" (1:8). As Luke finished his writing, the gospel had spread *that far*. Particularly in the last chapters of Acts, Luke shows the announcement of several specific prophecies and then documents their fulfillment (for example, 23:11, fulfilled in 28:23-31; and 27:24, 34, fulfilled in 27:44). Paul's preaching in Rome, at the end of Acts, demonstrated the reality of Jesus' *unbelievable* words: "to the ends of the earth." (Paul's Roman ministry also completed the prophecy recorded in 23:11, that Paul would reach Rome, and gave ultimate fulfillment of 9:15, that Paul would preach before **kings.** In Rome, Paul preached before the one whom the Roman world viewed as *the* king.) If Paul could preach in Rome, then there would be no place outside the reach of the gospel. Could there be any more fitting way for Luke to finish this story of God's power?[12]

Ironically, however, Paul was not the first to preach the gospel in Rome. Unnamed believers had founded the church there before his arrival. How do we know this? Aquila and Priscilla may have been believers before they were evicted from Rome (see commentary on 18:2). Luke, in 28:15, documents the previous existence of a church in Rome. He mentions **brothers** from Rome who heard Paul was coming. These believers walked miles[13] out of the city to meet Paul and accompany him on his "triumphal entry." Paul recognized their arrival as a gift from God (see 28:15). For him, their presence meant that (1) there were believers in Rome; (2) someone had told them about Paul; and (3) they saw him as a true brother in Christ, and not as a criminal deserving execution. No wonder Paul felt **encouraged** (28:15); a large group of supportive friends had arrived to walk the last miles with him.

Julius, the Roman centurion, who had successfully brought Paul to Rome, must have felt mixed feelings as he completed his task. Like Paul, he would have been relieved to reach the capital city. But he was probably sorry to lose a "prisoner-turned-friend." It appears that the centurion gave Paul a good reference, for in Rome, **Paul was allowed to live by himself, with** only **a soldier to guard him** (28:16).

Paul not only experienced the relative freedom of living in his own (**rented** [28:30]) home, but also was permitted to welcome guests. He undoubtedly enjoyed the company of believers. But the Christians in Rome disappear from the record after the first **three days** (28:17). It seems that from that time on, Paul turned his attention to those who did not yet know Jesus. As a prisoner, he was unable to visit the local Jews. Because Paul could not visit the synagogue, he invited the synagogue to visit him. Paul **called together the leaders of the Jews** (28:17). In one sense, this was not unusual. It was Paul's custom, when visiting a city for the first time, to visit first the local gathering of Jews. But the fact that he continued to minister to God's chosen people, even after the Jerusalem Jews had worked so hard to kill him, shows how thoroughly God's grace had transformed Paul.[14]

For this group of esteemed guests, Paul described himself as a loyal Jew and summarized how he had ended up in chains. Recording Paul's words on this occasion gave Luke opportunity to record one more "closing statement" in Paul's defense. Paul declared his innocence: **I have done nothing;** he had violated neither the Law of the Jews[15] nor the Roman law (28:17-18). Paul bore no grudges against the Jews and indirectly stated his faith in Roman justice (see 28:19). Through his past ministry, and even in his present desire to serve God in Rome, he merely wanted to maintain his loyalty to **the hope of Israel** (28:20).

The Jews' first response was a bit ironic. They knew of Christianity, for they had heard many people **talking against this sect** (28:22). But they had not heard anything, at least anything negative, about Paul (see 28:21). At minimum, they were open-minded regarding Paul's message. They were willing to hear more. Whether from enthusiasm or from doubt, when they returned, they came **in even larger numbers** (28:23). Paul gave them everything he had. **From morning till evening,** he showed them how God's recent actions (bringing **the kingdom**) had fulfilled **the hope of Israel** (28:20, 23). Paul pointed out to the Jews that they should not see this message as surprising, for it had been predicted in **the Law of Moses and from the Prophets** (28:23). (That last phrase was commonly used to describe what we call the Old Testament.)

As was common in Paul's earlier ministry (see commentary on 13:1-3; 15:36–16:10), the Jews' final response was mixed. Some believed and others did not (see 28:24).

On one hand, Paul would have been disappointed with the negative response. On the other, he had come to expect it. Paul knew that if Jesus had suffered this rejection, Jesus' followers would, too (see John 15:18-21). Jesus had seen the blindness of the Jews as fulfillment of Old Testament prophecy, quoting Isaiah's words to explain how some would never see (Isaiah 6:9, quoted in Luke 8:10). Here at the end of Acts, Paul experienced this rejection and, like his Master, quoted the same words from Isaiah (see Acts 28:26-27; Isa. 6:9-10). Both of Luke's heroes—Jesus and Paul—continued faithfully to the end, despite the mistreatment they received.

How easily some of us see rejection of our witness as a signal to keep quiet. Paul, even nearing the end of his life, would not give up. Polycarp was another early believer in a generation soon after the apostles. He was given opportunity to deny Jesus before being thrown to the lions. Polycarp stood firm: "For eighty-six years, Jesus has remained faithful to me. How can I deny him now?" Polycarp followed the pattern set by Paul and Jesus before him.

When the Jews rejected Paul, Paul did *not* keep quiet. Once again, Paul saw their turning away from him as the signal that he should preach to the Gentiles (see 28:28; also 13:46; 18:6; 19:8-9). For **two whole years, Paul preached the kingdom of God** (28:30). Luke passes over those years with little detail, but other New Testament clues help fill in the gap.

Reading the Prison Epistles sheds much light on this period.[16] For example, one man to whom Paul ministered during this time would have been the runaway slave Onesimus, the central figure in Paul's letter to Philemon. During this time, Paul took the opportunity to share the gospel with his Roman guards. The Philippian epistle mentions the saints of Caesar's household who sent their greetings (see Philippians 4:22). At least some of those believers would have been from among Paul's guard, the "congregation" chained to Paul (see also Philippians 1:13). Paul took time to reflect on his past. As he did so, he felt no regrets. All that had been to his profit, he was now willing to see as loss, for "the surpassing greatness of knowing Christ Jesus my Lord" (Phil. 3:7-8). Paul remained human. He struggled with temptation. He asked the Ephesians to pray for him, that "words might be given [him] so that [he] would fearlessly make known the mystery of the gospel, for which [he] was an ambassador in chains" (Eph. 6:19-20).

God answered that prayer. As Luke left Paul, he was facing the possibility of execution for his loyalty to Jesus. Yet Paul still **welcomed all who came to see him**, **boldly** teaching **about the Lord Jesus Christ** (Acts 28:30-31). As Paul later wrote to Timothy, "I am suffering [for the gospel] even to the point of being chained like a criminal. But God's word is not [cannot be] chained!" (2 Tim 2:9).

ENDNOTES

[1]Not only in Scripture, but among all ancient documents, Acts 27 offers one of the most detailed descriptions of ancient sailing. Even secular historians find it a helpful resource.

[2]This is the first use of **we** since 21:18. During the time of Paul's trials, Luke had stepped into the background. But the fact that he accompanied Paul as he entered Jerusalem and, two-plus years later, when he left Caesarea likely indicates that Luke spent that time in the area, not far from Paul. Perhaps Luke used this slow time for background research on both volumes of the work we know as Luke-Acts.

[3]William H. Willimon, *Acts* (Atlanta: John Knox Press, 1988), p. 184. This journey was, however, quite opposite from Jonah's. In the first story, God's man was running from God and risked the lives of the entire crew. Here, God's person was running *with* God. Paul's faithfulness contributed to the rescue of all on board.

[4]William Barclay, *The Acts of the Apostles* (Philadelphia: The Westminster Press, 1955), p. 202. During this trip to Rome, Paul traveled on a number of grain ships. Although these ships were large (over 100 feet long and 30 feet wide), their equipment was not all that today's sailors would enjoy. The crew had no directional equipment other than the sun, moon, and stars. Ancient sailing vessels had no rudder with which to steer. The crew maneuvered the ship by means of two large paddles, one on each side. These ships had only one sail, making it impossible to sail into the wind. It's amazing that any ancient ship ever reached its destination.

[5]F. F. Bruce, *The Book of the Acts* (Grand Rapids, Michigan: Wm. B. Eerdmans Publishing Co., 1988), p. 481. Bruce presents evidence to argue that, the year of this trip, the Day of Atonement (**the Fast**) would have fallen on October 5. (Ancient calendars were not based on our 365-day years with twelve months. All their dates were fixed by twenty-eight-day lunar months.) The autumn period of dangerous travel went from the middle of September until the middle of November. After the second date, Mediterranean Sea travel was impossible.

[6]Ibid., p. 490.

[7]Ibid., p. 477. As a Roman citizen who had appealed to the emperor, Paul may have received some special treatment from the beginning.

[8]John R. W. Stott, *The Spirit, the Church, and the World* (Downers Grove, Illinois: InterVarsity Press, 1990), p. 389. Stott points out that, to this point, Luke has portrayed Paul as "apostle, . . . prisoner, and . . . defendant." During this voyage, however, Paul is "an ordinary man among men."

[9]Contemporary readers may appropriately compare their experiences in "the storms of life" with Luke and Paul's struggle in Acts 27. At the same time, we must remember that such "symbolic" meanings were not primary in Luke's mind when he wrote. Luke wrote to portray Paul's faithfulness and God's power in an actual historical situation.

[10]In the original Greek text, the last words Luke wrote were **boldly** and **without hindrance.** Luke saw such unhindered ministry in Rome as the climax of God's miraculous work in the middle portion of the first century.

[11]Contrast the positive spin Luke places on these two years with the two years in prison in Caesarea (24:27).

[12]It is possible that Luke left Acts a bit open-ended. Perhaps, in this way, he intended to say something like this: "Paul reached Rome. But he had hoped to get on to Spain. We believers have come much farther than some would have dreamed. But we now must carry on the unfinished work of taking the good news 'to the ends of the earth.'"

[13]I. Howard Marshall, *Acts* (Grand Rapids, Michigan: Wm. B. Eerdmans Publishing Co., 1980), p. 419. Luke mentions two points where **brothers** met Paul: **the Forum of Appius,** and **the Three Taverns** (28:15). These were, respectively, forty-three and thirty-three miles from Rome.

[14]Barclay, p. 211.

[15]Law refers to either the Levitical Code (all God's rules and regulations), the Ten Commandments, or the Pentateuch (the first five books of the Old Testament: Genesis, Exodus, Leviticus, Numbers, and Deuteronomy); it is often capitalized when it means the Pentateuch or the Ten Commandments.

[16]The Prison Epistles are those Paul wrote to the churches in Ephesus, Philippi, and Colossae, and to a friend named Philemon. These letters were most likely written during the Roman imprisonment Luke describes in Acts 28:30.

SELECT BIBLIOGRAPHY

Barclay, William. *The Acts of the Apostles*. Philadelphia: The Westminster Press, 1955, 1976.

Barker, Kenneth, ed. *The NIV Study Bible*. Grand Rapids, Michigan: The Zondervan Corporation.

Bruce, F. F. *The Book of the Acts*. Grand Rapids, Michigan: Wm. B. Eerdmans Publishing Co., 1988.

Bruce, F. F. *Paul: Apostle of the Heart Set Free*. Grand Rapids, Michigan: Wm. B. Eerdmans Publishing Co., 1977.

Carpenter, Eugene and McCown, Wayne. *Asbury Bible Commentary*. Grand Rapids, Michigan: Zondervan Publishing House, 1992.

Filson, Floyd. *A New Testament History*. Philadelphia: The Westminster Press, 1969.

Goodwin, Frank. *A Harmony of the Life of St. Paul*. New York: American Tract Society, 1895.

Guthrie, Donald. *New Testament Introduction*. Downers Grove, Illinois: InterVarsity Press, 1970.

Harrison, Everett F. *Introduction to the New Testament*. Grand Rapids, Michigan: Wm. B. Eerdmans Publishing Co., 1971.

Jeremias, Joachim. *Jerusalem in the Time of Jesus*. Philadelphia: Fortress Press, 1969.

——. *Luke: Historian and Theologian*. Grand Rapids, Michigan: Zondervan Publishing House, 1971.

Marshall, I. Howard. *Acts*. Grand Rapids, Michigan: Wm. B. Eerdmans Publishing Co., 1980.

Martin, Ralph. *New Testament Foundations*. Grand Rapids, Michigan: Wm. B. Eerdmans Publishing Co., 1978.

Metzger, Bruce. *The New Testament: Its Background, Growth, and Content*. Nashville, Tennessee: Abingdon Press, 1983.

Morgan, G. Campbell. *The Acts of the Apostles*. New York: Fleming Revell, 1924.

Munck, Johannes. *The Acts of the Apostles*. New York: Doubleday and Company, Inc., 1967.

Ramsay, William. *St. Paul the Traveler and the Roman Citizen*. London: Hoder and Stoughton, 1907.

Robertson, A. T. *Types of Preachers in the New Testament*. Grand Rapids, Michigan: Baker Book House, 1972.

Sherwin-White, A. N. *Roman Society and Roman Law in the New Testament*. Grand Rapids, Michigan: Baker Book House, 1963.

Stott, John R. W. *The Spirit, the Church, and the World*. Downers Grove, Illinois: InterVarsity Press, 1990.

Willimon, William H. *Acts*. Atlanta: John Knox Press, 1988.